Scotland and
the 19th-Century World

Scottish Cultural Review
of Language and Literature

Volume 18

Series Editors
Rhona Brown
University of Glasgow
John Corbett
University of Macau
Sarah Dunnigan
University of Edinburgh
Ronnie Young
University of Glasgow

Associate Editor
James McGonigal
University of Glasgow

Production Editor
Amy Wright

SCROLL

The Scottish Cultural Review of Language and Literature publishes new work in Scottish Studies, with a focus on analysis and reinterpretation of the literature and languages of Scotland, and the cultural contexts that have shaped them.

Further information on our editorial and production procedures can be found at www.rodopi.nl

Scotland and
the 19th-Century World

Edited by
Gerard Carruthers, David Goldie
and Alastair Renfrew

Amsterdam - New York, NY 2012

Cover image: Josephine Haswell Miller , Memories of the Sea (1936).
Reproduced courtesy of History of Art, School of Culture and Creative
Arts, University of Glasgow and with the kind permission of Silvia Percival
Prescott.

Cover Design: Inge Baeten

The paper on which this book is printed meets the requirements of "ISO
9706: 1994, Information and documentation - Paper for documents -
Requirements for permanence".

ISBN: 978-90-420-3562-1
E-Book ISBN: 978-94-012-0837-6
© Editions Rodopi B.V., Amsterdam - New York, NY 2012
Printed in The Netherlands

*This collection is dedicated to Douglas Gifford
on his 70th birthday*

Contents

Contributors

Gerard Carruthers holds a personal chair in 'Scottish Literature since 1700' at the University of Glasgow. He is General Editor of the new Oxford University Press edition of the works of Robert Burns. Recent publications include *Scottish Literature, a Critical Guide* (EUP 2009) and the co-edited (with Liam McIlvanney) *Cambridge Companion to Scottish Literature* (CUP 2012).

Sarah Dunnigan is Senior Lecturer in English Literature at Edinburgh University. She has published on medieval and Renaissance Scottish literature, Robert Burns, ballads, and contemporary Scottish women writers, and is presently writing a book about Scottish fairy tales from the medieval to Romantic periods.

Richard Finlay is Professor of History at the University of Strathclyde. His recent books include, *Modern Scotland 1914–2000* (2004) and with E.J. Cowan, *Scottish History: The Power of the Past* (2002). He has published many essays on the politics and culture of nineteenth- and twentieth-century Scotland.

Michael Fry pioneered the study of the Scots' worldwide imperial activities with his book *The Scottish Empire* (2001). He is the author of seven other works on the history of Scotland since 1707, as well as of numerous articles and contributions to scholarly collections.

Douglas Gifford is Emeritus Professor of Scottish Literature and Senior Research Fellow at the University of Glasgow. His publications include studies of James Hogg, Neil Gunn and Lewis Grassic Gibbon, and essays across the range of nineteenth- and twentieth-century Scottish writing. He edited *The History of Scottish Literature* Vol. 3: *The Nineteenth Century*, *A History of Scottish Women's Writing* (with Dorothy McMillan) and *Scottish Literature* (with Dunnigan and MacGillivray). He is Honorary Librarian for Walter Scott's library at Abbotsford.

Suzanne Gilbert lectures in Scottish literature, Romanticism, and oral traditions at the University of Stirling. Along with articles in these areas, she has edited two volumes of the Stirling/South Carolina Research Edition of *The Collected Works of James Hogg* (Edinburgh University Press), *Queen Hynde* with Douglas Mack (1998) and *The Mountain Bard* (2007), and serves as the edition's Associate General Editor. Currently she is editing a third volume, Hogg's *Scottish Pastorals, Together with Other Early Poems and 'Letters on Poetry'*; co-editing a collection of essays on Scottish traditional literatures (EUP); and completing a monograph on the ballad as a genre (Routledge).

David Goldie is senior lecturer and head of the School of Humanities at the University of Strathclyde. He is the author of *A Critical Difference* (1998) and joint editor, with Gerard Carruthers and Alastair Renfrew, of *Beyond Scotland* (2004).

Andrew Hook, Emeritus Bradley Professor of English Literature at the University of Glasgow, is a Fellow of both the British Academy and the Royal Society of Edinburgh. He has published widely on English, Scottish, and American literature. His seminal work *Scotland and America: A Study of Cultural Relations 1750–1835* appeared in a second edition in 2008. The Andrew Hook Centre for American Studies at Glasgow is named in his honour.

Susan Manning is Grierson Professor of English Literature, and Director of the Institute for Advanced Studies in the Humanities at the University of Edinburgh. She works on the Scottish Enlightenment and on Scottish-American literary relations, the topics of her comparative studies *The Puritan-Provincial Vision* (1990) and *Fragments of Union* (2001). She is one of the editors of the *Edinburgh History of Scottish Literature*, 3 vols. (2006), and has co-edited the first *Transatlantic Literary Studies Reader* (2007). She is currently completing a book on transatlantic character.

Pam Perkins teaches eighteenth-century and Romantic literature at the University of Manitoba. Her main current areas of research are women's writing of the late-eighteenth- and early-nineteenth centuries and Scottish travel writing. She has recently edited (for Humanities EBooks) two previously unpublished travel journals by Francis Jeffrey.

Alastair Renfrew taught at the universities of Strathclyde and Exeter before moving to Durham as Reader and Head of Russian in 2007. His main area of research specialisation is critical and literary theory, with particular emphasis on the Soviet 1920s. He has published widely on Mikhail Bakhtin and the so-called Russian Formalists, including the monograph *Towards a New Material Aesthetics* (2006) and the recent collection *Critical Theory in Russia and the West* (2010), and is currently completing an introduction to Bakhtin for *Routledge Critical Thinkers*. He has also taught and published on Russian and Scottish fiction, Russian and Soviet Cinema, and is currently developing a project on the history of political violence in Russian literature and culture. He is Director of Research in the School of Modern Languages & Cultures and Editor of the journal *Slavonica*.

Ritchie Robertson is Taylor Professor of German at Oxford University and a Fellow of Queen's College. His books include *Kafka: Judaism, Politics, and Literature* (1985), *The "Jewish Question" in German Literature, 1749–1939: Emancipation and its Discontents* (1999), and *Mock-Epic Poetry from Pope to Heine* (2009). He is currently working on a book entitled *Schiller and the Poetics of Conspiracy*.

Johnny Rodger has published several works of fiction, including *The Auricle* (1995), *g haun(s) Q* (1996), and *redundant* (1998). He has authored several full length critical works including *Contemporary Glasgow* (1999), *Edinburgh: A Guide to Recent Architecture* (2002) and edited the monograph *Gillespie, Kidd & Coia 1956-87* (2007), and the collection *Fickle Man: Burns in the 21st Century* (2009) together with Gerard Carruthers. He is editor of *The Drouth*.

Trevor Royle is an Honorary Fellow in the School of History, Classics and Archaeology in the University of Edinburgh. Recent books include *Flowers of the Forest: Scotland and the First World War* (2006) and *The Road to Bosworth Field: A New History of the Wars of the Roses* (2009).

Ken Simpson was Reader in the Department of English Studies at the University of Strathclyde and Founding Director of the Centre for Scottish Cultural Studies. He has twice (1999, 2005) been Neag Distinguished Professor in British Literature at the University of Connecticut and twice (1992, 2001) W. Ormiston Roy Fellow in Scottish Poetry at the University of South Carolina. Currently he is Honorary Professor of Burns Studies at the University of Glasgow. He has published on Sterne, Fielding, Smollett and Stevenson and Scottish writers of the eighteenth and nineteenth centuries.

Acknowledgements

The editors would like to thank Ronnie Young, Rhona Brown, Sarah Dunnigan, Jim McGonigal and John Corbett for their invaluable assistance in making this volume happen; thanks also to Gillian Sargent for compiling the index. We are also grateful to Silvia Percival Prescott for her kind permission regarding use of the Josephine Haswell Miller painting and to Marion Lawson for her expert assistance with the cover image.

Introduction

Gerard Carruthers, David Goldie and Alastair Renfrew

Scotland's engagement with the nineteenth-century world has often been read as one that threatened dire consequences for the national culture. A final surrender to cultural anglification, rampant industrialisation, a keen partnership in the British imperial enterprise are factors that might easily have inhibited the continued growth of a "native" literary tradition that had restored itself over the course of the previous century. The headliners of Scottish literature of the period, Scott and Stevenson, were, though, successful then and now precisely because of their very different abilities to articulate, mediate, and even perhaps sublimate the tensions produced by these unpropitious circumstances in a manner that was at once identifiably Scottish and at the same time consistent with an incipient "British" modernity. Elsewhere, away from the golden mean of a modern Scottish literature in English, literature in Scots proved to be marginalised or, worse, infantilised by its own context. The *Whistle Binkie* anthologies of poems and songs for the fireside (1832–90), for example, are emblematic of the stultified, cloying sentimentality that clogged the literary arteries of Victorian Scotland. There can be no better index of the sharp descent of literature in Scots since the time of Burns than the best known text from these hugely successful anthologies, "Wee Willie Winkie", a poem that put successive generations of fearful Scottish children safely to sleep, but which also placed the Scottish vernacular tradition into a coma from which it would not wake until deep into the twentieth century. Scott and Stevenson aside, the nineteenth century became a wasteland for Scottish literature, its despoliation of national identity contending even with that of the seventeenth.

And even the "mediations" of Scott and Stevenson come, by their very nature, with significant cost. The spectacular popularity and influence of Scott in the first decades of the century may be read as, at the very least, an ambivalent achievement: an inscription not of Scotland, but of "Scottland", a place of empty romantic history where indigenous causes, whether Covenanter or Jacobite, are doomed in the face of British Unionist progress. Scott, in this reading, merely performs the obsequies for the embalmed cadaver of a national culture, which is then picked over – Stevenson having in the end very little influence on his "native" tradition – by the "Kailyard" writers of the 1880s and 1990s. The Kailyard, in this view, seemingly confirming the deadness of Scots literature in its multiple failures to represent adequately the experience of a nation that has, by the end of the century, become one the most rapidly urbanising and industrialising countries anywhere in the world. The Kailyard's parochial setting and outlook, which ironically ensures its great popularity in England, Canada and America, seems to offer proof that Scottish literature, both as fact and as desire, had become a danger to itself, if not to others.

Why, then, return to the "wasteland" of nineteenth-century literature, other than as a proxy for the historiographical reconstruction of an episode in the long story of Scotland's decline and fall, a necessary preliminary, perhaps, to the story of its late-Modern revival? The most powerful answer might be that, from the current perspective, the charges laid against nineteenth-century Scottish literature appear to have very little do with nineteenth-century conditions or even the literature they produced; they are, rather, a product of what followed, a backwards projection of the over-determined impulse for "Renaissance", and are based, therefore, on an idealised, holistic version of "the nation" that few would subscribe to in the twenty-first century. We may now be less determined to impute a narrative of unsatisfactory "Scottishness" or "nation-ness" to the most kenspeckle parts of nineteenth-century Scottish literature than, say, that early twentieth-century idealist of national integrity, Edwin Muir, who did more than anyone to ingrain the idea of Scott as a "sham bard of a sham nation", a spurious Scottish artist writing in and of a Scotland that exists only in the imagination. Scott is accused by Muir and many others of escapism, of representing Scotland as a place bereft of self-determining possibility; his faux laments for the passing of "old Scotland" contributing to the process they affect to describe. Scott, and the modern-day reader of Scottish literature or history, might retort that his depiction of the defeat of "rebellious" Scots, Covenanter or Jacobite, was justified on no more significant grounds than consistency with historical actuality. Scott may have broadly approved the Union of Scotland and England, but the "old Tory" displays the most nuanced form of ambivalence in his fiction of Whig Protestant history. In *The Heart of Midlothian* (1818), for example, corrupt crown rule in the early eighteenth century provokes mass unrest in Edinburgh, causing a Presbyterian milkmaid to venture out, Pilgrim's Progress-like, to assist "modern" Britain in finding its moral compass. The milkmaid, Jeanie Deans, wins a pardon for her sister, who is falsely accused of infanticide, directly confronting Queen Caroline (who is left sourly overseeing the state of the nation in the absence of her dissolute, whoring husband, the King). Here the popular voice is much stronger than the royal voice, Scott confirming a long-standing Scottish myth of demotic moral fibre. More than that, however, this is consistent with the sense in which Scott's fictional landscape is generally characterised by the *uncertainty* of authority, and by the active encouragement of scepticism towards it. Scott, in loose concert with other writers who coalesced around the publisher Blackwood's, such as James Hogg and John Galt, makes a huge contribution to the invention of the historical (and regional) novel, a genre very well suited to the new "democratic" age of the nineteenth century: able to dramatise both the operation of large ideological and institutional formations as well as the smaller-scale impact of local power on the lives of the ordinary folk (as in Galt's satires on Scottish burgh politics). In this, as in other ways, the Scottish novelists of the "Age of Scott" were not the unambitious, marginalised voices of a culturally-backward Scotland, insulated from the effects of Romanticism, but were, on the contrary, writers profoundly engaged at the very heart of the period's sense of unrest.

Perhaps the best example of this ambivalence of centrality and marginality is Hogg's *Private Memoirs and Confessions of a Justified Sinner* (1824), a tale of tortured Calvinism, in which the young Robert Wringhim's belief in his own predestination presages murder and rape under the cloak of an assumed moral impugnity. Wringhim's multiple ambivalences, and his eventual disintegration into suicide, are figured through the novels' oscillation between "psychological" and "super- natural" modes of narration. In one sense a "sympathetic" (because deeply psychological) dissection of the Scottish mindset, Hogg's novel is, at the same time, an "exotic" Gothic thriller of late Romanticism/early Modernity, which confounds assumptions about the post-Enlightenment period's comfortable dispensation with superstition and fanaticism. The 1820s emerge as a period with no less an appetite for the "other", for alternative views of their world, for tales of fanatics, and folk and ethnic mythologemes.

It is in this very particular and deeply contradictory environment that the modern short story takes on its definitive generic profile, fuelled by strongly pronounced folk and gothic elements, but fashioned for an increasingly urban readership, and delivered by such publications as *Blackwood's Magazine*. The Edinburgh that was home to *Blackwood's* quickly became one of the great publishing centres of the world, ideally situated to mediate the ballad, song and supernatural tale of the historic Scottish hinterland for the tastes of the early nineteenth-century western world. The "tales of terror" in which *Blackwood's* came to specialise are the product and embodiment of the complex, tension-filled interaction of at least three contextual layers: their origins in the oral, "supernatural", "folk" tale; their function as entertainment for an emerging mass market; their status as a deeply-felt response to the disappointments of Enlightenment – the brutal purges, judicial murder, and terror that followed hard on the heels of revolution in France, and the resulting European wars. "Tales of terror" are the emblem of humanity's recidivist tendency towards primitivism in the face of Enlightenment, which reads like an alternative definition of Romanticism, itself to a great extent "made in Scotland".

And this is just one of the many curious transactions that abound in the opening decades of the nineteenth century, from Scott's restoration of a taste for the medieval throughout Europe in his narrative verse, to Bonaparte's divination of heroic inspiration in James Macpherson's Ossianic tales. Or Thomas Carlyle's *The French Revolution* (1837), which purports to be history, but is in fact a declamatory, Orphic performance, described by John Stuart Mill as "an epic poem". Steeped in the worldview of German transcendental philosophy, Carlyle anticipates Modernity's excavation of desire and the other "drives" in finding that it is not rationality that is the prime motive force of human history, but the working of a dark, cyclical psychology. This inevitably evokes Stevenson, a truly international writer whose fame at the century's end matched Scott's at its beginning. *The Strange Case of Dr Jekyll and Mr Hyde* (1886), which did more than any of Stevenson's other works to occasion that fame, is often read narrowly – like Hogg's *Justified Sinner* – as a manifestation of a peculiarly Scottish split personality rather than as one of the foundational texts in the modern diagnosis of extra-rational human motivation. It is the combination of the particular – the local, the national – and the universal that identifies Stevenson as one of the key writers of the nineteenth century, not just in Scotland but well beyond it.

Poetry in Scots, too, as isolated revisionists have recently come to realise, demands to be viewed in similar perspective; to be read above and beyond the stereotypes of its self-marginalisation and redundancy after Burns. The politically-engaged Scots poetry of the nineteenth century found only a restricted audience because of the limitations on the place and scope of its publication, though it impinged in diluted form on the emergent national and international mass markets through the *Whistle Binkie* anthologies to which we have referred. These formed a platform that was not always as debilitatingly conservative as might first appear, providing a sometimes unexpected outlet for the potentially unsettling demotic voice and, even, the lost revolutionary poetry of Burns. The influence of Burns remained strong, but as the nineteenth century progressed it was Wordsworth, then Tennyson, and then Whitman who might be regarded alongside Burns and Tannahill and their like as the major influences on Scottish poets working in English and in Scots.

In all of this, it is clear that Scotland, at worst, speaks to and keeps pace with the nineteenth-century world; or, to put it more boldly, propels it forward, qualifies its worst contradictions, and anticipates its terminal crises. Scottish literary culture, far from being the "wasteland" generations of critical introspection has conjured from fear of our "selves", contributes to the sweep of European Romanticism, and thus prepares itself for the onslaught of Modernity. The nineteenth-century Scottish world and its engagements with the world beyond are as complex and contradictory as might be expected of any culture involved in negotiating the processes we identified at the outset, namely the cultural anglification, rampant industrialisation, and willing partnership in British imperial enterprise that constitute the particular, though never unique, characteristics of Scottish experience of the onset of Modernity. The new age of explicit cultural nationalism that followed, and which reached a peak of national self-absorption in the 1920s and 1930s, sought to deny this alternative history of cosmopolitan engagement with the "world process"; in fact, it was compelled to do so, because its primary target was the lack of cogent, recognisably "national" expression it identified in nineteenth-century Scottish literature. The curious and itself contradictory "nationalist Modernism" of the early twentieth century was compelled to jettison all the achievements of the previous century in the name of prosecuting what it identified as a single, central failure – Scottish literary culture's lack of belief in the viability of a return to an independent Scotland. The concern of Scottish writers of the nineteenth century with the world beyond Scotland, anchored by Romanticism and washed over by the currents of international poetry, was characterised simply as a lack of concern with Scotland itself. This determination to sacrifice the "international" past for a "national" future inevitably blinded the cultural nationalists of the "Renaissance" to such longer-term developments as, for example, the legacy of the novelists of the age of Scott to the rise of the historical novel in America and Europe, or at least to the value of such a legacy. What business, after all, had Scottish literature in bestowing its gifts on the nineteenth-century world rather than on the implicitly needy and deserving native tradition? Literary traditions, like charity, must begin – and perhaps end – at home.

This complaint of twentieth-century Scottish cultural nationalism against its own nineteenth-century literary culture begins to look, from the perspective of the twenty-first, like something approaching self harm, a disavowal not only of internationalism, but also, paradoxically and self-defeatingly, of the national dimension that is a necessary condition of its possibility. The present book seeks to do no more than add its many voices to the steadily growing chorus declaring the falsity of this opposition so mercilessly imposed on Scotland and the nineteenth-century world.

Preparing for Renaissance: Revaluing Nineteenth-Century Scottish Literature

Douglas Gifford

Nineteenth-century Scottish literature represents a far richer field than a previously negative version of Scottish literary history suggested. Recent revisionist exercises unearthing this achievement, especially of a "regional" nature, show dynamic engagement with many pressing local, national and international themes and issues. The reassessment of nineteenth-century Scottish literature ought to cause also the reappraisal of the effects of the Scottish Enlightenment in the period immediately prior to this period and the milieu of Scottish modernism (or "the Scottish Renaissance") in the early twentieth century, which has greater continuity with the nineteenth-century period than has often been thought. The nineteenth century sees Scotland continuing to have a literature of both national and international importance.
Keywords: Revisionist disinterment; fiction of alienation; rural fiction; religious scepticism; national scepticism; gender writing; internationalism; parody.

This chapter seeks to question certain orthodoxies of literary history with regard to later nineteenth-century and *fin de siècle* achievement in Scotland, and its formative influence upon "The Scottish Renaissance" of the years between the first and second world wars.[1] I begin with an admission of previous failure. In the late 1980s I edited *The History of Scottish Literature: Nineteenth Century* (Gifford 1988), the third volume of the Aberdeen University press four-volume edition. This proved to be a learning experience, but one which is far from being complete, and one which has in the years since left me feeling (as many editors must feel) that I would like to do it again. Current revaluation of Scottish history and literature is moving with great rapidity; and I recognise now the limitations of that volume. For all that it gave perhaps unusual emphasis to writers like James Hogg, John Galt, George MacDonald, and indicated the many areas which called for urgent research, such as the late nineteenth-century popular press, as editor I failed to recognise sufficiently the achievement of women like Susan Ferrier and Margaret Oliphant, or to place

---

[1] This chapter, while freestanding, also forms a prequel to Gifford. 2004. "Remapping Renaissance in Modern Scottish Literature" in Carruthers, Gerard, David Goldie and Alastair Renfrew (eds) *Beyond Scotland: New Contexts for Twentieth-Century Scottish Literature*. Amsterdam: Rodopi. 17–38.

significantly in the centre of the period the huge figures of Thomas
Carlyle and Hugh Miller; or to emphasise sufficiently the achievement
of poets like the post-Burns radicals, such as Alexander Wilson,
Alexander Rodger, John Mitchell and Alexander McGilvray; or the
later nineteenth-century Dundee disciple of Walt Whitman, James
Young Geddes; or John Davidson, or the major and deeply satirical
reassessment of the Highlands in the fiction of Neil Munro; or the
massive, if uncertain achievement of writers such as John Buchan and
S.R. Crockett – not to mention the need for perhaps less positive yet
important revaluation of "decadent" movements such as the Kailyard
and the Celtic Twilight.

Later critics have begun to reveal the richness of neglected areas.
Many original and neglected radical poets were rescued, for example,
by Tom Leonard in his groundbreaking anthology *Radical Renfrew*
(Leonard 1990). Critics are becoming interested in the cultural
influence of philosophers and thinkers like Sir James Frazer and Hugh
Miller, and previously sidelined writers such as Neil Munro are being
more positively reassessed. And along with this we must take stock of
recent reassessments of a whole range of writers like Oliphant,
Macdonald, Stevenson, James Barrie, Buchan and Davidson, at the
same time exploring more fully what we mean by "Kailyard" writing
and culture. We must listen also to William Donaldson and his tireless
urging in studies like *Popular Literature in Victorian Scotland*
(Donaldson 1986) that we explore the neglected areas of our literature
to be found in the huge number of local papers and publications which
burgeoned following the repeal of Stamp Duty in 1855.

This project of revaluation is important not just for our understanding of the nineteenth century itself, but also for a diachronic
reassessment of the notion of literary "Renaissance", which depends
for its meaning on a sense of the achievement of writers who went
before. We should bear in mind that MacDiarmid and his contemporaries had very good reasons for undervaluing their predecessors, and
that Scottish education generally had little time for Scottish literature
and culture in its curricula; and this is perhaps the clearest reason why
the argument of the pioneering German critic Kurt Wittig, who
identifies a late nineteenth-century revival, "another spring" in
Scottish literature, "heaving again" with Robert Louis Stevenson, has
until recently been ignored (Wittig 1958: 257; see also Glen 1964;
Hagemann 1992). The outstanding characteristic of this revival – and

for much of the later literature, including that of the "Scottish Renaissance" – is a cathartic negativism expressed in a sustained critique of Scottish society and culture, presumably with the underlying aim of destroying what the revival's writers saw as the false mythologies of Kailyard and Celtic Twilight literature. This "positive negativism" characterises the work of many writers from Stevenson himself to that of Davidson, George Douglas Brown, John MacDougall Hay, Mary and Jane Findlater, Violet Jacob, and Catherine Carswell, and can be described as an attitude that takes as its main subject the deficiencies and distortions in Scottish social, cultural and religious values and behaviour, and which seeks to advance beyond these through satire and ironic exposure. And looking further back, we can see that novels such as *Waverley* (1814), *Old Mortality* (1816), *The Heart of Midlothian* (1818), *The Entail* (1823), *The Private Memoirs and Confessions of a Justified Sinner* (1824), *The Master of Ballantrae* (1888), and *The House with the Green Shutters* (1901) (with none of which Muir or MacDiarmid ever significantly engaged) are great precisely because they articulate successfully the divisions and oppositions of Scotland's Highlands and Lowlands, past and present, ironically and critically exposing the conflict of romance and realism.

In his *A Century of the Scottish People 1830–1950*, the historian T.C. Smout gave a graphic account of the horrors of industrialisation in nineteenth-century Scotland (Smout 1986). Unlike his earlier volume, *A History of the Scottish People 1560–1830*, with its rich coverage of society and culture, Smout explains in his introduction why his priorities here do not allow him to discuss Scottish culture at all (Smout 1969). For Smout, apart from a mention of Thomas Carlyle, and a (mistaken) description of William Alexander's *Johnny Gibb of Gushetneuk* (1871) as "a kailyard novel", Scottish culture and literature from 1830 to 1950 is not worthy of historical record. Smout's view seems to me to be unfair and damaging, and unfortunately too typical of the way Scotland's literature between Scott and MacDiarmid is generally viewed. I would suggest that the twenty years between 1835 and 1855 (with the Disruption of the Church of Scotland at its heart) were the real nadir of Scotland's immensely changing, and, for so many in the Highlands and the new cities, hugely unhappy nineteenth century. Industrialisation, Clearance, Scottish participation in and celebration of British Imperialism,

anglicisation of Scottish educational institutions – all these combine
with the eventual result of dissipating any core notions of national
culture, other than the pseudo-myths which filled the vacuum.

The end of the last great period of Scottish Enlightenment writers
is bounded by the deaths of Scott, Hogg and Galt in the 1830s. With
their deaths it is arguable that the uneasy compact between church and
state, which had managed to sustain itself from around 1750 until
arguments were rekindled over Patronage in the 1820s and 1830s, also
died. This was certainly the case by the time of the Disruption in
1843, when Scotland lost the power of the single voice of its powerful
General Assembly to speak up as a kind of State Assembly for its
interests. Andrew Noble has shown vividly the negative effects of
having Professor John Wilson succeed Scott as uncrowned king of
Scottish literature (Noble 1988). It could be argued that it is in the
period of the Tory hegemony and the international literary reach of
Blackwood's Edinburgh Magazine (beginning in 1817, but really
hitting its snobbish and anglicising stride from the 1830s) that Scottish
literature descended into its deepest doldrums, and came closest to
merging indistinguishably with British or essentially English culture.
This is the period of royal commissions on Scotland's Universities; it
is also the period when Scots and Gaelic language and culture were
most systematically ignored in schools and universities.

The real literary and cultural achievements of the second half of
the century were overshadowed by the dominance of Kailyard
romanticisation and sentimentalisation, which took a number of forms,
ranging from settings and subjects rural, Celtic, urban, military, and
even marine, as in Neil Munro's still-popular *Para Handy* series,
which ran from 1906 to 1931. Perhaps the popularity and success of
such cheerful romanticism stemmed from the reassurance it gave
against a background of Scottish and British fears of radical social
change and industrial blight, and not entirely incidentally fulfilling the
nostalgic desires of those transplanted from country to city, or exiled
abroad. Arguably the real originators of Kailyard, James Grant,
William Black, and Queen Victoria's chaplain Norman Macleod,
celebrants of Highlands, soldiers and empire, became the darlings of
the lending libraries of the English-speaking world. And from the time
of Wilson and *Blackwood's Magazine* to that of Stevenson, Davidson
and Buchan we find a recurrent tendency whereby these writers refer

to themselves as Englishmen, reflecting nineteenth-century Scotland's general acceptance of a kind of dual identity.

The diagnostician of Scotland's uneasy condition would note, however, that beneath a veneer of fashionable Britishness something was stirring. The 1850s saw the foundation of the National Association for the Vindication of Scottish Rights, initiating a Scottish home rule movement, led by Professor John Stuart Blackie, himself a poet and essayist (and the year 1855, brought the repeal of the crippling Stamp Tax on newspapers and periodicals, with astonishing results; see Donaldson 1986).

Recent revaluation of writers of the late nineteenth and early twentieth century has worked along broadly three lines, seriously reassessing writers like Macdonald, Oliphant, Stevenson, and Davidson, together with poets of the Great War period, and their women contemporaries such as the Findlater sisters, Jane and Mary, Violet Jacob, and Catherine Carswell. By the 1890s Munro, recognised as one of Scotland's foremost journalists and commentators on its Arts (who hated the Kailyard movement, and had a most uneasy relationship, still not fully understood, with the Celtic Revival), could argue that Scottish art and industry was in the middle of a great revival. With the Scottish Colourists, the Glasgow Boys, Whistler, and the Charles Rennie Mackintosh Circle in art, and the work of George Douglas Brown, Davidson, Buchan and Munro himself, together with the Patrick Geddes and Celtic Revival movement in literature, clearly something was afoot right across the range of arts and sciences (in Glasgow and the West, at the very least).

Munro's own cross-journalism at the turn of the century captures this mood well, as he mixes art and engineering, literature and technology. This was Glasgow's time as Second City of the Empire, with its many major exhibitions, including the most ambitious, that of 1911. Significantly, this Exhibition simultaneously celebrated Glasgow in science and art as central to Empire, but presented Scottish customs and traditions on a lavish scale, even down to an entire Highland village at its heart – and used its profits to found a Chair of Scottish History and Literature at Glasgow University. This was also a period when momentum was moving towards presenting a bill for home rule to parliament in 1914 – but, as international events showed, not at the most opportune moment.

The last two decades have seen substantial positive reassessment of Scottish writing in the period between 1850 and 1920. The lead given by critics such as Donaldson (1986), Leonard (1990), and Catherine Kerrigan in her *An Anthology of Scottish Women's Poetry* (1991), was followed by Edinburgh University Press' production of the first comprehensive survey of the field (Gifford and Macmillan, 1997). Non-fiction prose writers, quasi-philosophical, anthropological and theological, such as Thomas Carlyle, Henry Cockburn, Sir James Frazer, and David Masson, are being reintegrated into a more complete picture of Scottish culture in this period. In addition to the reassessments of hitherto neglected writers to which we have already referred, the work of many others merits re-examination, including poets like the early radicals of Leonard's anthology, and later poets like William Thom, Elizabeth Hamilton, James Young Geddes, Robert Buchanan, Lord Neaves, and "Moses Peerie".[2]

Additionally, there are the subversive arguments of modern Scottish writers like Leonard and James Kelman that for too long we have read our literature within the restrictive parameters of "Eng Lit", which they see as a state-reinforcing apparatus underpinning snobbery, privilege and Britain's outmoded political arrangements. Leonard as early as 1973 argued in *Scottish International* that

[T]he "beauty" of a lot of English poetry (particularly the Romantics) for many, is that the softness of its vowel enunciation reinforces their class status in society as the possessors of a desirable mode of speaking. (Leonard 1988: 65)

Leonard attacked the way Scottish and British education, and universities in particular, dismissed local dialect and working-class culture. Writing about "the wee game" going on between writer and reader in 1985, Kelman implied that for too long "English" literary assessments have been made on very dubious premises (McLean 1985). At the very least their arguments suggest that we need to reconsider the bases on which accepted judgements have been made in the past, and ask how class and political issues have shaped them.

---

[2] In addition to Craig 1999, Donaldson 1896, Leonard 1990 and Kerrigan 1991, recent individual studies of pre-1920 authors include Anderson 2001, Jack 1993, Leonard 1993, Renton and Osborne 2003, Robb 1987, Sandison 1995, Sloan 1995, and Williams 1986.

All this leads to an assertion I cannot hope to substantiate here, not only because of the sheer scale of the project of revision it implies, but also because it involves the unfashionable business of arguing that the primary concern is the aesthetic quality of the literature being reassessed. The assertion should nevertheless be made – namely that a country which can, between 1880 and the time of the early lyrics of MacDiarmid in the 1920s, produce writers of prose of the stature of Oliphant, Macdonald, Alexander, Stevenson, George Douglas Brown, Munro, Barrie, Crockett, the Findlater sisters, Davidson, Buchan, Jacob, John MacDougall Hay, Robert Cunninghame Graham (not to mention "Fiona McLeod" [William Sharp], whose enormously popular pseudo-Celtic fictions deserve attention on socio-cultural grounds), and in poetry, James Young Geddes, Robert Buchanan, James Thomson, Davidson, the War poets, Jacob and Angus (to name only an outstanding few), is hardly in decline – indeed, may rightly be seen as being in a state of revival.

Bearing in mind Wittig's notion of Scottish literature "heaving again" in the late-nineteenth century, we might shift our view to a more general consideration, from a contemporary perspective, of what a mature Scottish literature (or any mature national literature) might be expected to have achieved. Arguably, amongst many considerations, a full and mature national literature would represent, explore and criticise its social and historical contexts, while not necessarily celebrating national historical achievement, and certainly no longer seeking to discover or place value on characteristics and qualities of essential national identity. Rather, it would express the uncertainties, dilemmas, and challenges of its social and historical contexts. It would seem to me that in a post-modern and post-Bakhtinian age we should now appreciate the diversity of our older voices, and rather than blaming them for their uncertainties of subject, perspective and identity, read them as articulating their fragmented and displaced situations and times. Just because so many – and arguably most – of Scotland's major writers moved beyond Scotland in the second half of the nineteenth century does not mean that they do not speak to Scottish issues and predicaments, or cease to be Scottish as they look further afield. It is true, however, that they speak with mainly negative voices, to the point that they could be seen as generally unhappy and disillusioned with what Scotland had become. Where they deal explicitly with Scotland, it is in terms of clearing out old ideas, old values, old shibboleths of community and culture. "Heaving again" takes on a new and purgative connotation.

What are the principal features of the writing of the period? Not, admittedly, industrialisation or urbanisation, Clearance or emigration. Poetry, with a very few honourable exceptions, such as in the work of Alexander Smith, William Thom, Elizabeth Hamilton, and James Young Geddes (whose magnificent long poem "Glendale and Co" stands out as the most achieved and substantial nineteenth-century treatment of the complex social effects of industrialisation), was in fact preoccupied with religious debate. Until Barrie, Scottish drama was preoccupied with the adaptation of the fiction of Walter Scott; and it has long been recognised that fiction, which of all modes might have been expected to deal with the consequences of industrialisation and urban poverty, had before Grassic Gibbon's *Grey Granite* (1934) and George Blake's *The Shipbuilders* (1935) largely ignored such consequences, as it had also ignored the realities of Highland economic cultural decline and emigration, which had to wait until novels like Gunn's *The Grey Coast* (1926), *The Lost Glen* (1931) and *Butcher's Broom* (1934) and MacColla's *The Albannach* (1932).

Omission or evasion of these two important problems does not mean, however, that deeply serious Scottish issues were not aesthetically addressed. These cannot be discussed in full here, but a preliminary survey of a range of important and qualitatively impressive writers reveals a significant consistency of preoccupation and response. The tentative findings of that survey are presented under seven main headings, each of which represents what I consider to be a recurrent issue for most of the most important writers. The order in which they are listed is not hierarchical: individual writers present their critical views of Scottish society and culture with different emphases, so that, for example, where Douglas Brown shows his antipathy towards Lowland Scottish community in terms of almost total disgust, Munro's view of his Argyllshire society is more delicately balanced between antipathy and love. That said, I would argue that the following observations have a general validity and suggest overall that Scottish literature between Stevenson and MacDiarmid is far richer in its depth and subtlety of social and cultural analysis and debate than has hitherto been recognised. My summary of thematic concerns is as follows:

[1] An authorial expression of personal alienation from community and society generally, together with the expression, through central fictional protagonists, of uncertainty of identity and cultural allegiance and a feeling of being imaginatively stifled. In fiction, the figures of Barrie's sentimental Tommy, Munro's Gilian, Douglas Brown's young John Gourlay, and MacDougall Hay's Eochan Strang (of *Gillespie*) stand out: all are deeply sensitive and creative, all are at odds with their family and/or community, all represent creative talent which is either destroyed or warped through the failure of their culture, society and country to recognise their potential. The handling of this same issue in women's fiction is just as impressive: Oliphant's Kirsteen is forced to flee her patriarchal Argyllshire family; the Findlater's Alexandra Hope (from *Crossriggs* in 1908) is shown wasting her enormous human and creative talents on looking after her father and her sister's children, while destroying her own chances of fulfilment; and the heroines of Carswell's two novels, Joanna Bannerman (*Open the Door!*, 1920) and Ellen Carstairs (*The Camomile*, 1922), are shown as trapped by their family's and society's limitations. In poetry it is clear in the work of Young Geddes, James Thomson [B.V.], Buchanan and Davidson that they too feel alienated from the predominant religious and social values of the Scotland of their time.

[2] A recognition of fundamental sickness in the rural community, with its narrow-minded introversion and malicious gossip, which is in direct opposition to the nostalgic praise of Kailyard poetry and fiction. Poets such as Buchanan and Davidson reject Scottish community through exile, with a few side swipes, such as in Davidson's marvellous presentation of an alienated rural, now urban Scottish poet turned to drink and self disgust in "Ayrshire Jock". Trenchant satirical treatment of malicious gossips and warped community is a major focus of fiction from William Alexander's *Johnny Gibb of Gushetneuk* (1871) and George MacDonald's many Scottish community novels, through Stevenson's *The Master of Ballantrae* (1888) and "Thrawn Janet", to the novels of Brown, Munro, Barrie, the Findlaters, and Hay, together with Jacob's dark stories of community gossip and betrayal (published together for the first time in *The Lum Hat* in 1982); this recurs with unexpected ferocity in the later work of Buchan, like *Witchwood* (1927), with its revelations of demonic activity behind the façade of community

respectability. All of these anticipate the outstanding satirical treatment of such community backbiting and intolerance in village and town in Grassic Gibbon's *A Scots Quair*.

[3] A fierce antipathy towards dogmatic and secularised religion. These categories often overlap, so that the criticism of community discussed under the previous heading can be seen here to focus on the narrowness of belief and consequent intolerance. The attack on dogmatic religion is most clearly expressed in the savagely explicit poetry of Thomson, Buchanan and Davidson, and (with equal seriousness, but also with hilarious satire) in the poetry of Geddes, such as "The New Jerusalem", "The New Inferno", and "The Second Advent", where Christ returns, to be rejected by modern church and society. In fiction, Stevenson attacks dogmatism directly in his wonderful presentation of a tormented zealot in the Reverend Murdoch Soulis of "Thrawn Janet", and indirectly in his subtle portraits of dour Calvinists, like the demonic wrecker of ships, Gordon Darnaway, in *The Merry Men* (1887), or the devious and "unco guid" house steward, Ephraim McKellar of *The Master of Ballantrae*.

The work of Oliphant and MacDonald, whether fantasy or realism, was devoted to lessening the bonds of Scottish Presbyterian dogmatism, to the extent that MacDonald was forced to resign as Church of Scotland minister, as was the later genial minister and novelist Crockett. Douglas Brown's *The House With the Green Shutters* shows by omission his contempt for the role of the church; MacDougall Hay, again a minister, appeals for a hugely more compassionate religion for humanity in *Gillespie,* as in many novels do the Findlaters, daughters of the manse whose values transcend their upbringing.

[4] A sceptical reassessment of Scottish history, society, and culture. Once again, this can be found throughout the work of the writers already discussed, as they repudiate the claims of traditional laird, minister, dominie and community. More specifically, Alexander's *Johnny Gibb of Gushetneuk* presents a revisionist view of the supposed narrowness of Free Church values; while in Stevenson and Munro the Highlands and their romantic history and heritage are consistently undermined through revelation of far from romantic double-dealing and cruelty in novels like *Kidnapped* (1885), *Catriona* (1893), *The Master of Ballantrae, John Splendid* (1898), *Gilian the Dreamer* (1899), and *The New Road* (1914). A similar reduction of

romanticised history is found in Violet Jacob's account of divided and hypocritical loyalties in *Flemington* (1911), as also in much of the early fiction of Buchan, as well as the later *Witchwood*. All of this more than anticipates the revisionist views of "Renaissance" writers such as Gunn, Gibbon, and Mitchison.

[5] An awakening sense of gender and of the limitations and predicaments of women. Clearly here the major achievements are with Oliphant, the Findlaters, the fiction and poetry of Jacob and Angus, and Carswell. For the first time since the early nineteenth-century novels of Susan Ferrier, the women of Scottish literature confront the limitations that Scotland's male-dominated society places on women, and comment perceptively on the snobberies and divisions of class which had intensified throughout the century. It is a comment on the limits of MacDiarmid's interests, sympathies and vision that he failed to recognise the significant and aesthetically impressive achievements in these areas in novels like Oliphant's *Miss Marjoribanks* (1866), *Hester* (1883), *Kirsteen* (1890), Mary Findlater's *The Rose of Joy* (1903), *The Ladder to the Stars* (1906), and (with Jane) *Crossriggs,* Carswell's *Open the Door!* and *The Camomile*, as well as the poignant and perspective explorations of the phases and complexities of womanhood in the poetry of Jacob and Angus. Arguably, if MacDiarmid's *desiderata* for Scottish renaissance included mature and philosophical exploration of human issues (as opposed to Kailyard and Celtic Twilight simplification and sentimentalisation), and a merging with and use of the best features of European thought and methodology, then he should have realised the importance of Carswell's achievement in her profound exploration of womanhood in *Open the Door!* With its awareness of the treatment of women in European fiction in the manner of *Madame Bovary, On the Eve, Middlemarch* and *Anna Karenina*, and its use of a subtle symbolism throughout, together with an authorial voice as Modernist as (and indeed working consciously with) D.H. Lawrence's, it is Carswell's novel of 1920 that deserves to be seen as the real harbinger of a Scottish Modernist Renaissance. It would also be fair to note, however, that men's writing of the period acquires a greater perceptiveness and sympathy in the representation of women, as in Stevenson's Kirstie from *Weir of Hermiston* (1896), in the often striking women of the novels of Munro, who indeed tries gamely to understand and present changes in modern women and their treatment

in his novel *The Daft Days* (1907), with its striking young American, the new woman Bud, shaking up dry Scottish values; and this is a theme to which he returns even more seriously in *Fancy Farm* (1910).

[6] A surprising degree of international awareness. If on one hand it is true that from the 1840s on most major Scottish writers, from Carlyle to Grassic Gibbon, chose to leave Scotland, this led, on the other hand, to their direct contact with the wider world. Young Geddes is an exception, yet even he, deeply involved in community in Dundee and Alyth all his life, shows remarkable awareness of writing elsewhere in the world – in his case adapting the voice and style of Walt Whitman to become the most innovative and original Scottish poet of his time. Oliphant, MacDonald, Stevenson, Buchanan, Thomson, Davidson, the Findlaters, Cunningham Graham, Buchan, the Great War poets, and Carswell are very much in touch with the best of European and American writing. MacDonald is inspired by the mysticism of Jakob Boehme and Novalis. Stevenson conducts an important debate on the nature of fiction with Henry James. Thomson draws on Dante, Albrecht Dürer and his engraving *Melencolia I*, and the eighteenth-century scepticism of Giacomo Leopardi's *Operette Morali* as the inspiration for his greatest poem. The Findlaters keep an extensive diary of their American travels, meeting William James, Amy Lowell, and the Emersons. Cunninghame Graham ("the Gaucho") writes extensively of South America. Buchan's fiction ranges across the world, while what many believe to be his greatest novel, *Sick Heart River* (1941), fuses his Scottish and Canadian experience in a fiction of enormous canvas. Carswell's novels move their characters across Europe, while the neglected work of the Scottish Great War poets like Roderick Watson Kerr, Charles Hamilton Sorley, Ewart McKintosh, and Joseph Lee, in its radical challenge to narrow jingoism and false patriotism, shows how the profound experience of the horrors of international war shaped their very twentieth-century and Modernist attitudes.

[7] A wide range of innovatory methods and attitudes, including parody and pastiche, a willingness to cross genres, to use symbolic fantasy and allegory. MacDonald, Oliphant and Stevenson all explore the possibilities of fantasy, but always with ambitious spiritual implications. Barrie's work is increasingly discussed in terms of the need to question its belonging to the Kailyard; recent critics have pointed to the subtle psychological symbolism and profoundly un-

childish meanings of his work, from *Peter Pan* (1904) and the plays, to *Sentimental Tommy* (1896) and *Tommy and Grizel* (1900). Similarly, we need to reassess the subtle parodic implications of Munro's treatment of Gaeldom in *The Lost Pibroch* (1896), where the traditional storytelling voice of oral culture – as collected by J.F. Campbell in his *Popular Tales of the West Highlands* (1860–62) – is deployed to satirise and expose Highland failings. The unique new voice of Young Geddes has already been mentioned, while critics of Davidson consistently remark on the sheer variety and range of voices and registers as one of the most striking features of his poetry, as he ranges from traditional ballad to contemporary cockney, and from English folk song to the ratiocinative and extensive series of the formidable *Testimonies*. The strikingly original blend of tradition and modern exploration of the nature of womanhood in the work of Jacob and Angus we have already noted as inspiring MacDiarmid in his early lyrics. The "Renaissance" can be seen at the very least as having a wide range of diverse, original and innovatory voices to learn from.

Leaving aside for a moment the quite legitimate demands of veracity that any literary history must make of itself, we are entitled nonetheless to ask why this revaluation of the period between Scottish literature's "fall" from Enlightenment (or earlier) and its "Renaissance" in the twentieth century should be of such pressing concern. The answer, as is the case with so much of Scotland's modern literary and cultural history, lies in the valences of the term "Renaissance" itself. As I have argued elsewhere (Gifford 2004), the resurrectionist rhetoric implied by the term, its evocation of a resurgent, if ambivalent, sense of cultural autonomy, has come latterly to obscure the other side of the rhetorical coin: what is to be resurrected or regenerated must, by definition, have perished. The rhetoric of "Renaissance" must also be a rhetoric of endemic failure and underachievement, conclusions that do not survive even the brief survey of the preceding period offered here. It is also a rhetoric of exceptionalism, not in the conventional sense of a national, ethnic or cultural insistence on its own originary uniqueness – the narcissism of minor differences – but in the temporal sense, and *within* the boundaries of a particular literary tradition. In its common currency in Scottish literary history "Renaissance" implies either a single, Golden Age for native writing, conveniently projected back onto the Middle Ages; or, in an ostensible admission of the "exception" that confirms the validity of the overall thesis, it admits of a period of "revival" in the eighteenth century, the final burst of ambivalent vitality of a culture facing terminal contradiction. Everything else, in confirmation of Eliot's dismissal of the Scottish Literary Tradition, is, at best, "minor".

We can see from this vantage point how intimately this rhetoric of Renaissance is related to Eliot's theory of "dissociation of sensibility", the dynamics of which it seeks to reverse, but, unwittingly or otherwise, ends by reinforcing. The idea of a "Renaissance" thus risks colluding in precisely what it strives to overturn, locating Scottish literature and culture in the subject position of the Slave who internalises the dominant discourse of his Master. This may be the ultimate explanation for the paradox I have described as "positive negativism", which seeks, but can never attain, catharsis.

We also begin to see, however, in the varied and mature ways in which Scottish writing between 1855 and the Great War mediates its themes of alienation – of the self, of community, of faith, gender and nationality – that these strategies were not unavoidable, and were indeed provoked by factors more wide-ranging than considerations of the "rise and fall" of a national literary tradition. A thoroughgoing revisionist position on the transitions undergone by Scottish literature from the late-nineteenth into the twentieth century would regard the "Scottish Renaissance" as a *movement*, as a limited-scale "fact" of literary history, rather than as a suggestive proxy for a global conception of Scottish literary history as such. This is not, in fact, to restrict the significance of the "Renaissance", but rather to expand upon it, and to restore to it a greater sense of continuity with the rest of Scottish literary history – not only with what comes after, but also, less fashionably, with what came before.

Bibliography

Anderson, Carol (ed.) 2001. *Opening the Doors: The Achievement of Catherine Carswell*. Edinburgh: Ramsay Head Press.

Craig, Cairns. 1999. *The Modern Scottish Novel: Narrative and the National Imagination*. Edinburgh: Edinburgh University Press.

Donaldson, William. 1986. *Popular Literature in Victorian Scotland*. Aberdeen: Aberdeen University Press.

Gifford, Douglas (ed.) 1988. *The History of Scottish Literature: Nineteenth Century*. Aberdeen: Aberdeen University Press.

—. 2004. "Re-mapping Renaissance in Modern Scottish Literature" in Carruthers, Gerard, David Goldie, and Alastair Renfrew (eds) *Beyond Scotland: New Contexts for Twentieth-Century Scottish Literature*. Amsterdam & New York. Rodopi. 17–37.

Gifford, Douglas & Dorothy Macmillan (eds). 1997. *A History of Scottish Women's Writing*. Edinburgh: Edinburgh University Press.

Glen, Duncan. 1964. *Hugh MacDiarmid and the Scottish Renaissance*. Edinburgh: Chambers.

Hagemann, Susanne. 1992. *Die Schottische Renaissance*. Frankfurt: Peter Lang.

Jack, Ronald. 1993. *The Road to Never-Neverland: a Reassessment of J.M. Barrie's Dramatic Art*. Aberdeen: Aberdeen University Press.

Kerrigan, Catherine (ed.) 1991. *An Anthology of Scottish Women Poets*. Edinburgh: Edinburgh University Press.

Leonard, Tom. 1988. "The Proof of the Mince Pie" in *Intimate Voices 1965–1983*. Newcastle upon Tyne: Galloping Dog Press.

—. (ed.) 1990. *Radical Renfrew*. Edinburgh: Polygon.

—. 1993. *James Thomson: Places of the Mind*. London: Jonathan Cape.

McLean, Duncan. 1985. "James Kelman Interviewed" in *Edinburgh* Review 71: 64–80.

Noble, Andrew. 1988. "John Wilson (Christopher North) and the Tory Hegemony" in Gifford, Douglas (ed.) *The History of Scottish Literature: Nineteenth Century*. Aberdeen: Aberdeen University Press. 125–52.

Renton, Ronald and Brian Osborne (eds). 2003. *Exploring New Roads: Essays on Neil Munro*. Colonsay: House of Lochar.

Robb, David. 1987. *George MacDonald*. Edinburgh: Scottish Academic Press.

Sandison, Alan. 1995. *Robert Louis Stevenson and the Appearance of Modernism*. Basingstoke: Macmillan.

Sloan, John. 1995. *John Davidson: First of the Moderns*. Oxford: Clarendon.

Smout, T.C. 1969. *A History of the Scottish People 1560–1830*. London: Collins.

—. 1986. *A Century of the Scottish People 1830–1950*. London: Collins.

Williams, Merryn. 1986. *Margaret Oliphant*. Basingstoke: Macmillan.

Wittig, Kurt. 1958. *The Scottish Tradition in Literature*. Edinburgh and London: Oliver & Boyd.

Scotland, the USA, and National Literatures in the Nineteenth Century

Andrew Hook

Early nineteenth-century America's tensions with Britain caused America much cultural anxiety, not least because of the inclusion of attacks on the idea of American literature from a periodical press largely based in Edinburgh. Washington Irving and James Fenimore Cooper observed this phenomenon and discussed how best to respond. For Cooper, American literature ought to model itself on English literature. Other commentators proposed the period of Scottish literary romanticism from Allan Ramsay to Walter Scott. John Neal saw Scottish literature's concentration on indigenous landscape as the way forward for American literature and, in practice, Walter Scott's Waverley novels were most influential here. The development of a nineteenth-century American fiction of romance owes much to this period; in following Scott's example, writers of American romance fiction bring forth an imaginative landscape that features complex iterations of the civilised and the primitive.
Keywords: Anglo American War (1812); Washington Irving; James Fenimore Cooper; provincialism; civilisation; primitivism; *Edinburgh Review*; Sydney Smith; *Blackwood's Magazine*; defining American Literature; Scottish literary romanticism; Walter Scott; John Neal; American romance.

When America declared and successfully defended its independence from Great Britain a new situation was created for its culture, including its literary culture. In the colonial period, American writing could legitimately be seen as an off-shoot of English Literature. After independence the exact position of American literature was much more problematic. The connection with English literature – its language, forms, traditions – remained as before. English literature, as a source of models or paradigms, was no more or less available to American writers after 1776 than before. Nonetheless, with the emergence of the United States as a country in its own right, American writing automatically acquired a new status. What had been a colonial literature became a national one. Such a transformation was unavoidable, and with the passage of time the development of an American literature moving in new, distinctive directions, and eventually establishing its own forms, traditions, and even linguistic usage, was certainly inevitable. But this was not quite what happened.

A set of particular historical and cultural circumstances required that a national American literature be established, as it were, overnight.

What were these circumstances? On the historical side, they involve the recognition that the cessation of military and political conflict between Britain and America in 1783 did not mean that relations between the two countries thereafter were all sweetness and light. The defeat of British arms, and the loss of her first empire, were immensely bitter pills for the British ruling class to swallow. And the presence in England and Scotland of large numbers of former Loyalists from America demanding reparations for the losses their loyalty had brought them, ensured that in government circles and beyond the American question remained very much alive. Only a small minority of British liberals saw anything to welcome in the Americans' successful defence of what, from some points of view, could be seen as the principles of freedom and the rights of man. Not even in those working-class circles where sympathy for the Americans and their cause might have been expected to flourish is there much evidence of widespread or enduring support for the newly established American republic. In the early decades of its existence then, the United States was regarded by most sections of British society with feelings of bitterness and hostility. Nor were things different on the other side of the Atlantic. Few Americans appear to have been ready to forgive and forget imperial Britain's resorting to military might to crush their demands for justice and liberty. The Federalist party may have been inclined to try to maintain reasonable relations with British governments, but their Republican opponents were much less conciliatory. And it is clear that a great many ordinary Americans, including recent immigrants, continued to regard the British, and everything they stood for, as their natural enemy.

In these social and political circumstances it would have been surprising had cultural relations between the imperial power and its lost colonies been anything other than distinctly troubled. And the truth is that between independence and the middle of the nineteenth century at the very least, Anglo-American cultural relations were never other than tense. The best evidence is the least remarked: what one of its most recent and authoritative historians has called "A Forgotten Conflict" (Hickey 1990). Conventional accounts of the causes of the War of 1812 between Britain and America focus on the damage to America's trading economy occasioned by the British

Orders in Council – designed to prevent neutral countries from trading with Napoleonic Europe – the impressment of British (and sometimes American) seamen from American vessels to serve in the British Navy, and American hopes of absorbing Canada. But it is hard to believe that these reasons alone are enough to explain the decision by the two countries, less than a generation after the conclusion of the original Revolution, to descend once again into the violence and anarchy of war. Rather, looked at from the widest of perspectives, the War of 1812 may be seen as in essence a cultural war. Such a view is perhaps implicit in Hickey's description of the war as an event which "reinforced the powerful undercurrent of Anglophobia that had been present in American culture since the Revolution" (Hickey 1990: 3). Hickey is certain that the Republican party at least saw the conflict as one "that would vindicate American sovereignty and preserve republican institutions by demonstrating to people both at home and abroad that the United States could uphold its rights" (Hickey 1990: 47). The war, that is, Hickey insists, had a powerful ideological dimension. The question that needs to be asked, however, is in what sense had American ideology, and America's republican institutions, been challenged or threatened in the years leading up to 1812? The answer is in the cultural war involving Britain and America that had been running since America's triumph in the Revolution. Seen in this context, the War of 1812 was but the most powerful of symbolic expressions of the depth to which Anglo-American cultural relations had sunk; the war emerged out of a generalised sense of mutual dislike and hostility which had been most widely focused, disseminated, and debated in cultural terms. The burning of the American Capitol in Washington by British troops in 1814 may not have been seen at the time as an attempt to punish the Americans for their temerity in "killing" George III in the Declaration of Independence, but in symbolic terms that is what it probably meant.

That the suggested interpretation of the ultimate *casus belli* of the War of 1812 is not to be dismissed as entirely fanciful is indicated by the views of at least one contemporary American writer. In *The Sketch Book of Geoffrey Crayon, Gent.* (1819), Washington Irving included an essay entitled "English Writers on America". Irving's opening sentence indicates in the clearest possible terms what his subject is: "It is with feelings of deep regret that I observe the literary animosity daily growing up between England and America" (Irving 1819: 57). In the body of the essay, Irving's focus is on British travellers' accounts of America and the damaging consequences of their prejudicial, narrow-minded, and purblind writings. He is disdainful and dismissive of the authors in question: "it has been left to the broken-down tradesman, the scheming adventurer, the wandering mechanic, the Manchester and Birmingham agent to be [England's] oracles respecting America" (Irving 1812: 58). But his topic is less the inaccuracies, misrepresentations, and biases of these English writers – "this irksome and hackneyed topic" as he calls it – than the dangers inherent in American over-reactions to such attacks. (Irving 1812: 60). Two countries with so much in common could end up permanently divided. Friendship will be replaced by "rivalship and irritated hostility". And in dwelling on this point Irving seems to have the War of 1812 in mind:

> Every one knows the all-pervading influence of literature at the present day, and how much the opinions and passions of mankind are under its control. The mere contests of the sword are temporary; their wounds are but in the flesh, and it is the pride of the generous to forgive and forget them; but the slanders of the pen pierce to the heart; they rankle longest in the noblest spirits; they dwell ever present in the mind, and render it morbidly sensitive to the most trifling collision. It is but seldom that any one overt act produces hostilities between two nations; there exists, most commonly, a previous jealousy and ill-will; a predisposition to take offence. Trace these to their cause, and how often will they be found to originate in the mischievous effusions of mercenary writers; who, secure in their closets, and for ignominious bread, concoct and circulate the venom that is to inflame the generous and the brave. (Irving 1812: 61)

Reading such a passage, and attending to the closing sentences in particular, one can hardly not recognise that the example in Irving's mind of the path to war he is describing is indeed the War of 1812. The "mercenary writers" are those he has just been describing – the English travellers in America. And in the second paragraph following this one, he actually refers to "the late war" suggesting there were "generous spirits" in America who even then "kept alive the sparks of future friendship" (Irving 1819: 62).

Whatever its ultimate cause, the War of 1812 solved nothing. If anything, it served only to exacerbate the existing bitterness in Anglo-American social and cultural relationships. Neither side had much to feel good about at the war's conclusion. If the British derived satisfaction from the destruction of the Capitol, American pride and self-esteem were firmly re-established by Andrew Jackson's shattering defeat of the vaunted British army at the Battle of New Orleans. The War of 1812 was formally over before that battle even took place. But the cultural war out of which it arose still had decades to run.

1

What then was the precise nature of the cultural animosity which characterised Anglo-American relations in the early decades of the new republic? In terms of literary history the phenomenon in question has traditionally been called the "literary quarrel". It broke out within a few years of the conclusion of the American Revolution. It reached boiling point in the first three decades of the nineteenth century, but simmered away for quite a time after that. From the beginning, Scotland and Scottish writers played a crucial part in this literary conflict. For example, the most famous of shots fired in the course of the war had a Scottish source. In 1820 the little question that Sydney Smith asked in the mighty *Edinburgh Review* – a journal, ironically enough, nowhere attended to with greater respect and care than in the United States – "Who reads an American book?" echoes as loudly round America as the shot fired at Lexington is supposed to have echoed around the world (*Edinburgh Review* 1820: 33: 79). So much so that in 1824 the *Edinburgh Review* felt obliged to defend itself, as deftly as possible, from the American hostility that Smith's remark had helped to stir up. The American reaction was such, wrote the *Review,* that

We really thought at one time they would have fitted out an armament against the Edinburgh and Quarterly Reviews, and burnt down Mr Murray's and Mr Constable's shops, as we did the American Capitol. We, however, remember no other anti-American crime of which we were guilty, than a preference of Shakespeare and Milton over Joel Barlow and Timothy Dwight. (1824: 432)

This quotation from the *Edinburgh Review* implies that the literary quarrel centred around British criticisms of American literature. Such criticisms, often still more condescending and dismissive in tone, were indeed an important factor in the cultural situation, and they were destined to go on appearing to the end of the nineteenth century and beyond. (Oscar Wilde, for example, in A *Woman of No Importance,* must have been sure that his throwaway definition of American dry goods as American novels would be good for a laugh.) But in fact the quarrel had much wider ramifications than merely literary criticism.

Most important of all, as a source of the smouldering ill-feeling between Britain and America, exactly as Irving suggested, were the descriptive accounts published by a series of British travellers in America. Inevitably, the commentaries of these travellers extended out into considerations of the entire range of American manners and customs, and especially of America's distinctive social and political arrangements and institutions. In the end the literary quarrel was about the very nature of American society itself rather than about individual works which could be seen as representative of American culture. Ultimately it was America itself which was on trial in the literary quarrel. Whatever the apparent subject, this was the underlying reality, and it is this that explains the virulence of the exchanges between the two countries. Perhaps in the early nineteenth century such conflict between Britain and America was inevitable. If the new American society and its republican institutions had received an entirely favourable press that would have implied the Old World's acceptance of its own limitations and shortcomings. The United States of America had come into being through a deliberate breaking away from Britain and Europe. If the consequences were only good, the implied criticism of all of established European society was only too clear. Such a conclusion could only have been repugnant to anyone of conservative feelings in Britain or elsewhere in Europe. For anyone who believed that the traditional social and political arrangements of the Old World represented an admirable and defensible ideal, the new American model had to be repudiated. But there were boastful transatlantic voices more than willing to trumpet their own superiority over things British and European, in social and political terms above all. Inevitably then, the cultural wars between Britain and America were from their outset inextricably caught up in the ideological patterns of internal British politics.

In this context, one needs to keep in mind the historical reality that the decades in the early nineteenth century when the quarrel between Britain and America raged most violently were ones in which counter-revolutionary forces were in the ascendant in Britain. The French Revolution and its aftermath, and the long drawn-out war with

France, had produced a situation in which even the idea of change in any aspect of British society and its institutions had been made to appear unacceptably unpatriotic. Reform was delayed for an entire generation. However, after 1815 and the defeat of Napoleon, one apparently successful revolutionary society survived: the USA. Thus, when the pressure for change and the reform of Britain's political institutions began to re-emerge in the post-war period, America became an important battleground. If the American experiment could be portrayed as a success, then the case for reform elsewhere could be strengthened; if on the other hand the new America could be shown to be inferior to Europe on every count, then the position of *anciens régimes* everywhere was reinforced.

The literary quarrel between Britain and America thus always carried a powerful ideological dimension. Neutrality was not an option. Everything depended on the critic's or commentator's or observer's own political persuasion. This is why the *Edinburgh Review,* with its consistent support of more liberal, Whig principles, and despite all the furore occasioned by Sydney Smith's question, remained at bottom well-disposed towards America and its emerging culture. The *Quarterly Review* and *Blackwood's Magazine,* on the other hand, fully committed to conservative, Tory values, were long deeply hostile to everything American. The books of British travellers in America – like the reviews of their works appearing in the major, widely-read journals – simply reflect the same defining political divide. If the traveller was broadly sympathetic to the cause of reform in Great Britain – like George Birkbeck or James Stuart (Dugald Stewart's grandson) – then his account of America tended to be largely favourable. If there were problems they were occasioned by the newness of the country; a new kind of society was still in the process of being forged. For the moment, practical activities had to take precedence over cultural ones; the achievements of American culture exist in the future rather than the past; politics, commerce and material development have so far necessarily absorbed the American genius. (A cultural version of the Scottish Enlightenment's favourite stadial view of history seems to underline all these accounts.) But Britain and Europe should welcome the dawning of this new, democratic, western civilisation.

If, on the other hand, the British traveller were a Tory, committed to a "Church and King" vision of society, and hostile to any major change in Britain's political institutions, then their account of republican America emerged largely as an essay in detraction and abuse. If for liberal opinion in Britain the United States was an example of how society could flourish after revolutionary change, for those of a conservative frame of mind the same country was a dire warning of the costs of precisely such radical change. Hence hostile Tory travellers such as Mrs Trollope, Basil Hall and Thomas Hamilton (brother of the philosopher William Hamilton) return again and again to the same topics, launching identical attacks: American roads and inns are deplorable; American servants do not know their place; American manners in eating, drinking, and, worst of all, spitting, are uncivilised; American religion, lacking an established church, is unpredictable and various; American law and politics are corrupt; American newspapers are libellous. These defects are the sum-total and true consequences of America's "democratic experiment".

To illustrate just how bitter and divisive the issue of America could be – and could be seen to be – let me quote a single passage from *Blackwood's Magazine*. The date is 1832 and the controversy over Britain's first Reform Bill is at its height:

We therefore hope that all true Britons hate American manners, and, to the full extent of their influence, the American people. They must either do that, or hate their own manners, and themselves; for manners are not matters of indifference, but of mighty importance to the whole moral and intellectual character. "Manners maketh man" is a wise old adage; and it is painful to see what they have made of the Americans. (1832: 93)

Even if we regard *Blackwood's* as representing no more than a kind of lunatic fringe – unjustly I suspect – the general context of the literary quarrel in the first half of the nineteenth century was clearly not one in which America's developing literary culture was likely to get an objective hearing. Too much was at stake – in social, political, and even religious terms – for this to be possible.

2

As Smith's "Who reads an American book?" indicates, America's possession – or lack – of a viable literary culture became a central issue of the literary quarrel. For European countries, a national culture, and particularly a national literary culture, was crucial to national identity. A country without a defining national literature was not really a country at all. Recognising this, the proponents of anti-American feeling in nineteenth-century Britain seized every opportunity to belittle and condemn American writers; in so doing they were attempting to sustain the view that America was at best a nation of uncultured shopkeepers. Americans, on the other hand, from the earliest years of the new republic, began to call for the creation of a national American literature. The emergence of such a literature would help to refute the Old World's critics.

Of course the call was a quixotic one. The creation of any national literature is an evolutionary process. And for American writers there was the additional problem of the unavoidable and dominating existence of English literature. Writing in the same language, how could they be other than subservient to English models and forms? As Irving put it in 1819: "We are a young people, necessarily an imitative one, and must take our examples and models in a great degree, from the existing nations of Europe" (Irving 1819: 64). Irving is alluding to a wider range of examples and models than purely literary ones, but, as his own writing makes clear, the relevance to literature is clear. A few years later, James Fenimore Cooper made the same point quite explicitly: "It is quite obvious that, as far as tastes and forms alone are concerned, the Literature of England and that of America must be fashioned after the same models [...]" (Cooper [1830] 1991: 342). But if the new American literature was to be so closely modelled on English literature how was its individual, national identity to emerge? Cooper's answer was in terms of the new political ideology that American literature would promote. But if the existing forms of English literature reflected at bottom the structures and manners and values of English society, it was difficult to see how, employing such models, a recognizably American national literature could emerge. It was precisely here that the Scottish literary paradigm became important. For a time in the early nineteenth century some American critics and commentators, at least, saw contemporary Scottish literature as pointing the way forward to the creation of a truly national American literature.

Just how widespread this recognition of the example of Scottish literature actually was in America may be open to question, but general American appreciation and admiration of eighteenth-century and early nineteenth-century Scottish writing is not. Scottish literary romanticism, from Allan Ramsay to Walter Scott, was received as enthusiastically in America as in any other part of the Western world. Scholars today readily acknowledge that colonial, Revolutionary, and post-Revolutionary America was exceptionally receptive to the writers and thinkers of the Scottish Enlightenment. But this American receptiveness to Scottish philosophical, intellectual, and educational traditions was matched by a parallel enthusiasm for Scottish literary productions. Ramsay's *The Gentle Shepherd,* Home's *Douglas,* Beattie's *The Minstrel,* Macpherson's *Ossian,* the poetry of Burns and Campbell, Scottish ballad and song, and above all Scott's poetry and Waverley Novels, all found a large and receptive audience in America.[1]

In relation to the demands for a national American literature, however, it was not simply the successful emergence of Scottish literature that was in question, but also the speed with which that success had been achieved. In 1814, an article on American literature, in the Philadelphia magazine *Port Folio,* cited Scotland's literary achievement as a perfect example of how a national literature could develop quite suddenly:

> [...] until within little more than the last fifty years, Scotland had scarcely a poet or a dramatic writer, to balance against Chaucer, Spenser, Shakespeare, Jonson, Cowley, Milton, Dryden, Pope, and twenty others, produced in England, except Allan Ramsay, a name that would hardly have risen to notice, if it had belonged to the other part of the Island. Yet, since that time, Scotland has produced its full quota of literary genius. In a very dignified species of composition, history, it is indeed unrivalled; and at the present day, the names of Campbell and Scott, stand higher on the list of poets, than any of their cotemporaries in England. (1814: 5–8)

The historical and critical limitations of such an account are not the point. What matters is the emphasis on the perceived status of Scottish literature and its implications for a future American literature. If the Scots could pull it off, why not the Americans? A few years later, an article in Constable's *Edinburgh Magazine* (formerly the *Scots Magazine),* reprinted in America in the *Analectic Magazine,* similarly

---

[1] For a widely ranging account of the reception of Scottish literary romanticism in America see Chapters 5 and 6 ('Land of Romance' and 'Classic Ground') in my *Scotland and America, 1750–1835.*

saw in the contemporary triumph of Scottish literature a positive augury for future American success:

> England and America are both at this moment supplied, in great measure, with a literature of Scottish manufacture. We should not be much surprised were we to live to see the day when we, in our turn shall be gaping for new novels and poems from the other side of the Atlantic, and when, in the silence of our own bards and romancers, we shall have Ladies of the Lake from Ontario, and Tales of my Landlord from Goose-creek, as a counterpart to those from Gandercleugh. For our part, we have no kind of aversion to the augury; and we cannot but regard it as a most paltry and contemptible littleness, quite unworthy of the material majesty of England, not to look with an eye of love and delight upon all that is promising in the rising genius of America. (1820: 342–43)

Developing this allusion to the continuing Anglo-American literary quarrel, the article goes on to imply a kind of Scottish-American cultural togetherness in confronting English arrogance and prejudice. The Scots had to fight for cultural recognition – but the fight has been won. Now it is America's turn, but the outcome will be the same: "The literary glory of America is yet to come; but we doubt not that it is coming" (1820: 342–43).

In the references to Ladies of the Lake from Ontario and Tales of my Landlord from Goose-creek there is a hint of how precisely American writers might choose to emulate their Scottish contemporaries. Scottish literature had defined itself by focusing on Scottish scenes and landscapes, on Scottish customs and manners, on Scottish history and traditions and characters. American literature should do likewise. John Neal, an expatriate American who contributed a series of articles – in which he pretended to be British – on America's literary culture to *Blackwood's Magazine* in the mid-1820s, made this point quite explicitly. For Neal, the problem with American literature was that it was not American enough; and the reason for that was simply that "the writers of America will persist in writing after British models" (Neal, 1825: 324). Reviewing Cooper's novel *Lionel Lincoln* (1825), which Cooper himself regarded as the first of a planned series of national romances, Neal is highly critical, but still allows the book one praiseworthy dimension:

> It is not, as ninety-nine out of a hundred, of all the American stories are, a thing of this country [i.e. Britain] – a British book tossed up, anew; worked over, afresh; and sent back, with a new title-page. (Neal 1825: 323)

Neal summed up his view thus: "It is American books that are wanted of America; not English books [...] books, which, whatever may be their faults, are decidedly, if not altogether, *American*" (Neal 1825: 321). A few years earlier, another American reviewer had alluded to Scott's use of Scottish scenes and landscapes as a way of pointing out to American writers the potential native material they had available:

And as to the resources, which a poet might find for description of natural scenery, he whose mind recurs, – as whose does not when poetical description is named, – to the haunt of the northern muse, [...] must remember that compared with some of ours, Scottish rivers are but brooks, and Scottish forests mere thickets. (*North American Review* 1821: 484)

For Neal too, it is Scott above all who is the writer pointing the way forward for a national American literature. In relation to Cooper, he makes the point explicit: "[*The Spy*] was, at least, an approach to what we desire – a plain, real, hearty, North American story; a story, which, if we could have our way, should be altogether American – peculiarly and exclusively so, throughout; as much American to say all, in a word, as the Scotch Novels are Scotch [...]" (Neal 1825: 325). Neal, it is clear, was happy to describe Cooper as the "Sir Walter Scott of America."

Another Scottish work which can be seen as signalling the way forward for a national American literature was Thomas Campbell's poem "Gertrude of Wyoming" (1809). Campbell, a lifelong friend and admirer of the United States – in 1840 he declared "if I were not a Scotsman, I should like to be an American" – was widely read and admired in America (see Beattie ed. 1850: 499). "Gertrude of Wyoming", with its specific Pennsylvanian setting and semi-historical story of the American frontier, would have been enough to guarantee his American popularity. But the poem had an additional significance for America's literary culture. Writing a poem with an American setting and an American story, Campbell was highlighting a crucial difference between the New World and the Old – the comparative absence of literary and romantic associations in the New – but also indicating how American writers could begin to supply such a deficiency. In fact, just as Scott's pen was beginning to open up the Scottish Highlands, so Campbell's poem led Americans to seek out and experience its local setting. A Scots author can be seen as once again heralding the way forward for the creation of a national American literature.

Inevitably, however, it was the immensely popular Scott who most clearly indicated to Americans the distinctively national path to literary glory. Typical recognition of Scott's role appeared in an address by Rufus Choate, lawyer and statesman, delivered in Salem in 1833. The sub-title to Choate's speech shows the direction of his thinking with perfect clarity: "The Importance of Illustrating New England History by a Series of Romances like the Waverley Novels". Choate imagined a genius like Scott doing for New England what Scott had done for Scotland:

He would wish to see him begin with the landing of the Pilgrims, and pass down to the War of Independence, from one epoch and one generation to another, like Old Mortality among the graves of the unforgotten faithful, wiping the dust from the urns of our fathers, gathering up whatever of illustrious achievement, of heroic suffering, of unwavering faith, their history commemorates, and weaving it all into an immortal and noble national literature.

Beside the conventional, austere histories of a New England, Choate would like to see

[...] a thousand neat duodecimos of the size of "Ivanhoe", "Kenilworth", and "Mannion", all full of pictures of our natural beauty and grandeur, the still richer pictures of our society and manners, the lights and shadows of our life, full of touching incidents, generous sentiments, just thoughts, beaming images, such as are scattered over everything which Scott has written, as thick as stars on the brow of night. (Choate 1902: 202)

Romances such as the Waverley Novels, Choate argues, supply the deficiencies of standard histories by speaking directly to the heart and imagination of the reader. A series of North American or New England Waverley Novels would present a series of pictures "so full, so vivid, so true, so instructive, so moving, that they would grave themselves upon the memory and dwell in the hearts of our whole people forever". An outcome, Choate concludes, which would help to strengthen America's sense of national identity (Choate 1902: 209–22). Choate's recognition of the connections between Scott's literary achievement, Scotland's national identity, and America's need to acquire an enhanced sense of nationhood through a similar cultural medium, is particularly precise. But given the general American receptiveness to Scottish literary romanticism in the early nineteenth century, and the nation-wide enthusiasm for the Waverley Novels in particular, one may assume that there were many others who saw in Scotland's literary success a potential paradigm for American writers to follow. Rejecting imitation of standard English models, Scott and his predecessors, employing resources both old and new, had produced exactly what America was desperately in search of – a national literature. Where Scotland had led, why should not America follow?

3

In fact the attempt was made. Back in 1932, in one of the earliest volumes of *American Literature,* G. Harrison Orians published an article entitled "The Romance Ferment after Waverley", in which he describes the flood of American romances in the 1820s and 1830s more or less modelled on the Waverley Novels. The vast majority of these works of course now remain, no doubt justifiably, totally unread. From the beginning, doubts were expressed about the availability within America of the kind of material necessary for the success of the historical romance. And such views would soon feed into the more general opinion – shared even by major figures such as Cooper, Hawthorne and James – that the experience of New World America provided less in the way of material for the novelist's imagination to work upon than did the long-established societies of the Old World.

But if the romance ferment soon died down, the Scottish contribution to the creation of a national American literature was nonetheless decisive. The novelist who, whatever his deficiencies, was everywhere seen as offering readers an imaginative experience that was both new and distinctively American – and whose work therefore went a long way towards the creation of the loudly-demanded national American literature – was none other than the American Scott, James Fenimore Cooper. However much Cooper objected to this nickname, it was not without justification. In the Leatherstocking series of novels, Cooper created one of America's most powerful and enduring myths. But in his handling of the series' central theme – the clash between primitivism and civilisation, between frontier and established society, between settlers and native Americans – there is an obvious link with Scott's exploration of the contrast between the way of life, the customs and manners of the Scottish Highlands, and those of Lowland Scotland and England. Scott's Highland line becomes Cooper's frontier. And Cooper even seems to share Scott's ambivalence over the two conflicting ways of life and the value systems he describes. Like Scott, Cooper is intellectually a conservative, committed to the civilising values of law and order, but he too is drawn imaginatively to another, freer, more individual world, outside the constraints of modern, civilised society. Cooper saw Scott as a rival to be outdone; but it is clear that Scott helped Cooper to see what his true subjects were. In this sense at least, it was ultimately the example of Scottish literature that contributed most to the creation of a truly national American literature.

Bibliography

Analectic Magazine [New Series 1]. 1820.

Beattie, William (ed.) 1850. *Life and Letters of Thomas Campbell*. New York: II.

Neal, John. 1825. *Blackwood's Magazine* 18: 321–24.

Blackwood's Magazine. 1832. 32.

Choate, Rufus. 1902. "The Romance of New England History" in *Old South Leaflets V*. Boston.

Cooper, James Fenimore. [1830] 1991. *Notions of the Americans: Picked up by a Travelling Bachelor*. Albany: State University of New York Press.

Edinburgh Review. 1820. 33.

Edinburgh Review. 1824. 40.

Hickey, Donald R. 1990. *The War of 1812, A Forgotten Conflict*. Urbana and Chicago: University of Illinois Press.

Irving, Washington. 1812. *The Sketch Book of Geoffrey Crayon, Gent*. New York: Doubleday & Company. n.d.

North American Review. 1821. 12.

Port Folio [3rd Series, 4]. 1820.

Reviewing America: Francis Jeffrey, *The Edinburgh Review* and the United States

Pam Perkins

In the early nineteenth century, *The Edinburgh Review* evinced political sympathy for the American republic, though sometimes hostility towards American language and literature. A complicated exchange about American culture with the *Review*'s rival *Blackwood's Magazine* ensued through which competing British political ideologies were engaged. Eventually visiting America, the editor of the *Edinburgh Review*, Francis Jeffrey had a very strong sense of being an alien, feelings which Jeffrey records in his American journal. These experiences counterpoint sympathetic writing about America in the *Review* which is revealed, then, to be much more a lens through which the policies of the British Tory administration are criticised, rather than full-blown engagement with American culture.
Keywords: Francis Jeffrey; *Edinburgh Review*; Anglo-American War of 1812; Henry Brougham; *Blackwood's Magazine*; "Franklin James"; James Madison; James Monroe.

When Francis Jeffrey travelled to America in 1813, he did so strictly as a private citizen: he was making the journey in order to marry Charlotte Wilkes, an American woman he had met a few years before while she was accompanying her aunt and uncle on a journey through Scotland. Nor did he use his travels as the basis of any published account of the American landscape or people, as did so many British visitors to the United States in the last years of the eighteenth century and the first decades of the nineteenth. On the contrary, as Jeffrey's friend and biographer Henry Cockburn noted rather sadly, "his journal, though minute, records nothing, even in his favourite lines of reflection and speculation that would now interest others" (Cockburn 1852: 1: 226). Yet Jeffrey's travels, no matter how resolutely private they remained, were touched by some major public events. He was, after all, visiting a country at war with his own, thereby running a small but very real risk of being interned as an enemy alien, a point emphasised when his departure from the United States was impeded by his difficulties in obtaining the necessary papers. Writing in 1941, William Charvat, the author of the one significant twentieth-century account of Jeffrey's visit to America, comments that "obtuse officials [in New York] considered him an enemy alien, subject to internment in what would now be called a concentration camp" (Charvat 1941:

317). Despite the glaring infelicity of terminology – whatever Jeffrey faced would most emphatically not now be called a "concentration camp" – Charvat's comments suggest the very real problems Jeffrey might have encountered. The result, however, was not internment or even minor harassment, but rather invitations to meet the President and the Secretary of State, James Madison and James Monroe, both in private and at a state dinner. Moreover, as Jeffrey noted rather bemusedly in his journal, both men debated British policy with him, evidently considering the views of the editor of *The Edinburgh Review* a matter of real interest in the American political world. Even if Cockburn thought the journal offered little to engage later readers, the journey itself is something more than a curious literary footnote, offering as it does a glimpse not only of the way in which an influential Scottish literary figure saw America, but also, more indirectly, an indication of the role played by America in the world of early nineteenth-century Scottish letters.

There has been a great deal of work done on various aspects of Scottish-American cultural relations in the eighteenth and nineteenth centuries. As Henry May (1976) has shown, key aspects of American revolutionary thought are indebted to the Scottish philosophical tradition; Andrew Hook (1975), focusing more specifically on literary connections, has demonstrated both the influence and the popularity of Scottish writers in the revolutionary and early Republican eras. Likewise, work by Robert Crawford (1992; see especially chapter three) and, most recently, Susan Manning (2002), has explored the ways in which the intellectual worlds of the two countries were linked on levels ranging from the structure of their educational systems to a shared literary fascination with concepts of union and fragmentation. Even if one focuses simply on the writing about the United States that appears in the major Scottish periodicals of the early nineteenth century – that is to say, *Blackwood's* and *The Edinburgh Review* – the role of the country and its culture in the Scottish literary imagination is both obvious and complex. Jeffrey's fascination with America, if one judges by his published articles, long predated his travels there, although one could argue that he was much more interested in debating ideas about the country than he was in actually seeing it for himself, as he made the journey only with considerable reluctance and only when it became apparent that his marriage would be indefinitely delayed if he waited for Charlotte Wilkes to return to Europe. (Cockburn described the journey as one of "the greatest achievements of love" given Jeffrey's "nervous horror" of "all watery adventures" [Cockburn 1852: 1: 215].) Yet even if that were the case, Jeffrey would not have been particularly unusual: what one finds in much of the periodical writing is a sense that the United States is of interest to the Scottish writers observing it mainly insofar as it offers them a way of exploring their own cultural and political situation.

This idea that the views on America by periodical writers in general – and Jeffrey in particular – were more a reflection of the politics of the magazine than of any real knowledge of or engagement with the United States was also expressed by at least some writers of the day. The essayist Anne Grant, for one, claimed to hope that the *Review* would ignore her 1808 *Memoirs of an American Lady*, since she could have no expectation of a warm reception in it; given the reviewers' "love of Jefferson", she wrote in a letter to a friend, she feared that only "cruelty" would lead them to say anything at all about a book written from a perspective so different from their own (Grant 1808: f. 152–152v). A decade later, a young American visitor – apparently in Edinburgh as a medical student – was even more critical of the perspective that Jeffrey and the *Review* took on American subjects: he attacks the "Edinburgh reviewers", singling out Jeffrey for particular abuse, because of "[t]heir avowed enmity to our glorious country", which, he adds with lofty disapproval, "makes their pretensions to a love of freedom, look rather suspicious". Worse, he concludes, their opinions are formed in "profound ignorance" of America and shaped by the inevitable biases of men who are "little better than deists" (Didier 1822: 78–79). Initially, this complaint about Scottish "ignorance" of America might seem a little odd, given that it is made specifically in context of what *The Edinburgh Review* had chosen to publish on the subject. Even leaving aside Jeffrey's relatively brief visit to the country – by then some years in the past – and what might be presumed to be the enlightenment on the subject he could gain from his American-born wife, the fact remains that all of the *Review*'s writing on America was sparked by books or pamphlets on the subject, none of which, the writer, Franklin James Didier apparently assumes, would be sufficient to dent that "ignorance" about the country. The complaint, in other words, might seem better directed against the books being reviewed than the reviewers. Yet this assumption of ignorance in fact fits neatly with Grant's complaints about the limitations of the reviewers: however much they read about America, Didier implies, they see only a reflection of their own political and cultural concerns.

Of course, very much the same could be said about the reading practices of Didier himself, since in advancing his Tory arguments against *The Edinburgh Review* by denouncing its "enmity" to the United States, he was simply echoing the complaints of the *Blackwood's* reviewers, whose cultural politics were evidently far more in line with his own than those of the *Edinburgh*. His complaint about *The Edinburgh Review*'s deism is in fact lifted almost directly from John Gibson Lockhart's *Peter's Letters to his Kinsfolk*, Didier's main literary model. Perhaps even more to the point, Didier would have had to overlook a great deal of what the *Review* had actually published on the subject in the years during and prior to his stay in Edinburgh. As early as 1806, a review by Jeffrey of *The War in Disguise, or the Frauds of Neutral Flags*, suggests the willingness of *The Edinburgh Review* to give at least a moderately sympathetic ear to American grievances. Six years later, one finds much more than moderate sympathy in a lengthy article by Henry Brougham, published in the lead-up to the War of 1812, in which Brougham analyses one of the major causes of British hostility, the claims that American ships were violating the standards of neutrality in their dealings with France. The review is both trenchant in its criticism of English politics and warm in its interest in the American position. Those who say, Brougham argues, that the English have a right to protest American trade with France must also

be ready to maintain [...] that we have a just right to quarrel with an unoffending people, for the sake of plundering their ships and ransacking their warehouses. Now, England has sometimes swerved from the only path which a great nation can ever pursue, consistently with its honour and character. She has carried on the slave-trade, and defended it because it was lucrative. She has seized the property of her neighbours, while they confided in the subsisting relations of peace. She has, on some pleas of state-necessity, burnt the capital of a friendly state, in order to obtain possession of its warlike resources. But, to this period of time, she has never laid it down openly as a maxim, that all right, and all public law, is at an end – that interest alone is her guide – and that she has a title to despise all principles – to make a mock of every thing like justice among nations, as often as she can make a profit by such monstrous deeds of perfidy and violence [...]. Surely, if an American war is so dear to our rulers [...] they may find some less revolting pretext on which to found their measure. (Brougham 1812: 308–9)

Even if the article did not prove quite as controversial as the notorious 1808 review of Don Cevellos' commentary on the Peninsular War – which provoked the indignant exodus of *The Edinburgh Review*'s more conservative readers and contributors, including Sir Walter Scott – its pro-American temperature nonetheless runs very high, as it uses its loudly proclaimed sympathy with American wrongs to mark its opposition to British government policy. One can argue, easily enough, that the focus here is more on the failings of the Tory ministry than on the wrongs endured by the Americans, but even so, such polemic does undercut claims of any sort of consistent or vehement "enmity" towards America on the part of the *Review*.

That said, such sympathy with American political wrongs does not lead to a uniformly warm response to all matters connected with the United States, and one would find at least some grounds for Didier's views on Jeffrey and *The Edinburgh Review* by turning from the political articles to more literary topics. The vehemently sceptical tone that the *Review* took towards British policy during both the Peninsular War and the War of 1812 was not matched by any equivalent scepticism about the value of British culture, and the writing by Jeffrey and others in the *Review* on American literature would not have given much comfort to American readers seeking European validation of their cultural life as well as recognition of their political grievances. As early as 1803, in the *Review*'s second volume, Brougham had proclaimed with weary disdain that "Providence has denied" the "eloquence and power of fine writing" to Americans, who fall back instead on "language of the ludicrously sentimental class" even in their scientific writing (Brougham 1803: 353). A few years later, in an article probably by Macvey Napier, the *Review* casually announced that if all American writing, excepting only that of Benjamin Franklin,

were obliterated from the records of learning there would [...] be no positive diminution, either of the useful or the agreeable. The destruction of her whole literature would not occasion so much regret as we feel for the loss of a few leaves from an antient classic (Napier[?] 1810: 446; in the doubt about attribution I am following the *Wellesley Index*).

Nor was Jeffrey himself particularly sympathetic to American claims to culture, however ardently his magazine defended the country's political actions. He considered the fact that Americans had to wait until 1806 for the publication of the collected works of Franklin, "their only philosopher," a clear indication of "the singular want of literary enterprise or activity" in the United States (Jeffrey 1806: 327). His scornful account of American neglect of Franklin was matched by amusement at the sorts of writing that the United States was producing; in a review of Joel Barlow's very self consciously grandiose attempt to create a national epic in *The Columbiad*, Jeffrey did not hesitate to read signs of general cultural failure into the lapses of an individual poet and poem. He devotes a large part of the review to elaborating on his mocking contention that the poem is "the first [...] considerable work composed in the American tongue," a language that he reports is to English what "the Italian is [to] Latin" (Jeffrey 1809: 28). Any respect for the American "language" implied in that simile soon vanishes, however, as Jeffrey turns the body of the review into an attack on what he clearly saw as American literary infelicities. "These republican literati" he remarks, "seem to make it a point of conscience to have no aristocratical distinctions – even in their vocabulary. They think one word just as good as another" (Jeffrey 1809: 29).

This mockery of American "language" is of particular interest, given the anxiety of later eighteenth-century Scots about their own relationship to English, an anxiety marked by their desperate attempts to purge their written and spoken English of "Scotticisms". Of course, this then recent history of Scottish worries about language, which has been well documented by Robert Crawford, among others, gives a markedly ironic twist (probably unintended) to Jeffrey's magisterial dismissal of Americanisms. As a young man, Jeffrey was deeply anxious about his own command of standard English; Cockburn cites a letter that he wrote a friend during his one unhappy year at Oxford, in which he proclaims "[t]he only part of a Scotchman I mean to abandon, is the language; and language is all I expect to learn in England" (Cockburn 1852: 1: 46). Apparently, he was not entirely successful in this goal; in one of the better known anecdotes of Jeffrey, Thomas Carlyle quotes Lord Braxfield as saying, after Jeffrey's return to Scotland, that "the laddie has clean tint his Scotch, and found nae English" (Carlyle 1997: 375). Yet even if one does choose to read Jeffrey's evisceration of Barlow's poem as containing evidence – and perhaps even some submerged acknowledgement – of parallels between Scots and Americans as linguistic outsiders attempting to make a place for themselves in the realms of English high culture, there is no doubt that the review is, even more plainly, establishing the Scottish reviewer as the arbiter of proper English style and manner, with the cool evaluation of Barlow's tonal and stylistic failings forming a more or less explicit measure of Jeffrey's command of English literary culture. If political sympathy for America is a measure of *The Edinburgh Review*'s loudly proclaimed stance of Whiggish opposition to British government policies, the *Review*'s treatment of American cultural life simultaneously helps to establish its Scottish writers as arbiters of the English literary standards against which the previous generation of Scottish literati had so carefully measured their own prose style.

What all this suggests is the extent to which *The Edinburgh Review*, as Grant and Didier imply, did in fact use the United States as a way of demarcating its position in specifically British debates. Its political support for America signals its opposition to government policy, while its hauteur about American culture marks its own attempts to distance itself from literary or linguistic provincialism. Yet contrary to what Didier implies as he uses *Peter's Letters* and John Gibson Lockhart as a stick with which to beat Jeffrey, the *Review* was by no means alone in using America in this way. *Blackwood's*, while inverting the *Review*'s perspectives, mirrored exactly its practices. The fact that Jeffrey was presumed to dislike American literature was enough to make *Blackwood's*, in 1825, advertise its own superior aesthetic judgement by preening itself on being "the first in this country who did justice to the literary merits of the citizens of the United States". As the writer then goes on to proclaim, even if the magazine's "extreme good-nature" had led it to overrate some of that literature, at least it had "never, like many others, Mr Jeffrey, for example, attempted to undervalue genius and originality" ("Travelling" 1825: 422). Such self promotion notwithstanding, there is no question that *Blackwood's* was more than happy to abuse American learning and culture in other contexts: indeed, a long two-part article on American education that had appeared six years before concludes with a near plagiarism of *The Edinburgh Review*'s 1810 dismissal of Thomas Ashe. According to the *Blackwood's* reviewer, Franklin is the only American "philosopher whose discoveries have been of much importance to mankind; and if the whole stock of their literature were set on fire to morrow, no scholar would feel the loss" ("Means of

Education" 1819: 646). This *ad hominem* attack on Jeffrey for his treatment of American literature emphasises the degree to which views of America are part of the Scottish periodicals' internecine struggles for cultural authority.

Yet this was not simply a case of Scottish writers ingeniously transforming their writing about the United States into a way of talking about themselves. *The Edinburgh Review*, in particular, had an international audience, and Americans both read and responded to what Jeffrey and his fellow writers had to say about them. The growing phenomenon of literary celebrity meant that early nineteenth-century visitors to Scotland were eager to meet the famous writers of the day, and while there is no question that Walter Scott was the major attraction for literary-minded tourists in Edinburgh during the opening decades of the nineteenth century, Jeffrey also caught the eye of curious visitors. These literary tourists were not only American: accounts of Jeffrey – and Scott – appear in journals kept by, for example, an aristocratic Pole (see McLeod 2004), a Frenchman (see Pichot 1825), and, of course, in John Gibson Lockhart's *Peter's Letters*, the narrative of a fictional Welshman. Yet there is no question that American visitors assumed that readers back home would be interested in Jeffrey. A Professor Garscombe, for example, who visited Edinburgh in 1819, noted that Jeffrey is "so much of the public man, and has been so much talked of [in America], it seems scarcely necessary" to describe him. Even so, Garscombe took the trouble to describe him at length, mentioning, among other things, Jeffrey's physical appearance, his "fullness and readiness of thought," his prolific work in a range of fields, and his New York-born wife (Garscombe 1825: 178, 187–88). Didier was apparently unable to strike up a personal acquaintance with Jeffrey, but he did make a point of hearing him plead a case in court. Unsurprisingly, given his dislike of the *Review*, he was less impressed than was Garscombe, complaining first about Jeffrey's "intolerable Scotch accent" and then launching into a more comprehensive denunciation:

Here a lawyer is at the same time an attorney, a reviewer, a fashionable beau, and a virtuoso! In the morning, he deals out his jargon, under his wig with two hundred curls; when he gets his feet on his andirons at home, he scribbles quires full of criticism, or reads over the "last sweet novel," or involves himself in the mazes of the Lake poetry; in the evening, he appears in the ball room or in the saloon of fashion, "neat, trimly dressed, fresh as a bridesgroom." One would be apt to imaging that such a fellow was a finished Aristippus; but, if you pursue him with a critic's eye, you will find him a clumsy speaker at court; a dry writer at home, and an awkward beau in the modish circles. (Didier 1822: 67–68)

Of course, this minor letter by an unknown writer might seem a rather precarious basis on which to draw any conclusions about the attitudes held in the United States towards either Francis Jeffrey or *The Edinburgh Review*, except insofar as the simple fact that Didier finds Jeffrey of sufficient interest to attack at such length provides evidence of a sort to support Garscombe's claim about how familiar – and intriguing – Jeffrey was to American readers. Yet such very personal animus towards Jeffrey (and the sympathetic interest in Lockhart) does suggest the extent to which these early nineteenth-century literary debates taking place in Edinburgh did in fact resonate across the Atlantic, even as the periodicals absorbed trans-atlantic issues into their domestic disputes.

Nor, to make that point about the interest in Jeffrey, is it necessary to depend only on the evidence of American visitors to Scotland. As William Charvat has documented, when Jeffrey made his own visit to America, there was deep interest in and curiosity about it on the part of both the American press and the literary community, although both journalism and literary gossip managed to get some details wrong (see, for example, Charvat's citations from both an anonymous article in a New York newspaper and from an article by Washington Irving in the Philadelphia *Analectic* [Charvat 1941: 316–18]). Even Carlyle, in his decidedly disenchanted memoir of Jeffrey, commented that the journey had "made considerable noise in its time" (Carlyle 1997: 366). American acquaintances of Jeffrey were apparently interested enough in his views of their country to read his journal of the tour while it was still in the process of composition and then report – more or less accurately – on its contents. Charvat, who did not have access to the journal (and believed it lost), quotes one American source who spread word that Jeffrey had written that Madison looked like "a schoolmaster dressed up for a funeral" (Charvat 1941: 324) – a slightly damped down paraphrase of Jeffrey's actual description of Madison as having "altogether the air of a country school-master in mourning for ~~the death of~~ one of his pupils whom he had whipted to death" (Jeffrey 1813: 31 [44]).[1] The correction in phrasing suggests that Jeffrey took at least some amused literary pains in crafting this description, but Charvat, who doubts the accuracy of the gossip about Jeffrey's comments on Madison, also indicates Jeffrey's embarrassment at having his views attract such interest: he quotes a letter from Jeffrey to Wilkes, in which Jeffrey proclaims – disingenuously – that "there is nothing in it [the journal], as you know of, of personal ridicule either of Monro [sic] or of any other minister. I beg that you contradict it in my name" (Charvat 1941: 324).

That Americans were interested in what Jeffrey had to say about their country is of course not especially surprising; it was taken for granted at that time, both by British and American writers, that Americans were keenly interested in British reactions to the new nation. The Professor Garscombe who wrote so flatteringly of Jeffrey also reported on his meetings with Anne Grant, whom he describes as being "popular" with Americans precisely because of her "agreeable account" of their country (Garscombe 1825: 197). A rather more familiar, if somewhat later, example of this American interest in British opinion is the initial eagerness and subsequent intense outrage that greeted Frances Trollope's *Domestic Manners of the Americans*. Yet in many respects, Jeffrey's journal is, as Cockburn suggested, unremarkable in its account of the country, merely echoing what numerous other writers had already said, even at that early point in the United States' history. Jeffrey's comments on the American preference for wood as a building material, for example, which he thinks gives the architecture "an air of insufficiency and perishableness" (Jeffrey 1813: 6 [7]), recall Thomas Jefferson's lament, a generation before, that the rapid decay of wood meant that "every half century" America "becomes a tabula rasa" (Jefferson 1999: 160). Likewise, his glancing comments on American intemperance – as, for example, when he takes a glass of what he assumes to be lemonade at Dolly Madison's levee, only to discover "to my infinite horror [that it] was strong <u>punch</u>" (Jeffrey 1813: 35 [45]) – echo complaints made by travellers whose books had previously been reviewed by the *Review* (see for example Napier [?] 1810: 451). Nor, even if they were original, would Jeffrey's comments have given American patriots any

---

[1] References quote the pencilled page numbers on the original manuscript and, in brackets, the page of the (unpaginated) typescript also held by the NLS.

grounds for vanity. The journal is scathing about matters ranging from American technological know-how – as Jeffrey describes visiting the Patent Office and inspecting "several perpetual motions – but unfortunately all standing still" (Jeffrey 1813: 40 [52]) – to the lack of social graces among American women. Even though he was apparently somewhat taken by the "plump tall good humoured affable looking" Dolly Madison, liking the "native frankness of her disposition" (Jeffrey 1813: 31 [40]), Jeffrey anticipates and perhaps even outdoes Frances Trollope in his dismay at the manners of the younger American women, who, he complains,

in Dress manners and deportment would have discredited the lowest boarding school that takes charge of the daughters of mere tradesmen in England – They either sate tittering audibly on each others laps in a corner – or ran hoydening and jostling each other about the room with noises and motions of incredible vulgarity and impudence. (Jeffrey 1813: 34 [44])

Jeffrey later explains this "loud forward flippant manner" of American "female youth" by suggesting that it is an attempt, although misguided and inaccurate, to imitate "the elegant freedom of the old French society" (Jeffrey 1813: 44 [56]). In doing so, he implies not just, as Frances Trollope was later to cause so much offence by doing, that American society was unpolished, but also that it was both derivative and degenerate in that lack of refinement.

That Jeffrey would be critical in his responses to America is, of course, just as predictable as was American interest in what he had to say, as Jeffrey's supposed unwillingness to be pleased by anything was one of the standard bases for attacks by his enemies. As "Timothy Tickler" wrote in an open letter to Jeffrey in an early issue of *Blackwood's*, "you [...] greatly [...] overrate your own talents, and greatly [...] underrate the talents of others" ("Tickler" 1818: 75). This critical temper was also the subject of affectionate teasing by his friends. Sydney Smith, for one, offered a parody of Jeffrey's style in a letter to Jeffrey himself: "D–n the solar system!" Smith imagines Jeffrey proclaiming, "bad light – planets too distant – pestered with comets –

feeble contrivance; – could make a better with great ease" (Holland 1855: 2: 22).[2] Yet however inclined Jeffrey was to the *nil admirari* tone parodied by Smith, his views on America are by no means uniformly or reflexively negative. One of his most striking descriptions of American landscape is, in fact, far more disoriented than it is critical; it is an account of an evening's walk that he took while travelling between Washington and Baltimore. His party arrived at their inn, he reports,

> so long before dark that I had time to wander down to a little lonely wood and an eddying dark stream winding and gurgling thro' its sad and wintry shades, before the light faded quite away – as I stood on a crazy ~~dreary~~ timber bridge in the midst of this desolate and dreary scene, and saw nothing all round me but fallen trunks – withered and rotting leaves – naked fields, and the bare tops of more distant woods, crossing the faint gleam of the lonely sky to the West I was struck with a sense of desolation and distance from <u>home</u> that I had not felt in all my other wanderings, and which soon became so oppressive that I was glad to get rid of it by the crackling fire of our little parlour in Mr Ross's Inn. (Jeffrey 1813: 40–41 [53])

What appears to be happening here, and perhaps driving Jeffrey's homesickness, is a sudden awareness of the utter foreignness of his surroundings, an awareness that seems to lead to an inability to "read" them according to his usual standards of aesthetic judgement. The elements of the scene – trees, a river, a bridge – are banal and familiar enough, but Jeffrey's "oppressive" sense of being entirely out of place suggests an unsettling gap between the foreign and the familiar that prevents him from responding with any comfortable or assured critical analysis. While other elements of the American tour are easily and casually assimilated to and judged against British standards (the girls are more forward, the drink is more strong, the houses more flimsy), Jeffrey either cannot or will not analyse what it is about this dreary twilight landscape that makes him so disturbingly aware of the vast difference between America and "home".

Given the ways in which *The Edinburgh Review* and *Blackwood's* use writing about America to reflect or contribute to Scottish literary and cultural debates, this sudden, vertiginous sense of being in an alien world, brief and unexplored as it is, might in fact be of more

---

[2] This joke has had a curious afterlife in popular science. It was attributed to Jeffrey in Martin Rees' *Just Six Numbers* (2001) then cited in Michio Kaku's *Parallel Worlds* (2006).

significance than any of Jeffrey's more predictable criticisms of American landscape and culture, not least because it might also illuminate a much more obviously disorienting and very much more striking episode in Jeffrey's tour: his political debates with the President and Secretary of State. In both cases, what stands out is Jeffrey's inability to express in any direct or explicit manner the gap between the foreign and the familiar, even as he makes clear the uneasiness caused by that gap. In his account of his interactions with Madison, for example, Jeffrey is apparently on reasonably comfortable ground as long as he can read the experience according to the rules of British life. The food offered might seem to him inappropriate to a state dinner, more like "a mock feast in a nursery" (Jeffrey 1813: 39 [50]) than the sort of entertainment that one would expect the ruler of a country to provide, but he still has no difficulty in judging the meal by familiar standards. The ensuing conversation, however, is more unsettling. "I was a little surprised," Jeffrey writes of Madison's attempts to engage him in debate about English policy, "at this sort of challenge to discussion thrown out by a Sovereign to a private individual in his own drawing room" (Jeffrey 1813: 75 [96]). Jeffrey's sense of the extraordinary nature of this conversation is implied in the physical format of the journal itself: his report of the political discussions was written up separately after the fact, rather than forming part of his the day to day account of events, and then sewn into the back of the volume, following several blank pages, making it quite literally stand out from the rest of the narrative. He also notes that he had his father-in-law, to whom he had given an oral account of the meeting immediately after the fact, read through to verify the accuracy of his written version, then adds (in a note dated 22 Nov. 1819) that he is confident that he has not omitted anything material nor put down anything "that was not to the best of my understanding intended and expressed by one or the other of us at the time" (Jeffrey 1813: 74 [95]). The quasi-legal phrasing of this disclaimer, in a private journal not intended for either publication or extensive circulation – Jeffrey's justifiable embarrassment at even the toned down report of his description of Madison makes clear that the journal's audience would of necessity have been very limited – implies Jeffrey's own sense that these political conversations are different in kind from his accounts of American landscapes or private social gatherings and much more difficult to make full sense of.

That difference and difficulty arises in part, of course, because of the touchy political nature of the subject being discussed. Charvat presents some evidence to suggest that Jeffrey's meeting with Madison was given a political spin by the President's enemies; he quotes at length a second hand account of the meeting provided by the Bostonian Samuel Breck, a political opponent of Madison and his party. According to Breck, Jeffrey began the interview with a haughty proclamation of his unshakeable support for British measures "in all that relates to their disputes with you". Despite this unpromising start, Breck continues, Madison and Monroe then "shed tears of entreaty that [Jeffrey] would condescend to be their advocate" in Britain, only to find that – still in Breck's words – "[t]he young puppy […] gave them, instead of consolation or hope, the most undisguised expressions of scorn," making his visit "a shame upon the chief [Madison] and the party that put him in office" (cited in Charvat 1941: 325–6). Needless to say, Jeffrey's accounts of his meetings with both Madison and Monroe bear almost no resemblance at all to Breck's decidedly inventive reconstruction of them. In his journal, he reports himself as being nonplussed but polite in his refusal to agree with the American perspective on the war and to have been treated in turn in a "civil and even courteous" manner (Jeffrey 1813: 75 [96]), despite the irreconcilable differences in opinion. Nonetheless, the simple fact that it could be said and presumably believed, even if only by Madison's enemies, that the editor of a British literary magazine could reduce the President of an enemy nation to tears by his refusal to endorse the President's cause, reinforces what appears to have been Jeffrey's sense of the deeply strange nature of this interview.

Of course, given the strenuousness with which *The Edinburgh Review* had argued against the American war less than a year before, it is not entirely surprising that Madison might have thought that the magazine's editor would be a sympathetic sharer of his views. Nor would Jeffrey's more rabidly pro-government countrymen necessarily have been astonished had he given what they would undoubtedly have seen as treasonous "consolation" and "hope" to an enemy. Indeed, the idea of treason in connection with *The Edinburgh Review* had been floated only a few years before, following the publication of the Don Cevellos review, which was probably the joint production of Jeffrey and Brougham (see Schneider 1945 170–71 for attribution). Anne Grant, for example, reported gossip that an uncle of Jeffrey's was "so much enrag'd at this indecent attack on the constitution" that he thought the "whole set," his nephew presumably included, should be sent "to Botany Bay" (Grant 1808: f. 151). Yet Jeffrey himself, judging by his American journal, seems to have been mystified by the idea that the American President would either expect or want to persuade him to agree with him on the iniquities of British policy. Just as the moment in the woods outside Baltimore reminds Jeffrey of how intensely foreign the American landscape can be to his Scottish eyes, these interviews with Madison and Monroe seem to underline the cultural and political gap between the two countries, as what ought to have been familiar political arguments become more or less unrecognisable to both participants in the debate. For *The Edinburgh Review*, sympathy with American grievances offers a way to highlight what it presents as the Tory ministry's lapse from high British ideals; for the Americans, resenting those grievances offers a chance to show "the world that [the United States] had a government capable of wielding the power of a great nation" (Jeffrey 1813: 74 [95]). (While this comment was made by James Monroe, Jeffrey reports that Madison shared Monroe's views on the subject). Both in the Maryland woods and in the President's drawing room, America ceases to be readily assimilated to the aesthetic or political perspectives of Jeffrey and *The Edinburgh Review*, and, as such, it becomes for a moment a genuinely disorienting foreign world

None of this is to suggest that Jeffrey was in any way naïve in his expectations of America or in the comments that he makes about it, but rather that his transatlantic interests in *The Edinburgh Review* are, perhaps inevitably, used in service of Scottish and British cultural and political debates. Yet as his journal suggests, the idea of America that underlies articles by Jeffrey and others in *The Edinburgh Review* – and reactions against them in *Blackwood*'s – could not always be sustained in the face of his experiences in the country itself. Even if those moments of disorientation remain brief and are never fully explored by Jeffrey himself, they are striking enough to disrupt the more predictably satiric comments on American cultural failings. Yet they remained unpublished and private, appearing in print only in the fragmentary quotations that Cockburn chooses to provide. Jeffrey's private emotional responses, private political discussions, thus never became part of the public discourse of America in *The Edinburgh Review*, a point that perhaps emphasises more strongly than anything else how his lived experience of American life and politics remained secondary to the lively and divisive *literary* construction of America that appeared in the Edinburgh periodicals.

Bibliography

Brougham, Henry. 1803. Review of *Transactions of the American Philosophical Society* in *The Edinburgh Review* 2: 348–55.
—. 1812. Rev. of "The Crisis of the Dispute with America" in *The Edinburgh Review* 19: 290–317.
Carlyle, Thomas. [1881] 1997. *Reminiscences*. Oxford: Oxford UP.
Charvat, William. 1941. "Francis Jeffrey in America" in *The New England Quarterly* 14: 309–34.
Cockburn, Henry. 1852. *The Life of Lord Jeffrey*. 2 vols. Edinburgh: Adam and Charles Black, 1852.
Crawford, Robert. *Devolving English Literature*. Oxford: Clarendon, 1992.
Didier, Franklin James. 1822. *Franklin's Letters to his Kinsfolk, written during the Years 1818, '19 & '20, from Edinburgh, London, The Highlands of Scotland, and Ireland*. 2 vols. Philadelphia: J. Maxwell.
Garscombe, Professor. 1825. *Letters*. In *The Contrast: or Scotland as it was in the year 1745, and Scotland in the year 1819*. London: P. Wright & Son, and Edinburgh: J. Dick & Co.
Grant, Anne. 1808. Letter to John Hatsell 29 December 1809. University of Edinburgh Library La.II.357, ff. 151–53.
Holland, Saba and Sarah Austin, eds 1855. *A Memoir of the Reverend Sydney Smith, with a Selection from his Letters*. 2 vols. London: Longman, Brown, Green and Longmans.
Hook, Andrew. 1975. *Scotland and America: A Study of Cultural Relations, 1750–1835*. Glasgow: Blackie.
Jefferson, Thomas. [1785] 1999. *Notes on the State of Virginia*. Harmondsworth: Penguin.
Jeffrey, Francis. 1806. "Review of *The Complete Works, in Philosophy, Politics, and Morals, of the late Dr. Benjamin Franklin*" in *The Edinburgh Review* 8: 327–344.
—. 1809. "Review of *The Columbiad: A Poem*" in *The Edinburgh Review*, 15: 24–40.

—. 1813. *American Journal*. National Library of Scotland Acc. 11099, 1–2.
McLeod, Mona Kedslie. 2004. *From Charlotte Square to Fingal's Cave: Reminiscences of Journey through Scotland, 1820–1824, by Krystyn Lach-Szyrma*. Edinburgh: Tuckwell Press.
Manning, Susan. 2002. *Fragments of Union: Making Connections in Scottish and American Writing*. London: Palgrave.
May, Henry. 1976. *The Enlightenment in America*. New York: Oxford UP.
[Napier, Macvey?]. 1810. "Review of *Travels in America, by Thomas Ashe*" in *The Edinburgh Review* 15: 442–53.
"On the Means of Education, and the State of Learning, in the United States of America" in *Blackwood's Edinburgh Magazine* 4: 546–53 and 641–49.
Pichot, Amédée. 1825. *Historical and Literary Tour of a Foreigner in England and Scotland*. 2 vols. London: Saunders and Otley.
Schneider, Elisabeth, Irwin Griggs, and John D. Kern. 1945. "Brougham's Early Contributions to the *Edinburgh Review*: A New List" in *Modern Philology* 42: 152–73.

Alliance and Defiance in Scottish and American Outlaw-Hero Ballads

Suzanne Gilbert

Interesting similarities in character construction can be detected in American and Scottish outlaw characters in ballads and similar contexts. Both take cues from legendary English outlaw-hero characters such as Robin Hood in their politicisation. However, more pronounced qualities of "alliance" (kinship) and "defiance" (reckless endeavour) might be found in American and Scottish outlaws owing to an even greater uncertainty about the geographical location they inhabit, reflecting complexities of colonial and postcolonial history.[1]
Keywords: Outlaw legends; Walter Scott; Robin Hood; "Railroad Bill" ballads; Joseph Ritson; Rob Roy; Highland character; border reivers; Jesse James; "Billy the Kid"; Mexican-American disputes; Border "debatable lands" in Scotland; rescue narratives.

As scholars of the "Anglo-American ballad" tradition have frequently observed, ballads have proved to be ideal carriers of cultural information. During periods of emigration from Scotland to North America throughout the eighteenth and nineteenth centuries, ballads that crossed the Atlantic – whether transmitted orally by singers or printed in broadsides and chapbooks – retained markers of their Scottish origins while also adapting to new circumstances, a process aided by the ballad's combination of compelling themes and formal strategies for containment and transmission.[2] This chapter considers a particularly enduring strand of the tradition: the outlaw-hero ballad as developed in Scotland and the United States. Comparing Scottish and American outlaw-hero ballads reveals cultural factors that govern variation in the character type and its representations. And while acknowledging the common attributes of outlaws across cultures, this approach complicates the notion of an abstract, universal "social banditry".

Outlaw-heroes such as Robin Hood, William Wallace, Rob Roy, Jesse James, and Billy the Kid have stimulated the popular imagina-

---

[1] An early version of this essay was delivered at the American Folklore Society's conference in Albuquerque, New Mexico, 2003, as part of a panel on "Scotland and America".

[2] See, for example, the major studies in this field, Coffin 1950 and Laws 1957.

tion for centuries. While suggestive comparisons have been made between American and British legends, treatments of the outlaw-hero have focused mostly on Robin Hood, and the famed English outlaw is often enlisted to stand for "British" outlawry as a whole.[3] There are important differences between the Scottish and English legends, however, and understanding of Scottish outlaw-heroes benefits if we extricate them from a totalising Britishness in order to gauge the degree and character of the Scottish-American connections. In light of differences among outlaw legends within British culture and the transatlantic migration of structures and motifs from outlaw-hero narratives, a number of factors may be seen as contributing to both stability and variation in the character type. Ballads detailing the exploits of outlaws from both Scottish and American traditions turn in similar ways on the motifs of "alliance" and "defiance", which shape the narratives while also revealing differences in these distinctive figures and the cultural spaces in which they function. In these narratives, Scottish outlaws share with their American counterparts a reliance on relationship – on family or extended family – in their resistance to authorities perceived to be repressing their social groups. In addition, outlaws from both traditions operate around contested borders or within geographical spaces that are marked by conflict, often national or quasi-national in nature.

A major vehicle for transmission of outlaw legends over long periods of time and great distances has been the ballad, a narrative form whose longevity may be attributed to its peculiar combination of stability, adaptability to diverse subject matter, and popularity. At many points in history, the ballad has emerged as a dominant form for expressing popular dissent, even outright subversion of the dominant discourse. Famously, Andrew Fletcher of Saltoun asserted in 1703 that he knew "a very wise man" who believed that "if a man were permitted to make all the ballads, he need not care who should make the laws of a nation" (Fletcher 1744: 265). The flexibility of this form makes it an ideal carrier for outlaw-hero legends with their "capacity for endless change and re-appropriation, adopted in seemingly contradictory fashion by diverse political camps" (Phillips 2008: 3).

Walter Scott was familiar with the attraction of outlaws, much to his own dismay: "I am a bad hand at depicting a hero, properly so

---

[3] A recent collection of essays (Phillips 2008b) marks a shift towards analysis of a range of British outlaws; see also Knight 2008.

called", he wrote, "and have an unfortunate propensity for the dubious character of borderers, buccaneers, Highland robber, and all others of a Robin Hood description" (Lockhart 1839: 4: 175–76). Tracing Scott's fascination for outlaws, exemplified by his engagement with the Scottish reivers in *The Minstrelsy of the Scottish Border* (1802) and his recasting of the Rob Roy legend, Helen Phillips finds a constant at the core of the outlaw myth:

> one might call it the duality that unifies the tradition, the paradox of the good rogue. The paradox's power lies perhaps in the fact that it provides an attractive vehicle for the truth that issues of social good and bad, of law and resistance, are rarely clear-cut. The question to ask about any version of the outlaw myth is thus not only whether it is an adaptation for Left or Right but also how it treats the central paradox. (Phillips 2008: 3)

Implicit in the term "outlaw-hero" is the apparent contradiction that Phillips describes. The function of the outlaw-hero narrative is to negotiate the paradox, however unstable and dependent it may be on a specific audience.

Studies of the outlaw inevitably refer to Robin Hood. Stephen Knight's *Robin Hood: A Complete Study of the English Outlaw* (1994) offers the fullest and most nuanced analysis of this complex and changing figure.[4] Barbara Hanawalt (1992) compares Robin Hood legends to medieval accounts of English highwaymen, and Tim Lundgren (1996) traces the roots of the Robin-Hood tradition, finding earlier manifestations of the figure in medieval England. Understandably, critics of the American outlaw tradition have made connections between Robin Hood and American badmen such as Jesse James. W.E. Simeone (1958) traces the Robin-Hood legend in American tradition, and Kent L. Steckmesser (1966), also treating Robin Hood and western-outlaw narratives, observes similarities in individual traditions and historical contexts. Richard E. Meyer (1980) identifies twelve elements essential to the image of the American outlaw, making connections to Robin Hood while also arguing for the distinctiveness of the American tradition. John W. Roberts (1981) applies these elements to the African-American "Railroad Bill" ballads.[5]

---

[4] See also an earlier book-length study of Robin Hood, Dobson and Taylor 1976.
[5] For an extensive list of critical sources on outlaw-heroes, see the bibliography in Seal 1996.

While acknowledging the relevance of Robin Hood, most critics of the tradition have concentrated on legends within single cultures. In contrast, however, another critical strand has emerged, best represented by Eric Hobsbawm's *Bandits* (1969). His highly influential analysis presents the "social bandit" as a global phenomenon – the outlaw, who defies repressive authority and is supported, even cheered on by, his social group – and emphasises similarities in conditions which give rise to such a legend. Ranging over four hundred years, and drawing on outlaw legends from Europe, Africa, Asia, and the Americas, Hobsbawm describes social banditry as "one of the most universal social phenomenon known to history, and one of the most amazingly uniform" (Hobsbawm [1969] 2000: 21). Many others have concurred that the outlaw-hero shares attributes across cultures.

This uniformity of the tradition provides the starting point for Graham Seal's wide-ranging study, *The Outlaw Legend: A Cultural Tradition in Britain, America and Australia* (1996), which combines insights from the "universal" school of outlaw-hero criticism with an emphasis on the cultural specificity of such figures. Seal first acknowledges the consistency. Based on previous analyses, he catalogues ten "motifs or discrete but interacting narrative elements": The outlaw-hero is (1) a friend of the poor (or oppressed) and (2) is himself oppressed. (3) He has been forced into outlawry. He is (4) brave, (5) generous, and (6) courteous. He (7) does not indulge in unjustified violence, but (8) he is a trickster. Ultimately, (9) he is betrayed, but (10) lives on in one way or another after death (Seal 1996: 11). Moving beyond the similarities, and in line with the approach of anthropologists and folklorists, Seal then highlights "discontinuities" among outlaw-heroes from the three traditions he has identified, arguing that fieldwork on "specific outbreaks of banditry" shows that "local circumstances and pressures are what determine the degree of support for a bandit, rather than the operation of some abstract, meta-historical force tagged 'social banditry'" (Seal 1996: 12, 3).

While helpfully complicating Hobsbawm's argument, Seal's conclusions nonetheless serve to homogenise British outlaw-heroes; but there are discontinuities as deep between Scottish and English outlaws as those he describes between British and American ones. Seal concentrates on English outlaws (with some reference to Irish figures), but he argues that in British folklore the outlaw-hero is represented as "heroic individual" and that, in contrast, the American and Australian figure "has strong family ties and influences" (Seal 1996: 12).[6] It may be argued, however, that while the English outlaw Robin Hood is most frequently depicted as a heroic individual, for Scottish outlaws family-, clan-, or nation-based relationships are paramount; their actions are motivated and supported by alliance, and thus shaped by "local circumstances and pressures". Highlighting another feature, Seal asserts that one element found "only in the Australian manifestation of the outlaw hero is an articulation of discontent regarding the British monarchy" (Seal 1996: 14). But for Scottish outlaws a common *raison d'être* is opposition to the English monarchy or to its elite representatives.

In *Scottish Fiction and the British Empire* (2006), Douglas S. Mack applies to the Scottish situation an understanding of Ranajit Guha's distinction between "elite" and "subaltern" classes; and in so doing he summarises Guha's description of British colonial rule in India:

Writing about Indian society in the days of British Imperial rule, Guha suggested that a dominant elite then operated in tune with the interests of the British raj, and contained "foreign as well as indigenous" groups. The foreign elements included British officials, industrialists, merchants, financiers, planters, landlords, and missionaries, while the indigenous elements [...] included "the biggest feudal magnates, the most important representatives of the industrial and mercantile bourgeoisie and native recruits to the uppermost levels of the bureaucracy". At a more local level, the indigenous portion of the dominant elite could also include people belonging to "hierarchically inferior" social strata, who nevertheless acted in the interests of the elite *"and not in conformity to interests corresponding truly to their own social being"* [Guha's italics]. Guha stresses that the "subaltern classes", on the other hand, consisted of the "people", the dominated mass of the population in town and country. (Mack 2006: 1)

We find that many Scottish outlaw-hero legends enact defiance in the context of national or quasi-national conflict, with the role of the oppressor being played not only by the crown or central government directly, but by the elite, indigenous representatives of that power. This tension colours the narratives in very particular ways. Thus the Scottish ballads contribute much to an understanding of the outlaw-hero dynamic, particularly in their complex treatments of kinship,

---

[6] Philip Butterss takes issue with Seal's representation of Irish outlaws in a discussion of the Irish outlaw, Bold Jack Donahoe (Butterss 1989).

nation, and authority. In this light, they suggest closer parallels to American outlaw narratives than to Robin Hood legends.

This said, Robin Hood has certainly figured in Scottish tradition, though in very specific ways. The outlaw-hero is deeply embedded in Scotland's stories about itself, the prototype being the national hero William Wallace (1272–1305). Joseph Ritson noted the comparison between Robin Hood, "noble outlaws", and Wallace in his 1795 account of Robin Hood (Knight 2008: 106), but little research assessing the relationship between the English and Scottish legends had been published before Knight's essay "Rabbie Hood: The Development of the English Outlaw Myth in Scotland". [7] Pursuing the representations and development of the Robin-Hood figure within Scottish historiography and literature, Knight observes that Robin Hood activities took place in Scottish towns in the late Middle Ages, and that Scottish chroniclers and writers had a role in promulgating the English outlaw myth. Knight finds that "the Scottish reading of the outlaw figure is clearly not the same as the English, especially in terms of national significance" and, further, that "the concept of an outlaw from a Scottish viewpoint entails a political and nationalist identity for the figure" (Knight 2008: 111, 106). Indeed, Knight argues, the Wallace legend draws on Robin Hood but contributes new elements to the mix. The English Robin Hood in a Scottish context was "hybridized in various ways and then re-exported in a different and remarkably successful form", and "it was in fact the Scottish version which lay behind major changes in the tradition of the allegedly English hero, changes which of themselves helped make it still so popular today" (Knight 208: 99–100).

The national outlaw-hero is firmly established in the Scottish ballad of "Gude Wallace", classified in Francis J. Child's *The English and Scottish Popular Ballads* (1882–98) as 157A. [8] The ballad is based on a long poem, *The Actes and Deidis of the Illustre and Vallyeant Campioun Schir William*, written by Henry the Minstrel (known as Blind Harry) in the second half of the fifteenth century. This poem is the most substantial early account of Wallace's legendary exploits during the Scottish Wars of Independence over 150 years earlier. Knight observes that in the poem the "outlaw motifs in a fully

---

[7] Knight's research follows brief suggestions made by Spence 1928.

[8] References to ballads give in brackets the number that Child assigned, sometimes followed by a letter indicating the variant.

Scotticised form have a powerful political thrust now, embodying resistance to English imperialism" (Knight 2008: 112). Child takes his preferred text from a chapbook printed around 1745;[9] and it is striking that a ballad of the national hero Wallace is deployed in this popular form at the height of tensions surrounding the last Jacobite rising to restore the Stuart line to the throne, which if successful would potentially have redrawn the map of Britain.

Titled for the chapbook "On an honourable Achievement of Sir William Wallace, near Falkirk", this variant of "Gude Wallace" opens with the hero contemplating his role in the conflict with the "auld enemy":

"Had we a king," said Wallace then,
"That our kind Scots might live by their own!
But betwixt me and the English blood
I think there is an ill seed sown."

The narrative details Wallace's outwitting of a series of English pursuers and his defeat of them all, advised and assisted by Scots, his fellow-oppressed. In another variant (157G),[10] when his mistress is bribed by English soldiers to betray him but confesses her near-betrayal, the "gude Wallace" demonstrates his chivalry and humane forgiveness:

"Do you repent," said Wallace,
"The ill you've dane to me?"
"Ay, that I do," said that ladie,
"And will do till I die."

"Ay, that I do," said that ladie,
"And will do ever still,

---

[9] Variant A is based on the fifth book of Blind Harry's *Wallace*, and the eighteenth-century chapbook from which Child took the text is titled *Four New Songs, and a Prophecy*. This variant was also included in the 1853 edition of James Johnson's *Scots Musical Museum* and James Maidment's *Scotish* [sic] *Ballads and Songs* (1859) (Child 1965: 3: 265).

[10] Variant G is based on the fourth book of Blind Harry's *Wallace* (Child 1965: 3: 266). Child takes the text from Alexander Laing's *The Thistle of Scotland*, who reportedly collected it from "the repetition of an old gentlewoman in Aberdeenshire". It was also collected by William Motherwell (see his manuscript), communicated by Peter Buchan "who had it from an old woman in that neighborhood" (Child 1965: 3: 272).

And for the ill I've dane to you,
Let me burn upon a hill."

"Now God forfend," says brave Wallace,
"I shoud be so unkind;
Whatever I am to Scotland's faes,
I'm aye a woman's friend."

She helps Wallace by providing her clothes, with which Wallace dis-
guises himself and is able to trick his pursuers. A good outlaw-hero,
he is kind to his friends but a deadly opponent to his enemies:

"Now if there be a Scotsman here,
He'll come and drink wi me;
But if there be an English loun,
It is his time to flee."

Depending on the variant, Wallace demonstrates larger-than-life skills
in hand-to-hand combat, killing anywhere from fifteen to thirty
English soldiers.[11] Variant G, which was circulating in oral tradition in
the nineteenth century, also invokes the outlaw-hero's financial
generosity towards those with whom he is allied, a motif found in
Robin Hood narratives: Wallace gives a woman twenty pounds taken
from the representatives of authority (i.e. the Englishmen he has
slain): he takes from the rich and gives to the poor. As in other such
legends, the gift functions to demonstrate the outlaw-hero's chivalry,
and to justify his actions. In the Scottish context, it also resonates with
the importance of alliance; the outlaw as heroic individual serves the
wider community of the oppressed. Despite the high body count in the
ballad of "Gude Wallace" and the typically impersonal narrator's tone,
Wallace emerges from the ballad as heroic individual and national
hero, not criminal or murderer.

The motif of providing for the poor is rooted in the English
Robin-Hood legend, as seen in the final stanza of "A Gest of Robyn
Hoode" (117), a very early ballad:[12]

---

[11] See 157I, a variant of "Gude Wallace" from C.K. Sharpe's collection, entitled "An
old song shewing how Sir William Wallace killed thirty Englishmen" (Child 1965: 5:
242–3).
[12] For the complicated history of this ballad, see Child 1965: 2: 39–56; and Knight
1994: 70–81.

Cryst haue mercy on his soule,
That dyed on the rode!
For he was a goo d outlawe,
And dyde pore men moch god.

The rich-poor motif that features in both Robin Hood and Wallace legends appears in virtually every ballad celebrating the exploits of the American outlaw Jesse James (Meyer 1980: 103, 122),[13] as may be seen in this variant included by Margaret Larkin in *Singing Cowboy: A Book of Western Songs* (1931):

Jesse James was a lad who killed many a man.
He robbed the Glendale train.
He stole from the rich and he gave to the poor,
He'd a hand and a heart and a brain.

Employing a common ballad technique, the declarative narrator's voice juxtaposes ideas economically but powerfully. There is a disjunction between the first and second halves of the stanza, lines 1–2 presenting the "outlaw" James and lines 3–4 the "hero" James; the proximity of the two parts serves to justify James's crime without an overt statement. This structural device may be observed, but in reverse, in another stanza:

Jesse was a man, a friend to the poor.
He'd never see a man suffer pain,
And with his brother Frank he robbed the Chicago bank,
And stopped the Glendale train.

The motif recurs in variants of legends about other outlaws, among them Sam Bass and Pretty Boy Floyd. Woody Guthrie perpetuated the theme in his song "Pretty Boy Floyd"; Guthrie's outlaw pays the mortgages of starving farmers, gives a thousand-dollar bill to a beggar, and provides Christmas dinners for struggling families.

Cross-cultural Robin-Hood echoes are fairly obvious and serve to clarify certain features of an outlaw-hero, and it would be easy to stop there. Focus on the Scottish-American similarities, however, casts light on more ambiguous elements of outlaw-hero legends, mostly

---

[13] For reference to some of the many variants of this ballad, see Seal 1996: 218.

involving contested spaces and the alliances that emerge from these conflicts.

If Wallace functions clearly as an outlaw-hero operating within a struggle to gain national independence from England, less straightforward within a national framework is Rob Roy Macgregor (1671–1734), about whom legends formed during a period when Scottish independence was lost. The historical Rob Roy's life strad-dled the turbulent making of Britain, which was sealed by the 1707 Treaty of Union that joined Scottish and English parliaments, thus marking the end of Scottish sovereignty. Macgregor's resistance to what he perceived to be abuse of authority by the Duke of Montrose, combined with his reputation as strong defender of his clan and skilled cattle thief, cemented his reputation as an outlaw. *Highland Rogue* (1723), a novel about Rob Roy (published anonymously but often attributed to Daniel Defoe), further romanticised and enhanced Macgregor's legendary status.

The outlaws of the Border ballads present an even more ambiguous case. It could be argued that these colourful rogues do not qualify as outlaw-heroes, but rather as criminals, and sometimes murderers.[14] And indeed a very fine line separates outlaw-hero from murderer in any of these narratives, depending on who controls the narrative: it is the community that awards hero status. Wallace-the-outlaw serves as a heroic individual who is conferred status as a national hero, and the Border outlaws highlight the priority of loyalty to family, community, or social group.

Here the parallel between Scottish and American outlaw-heroes becomes clear. Attempting to discover what is "peculiarly American", what makes the outlaw "a distinctively, though not exclusively, American folktype", Richard E. Meyer foregrounds twelve elements (Meyer 1980: 94, 97–114), many of which may be applied directly to Scottish outlaws. The American outlaw-hero, Meyers says, is first

---

[14] In the *Motif Index of the Child Corpus: The English and Scottish Popular Ballad*, Border reivers are not generally classified as "outlaws"; rather, those committing crimes against "representatives of authority" are "criminals" and "murderers", without reference to motive or justification. See, for example, the classification of motifs for "Kinmont Willie" (186), "Jock o the Side" (187), "Archie o Cawfield" (188), and "Hobie Noble" (189). This is also the case with "Gude Wallace" (157), though "The Outlaw Murray" (305) is an exception. For the Robin Hood ballads, however, the term "outlaw" recurs (see Wurzbach and Salz 1995: 187–88, 170–71, 141–68, 246).

a "man of the people"; he is closely identified with the common people, and, as such, is generally seen to stand in opposition to certain established, oppressive economic, civil and legal systems peculiar to the American historical experience. (Meyer 1980: 97)

The feature of the outlaw-hero as "common" does not seem to originate with Robin Hood, who in most accounts comes close to gentry himself; as Knight observes, over the centuries Robin Hood came to be characterised increasingly as a gentleman, not only in terms of behaviour, but in terms of social class, though exiled because of his outlaw status (Knight 1994: 88–97; 2008: 103). It might be noted, however, that regardless of nationality the outlaw-hero reflects "gentlemanly" ideals by demonstrating fairness and acting courteously.

Allies and alliance are crucial to the Scottish outlaw-hero. As Tom Devine explains, clan structure operates in both Highland and Lowland cultures:

[T]he essence of the clan was a real or assumed kin relationship between chief, ruling families, cadet branches and followers. In the medieval and for much of the early modern period [...] such kin-based groupings were not unique to the Highlands. They were to be found throughout Scotland and were especially strong in areas such as the Borders and the north east where state authority was often at its weakest. It was common for noblemen and greater lairds to surround themselves with networks of lesser gentlemen who bore their name and promised loyalty and service in return for protection. Social structures throughout Scotland were designed for defence and security and the martial ethos was not confined to the Highlands. (Devine 1994: 5)

Governing both Highlands and Lowlands proved difficult, at times impossible. Another historian, Edward J. Cowan, observes that the unruly Highlanders and Borderers were characterised similarly:

One deeply entrenched convention that transcended the Highland/Lowland divide was reverence for the name. [...] By the 16th century central government detected little difference between Highland clans and certain Lowland families, particularly the southern margins of the latter. Indeed, exactly the same language was applied to the Borderers as to the Gaels. The rhetoric of Scottish government referred to the "clans" of the Borders, "companies of wicked men coupled in fellowship by occasion of their surnames or near dwellings together, or through keeping society in theft". (Cowan 2003: 6)

Cowan adds, "allegedly troublesome Highland clans were described as 'infamous bykes of lawless limmers' – wasp-nests of lawless rogues. The bandits of the southern frontier were meanwhile dismissed as 'gangs', the first usage of the modern term" (Cowan 2003: 6).

The Border ballads often labeled as "riding" or "reiving" ballads depict dramatic, even lurid, episodes of life on the shifting border between Scotland and England before the Union of Crowns in 1603: cattle-stealing, revenge murders, rescue raids. Many of these ballads originated in the Scottish West Marches, northeast of the Solway Firth, in the Tarras Moss and the "Debatable Land", and along the Rivers Esk, Sark, Wauchope, Liddel, and Hermitage. The Debatable Land is a ten-mile by four-mile strip of land between the Esk and Sark, the nationality of which was not officially established until 1552 (Reed 1973: 42). In this area, what governance there was fell to the elite representatives of both Scottish and English authority, as James Reed observes:

It was easy for family feuds to develop into political conflicts between the nations. [...] Both governments enlisted the help of the Border chiefs and their followers to protect the frontier, and by the sixteenth century an intricate system of Border administration had evolved, based largely on the appointment of powerful feudal families as Wardens, responsible to the Crown, of three districts or Marches, East, Middle and West, on each side of the frontier. (Reed 1973: 41)[15]

Traditionally common grazing land for both Scottish and English farmers, the debatable land became the subject of a bitter contest for ownership. It was home to fugitives, criminals, and outlaws – in fact, literally and legally without law. The Wardens of both Scotland and English issued a proclamation in 1551:

All Englishmen and Scottishmen, after this proclamation made, are and shall be free to rob, burn, spoil, slay, murder and destroy all and every such person or persons, their bodies, buildings, goods and cattle as do remain or shall inhabit upon any part of the said Debatable land, without any redress to be made for same. (Reed 1973: 42)

In 1552 an alternative proposal was agreed, that the district "should be wholly evacuated and laid waste", and the land was divided between

---

[15] On Border reivers, see also Scott 1802, Borland 1910, Watson 1974, MacDonald Fraser 1995, and McAlpine 2000.

the kingdoms (Reed 1973: 42).[16] The debatable nature of the land, and of Border outlaw-heroes, is encoded in the relationships depicted in the ballads.

Like the Scottish Border reiver, the American outlaw Jesse James (1847–82) emerged at the time of another bitter feud with national implications; his life was shaped by the violence that erupted on the border between western Missouri and eastern Kansas in the aftermath of the Civil War. After fighting a guerilla war for the Confederate cause as part of "Quantrill's Raiders", James, his family, and associates suffered economically and socially with the South's defeat in 1865. Post-war, the James-Younger gang identified as enemies any who took advantage of their social group: the banks, the railroad corporations, and the Pinkerton detective agency, who hounded the outlaws at the behest of the government. They targeted their enemies, and their robbing and killing spree quickly became prime material for legend.

Henry McCarty – better known as William H. Bonney and even better-known as Billy the Kid (1859–81) – gained outlaw status during the war among ranchers over the contested range in Lincoln County, New Mexico, during the latter part of the nineteenth century. Despite the less-than-sympathetic behaviour of the historical Bonney, folklore has preserved elements important for outlaw-hero credentials: allied with a small rancher, he opposed a group of bigger ranchers and traders who were in collusion with corrupt authorities, and he earned the support of small ranchers and Mexican-Americans in the struggle over the "debatable" rangeland.

In both Scottish and American ballads, then, the ambivalent nature of the outlaw-hero is underscored by contested geographical spaces: the border-shifting battles for Scottish independence, the clan-based territorial divisions of the Scottish Highlands, the rampant lawlessness of the Borders Debatable Land, the bloody feuds of the Missouri-Kansas border in the 1860s, the cattle-rustling wars of the American west. In these narratives, contested land is fertile ground for the actions of ambiguous heroes. By comparison, Robin Hood's "greenwood" is another ambiguous space where lore rather than law rules, but it is not a contested space in the same sense; rather, it exists

---

[16] See a contemporary literary account of Borders violence in the sixteenth-century by Scots judge Sir Richard Maitland in *Complaynt Aganis the Theivis of Liddisdail* (Reed 1973: 53–6).

as an ambiguous area on a property whose ownership is not at the heart of the dispute, rather than as the site of a national or quasi-national contest.

It is the nature of contested spaces that within them outlaw-heroes can flourish outside of externally imposed moral strictures – outside "law". They become as debatable as the spaces they occupy. A debatable form itself, the ballad provides an ideal structure for these narratives, with its gaps and leaps, its tendency towards variation, its relative disinterest in or judgment of motivations, and its borders which must be defined by the audience. In accord with ballad dynamics, narratives can transfer from one ballad to another, and markers such as names and places can fall away and be replaced, leading to further variation. Within the cultural situations shaping the ballads, outlaws do indeed appear to be heroes, if of a very ambiguous sort. Despite the very real damage inflicted by reiving in the Scottish Borders, and by robbing in the American west, the ballads tend to be unabashedly pro-outlaw, seeming to delight in their exploits.

Marked by a rhetoric of defiance – warning, riding, raiding, rescuing – the Border ballads celebrate defiance of law or restriction, and audacity is a key ingredient of the outlaw-hero formula. But these ballads also reflect a "Dodhead" (190), which describes one of the many raids to steal cattle on the Scottish and English Borders during the fourteenth, fifteenth, and sixteenth centuries, illustrates a feature common in ballads whereby the heroic defiance of authority is shared among members of the family or clan. Many kinsmen come to the rescue of Jamie Telfer, whose kye are being driven (cattle are being stolen) by the Captain of Bewcastle. The family names and places anchor the narratives, but perhaps more significantly, the "muster call", common in Border ballads, anchors the narrative in alliance, as exemplified by the variant that Scott collected for the first volume of the *Minstrelsy*:

"Gar warn the water, braid and wide,
Gar warn it sune and hastilie!
They that winna ride for Telfer's kye,
Let them never look in the face o' me!

"Warn Wat o' Harden, and his sons,
Wi' them will Borthwick water ride;
Warn Gaudilands, and Allanhaugh,
And Gilmanscleugh, and Commonside.

"Ride by the gate at Priesthaughswire,
And warn the Currors o' the Lee;
As ye cum down the Hermitage Slack,
Warn doughty Willie o' Gorrinberry." –

The Scotts they rade, the Scotts they ran,
Sae starkly and sae steadilie!
And aye the ower-word o' the thrang
Was –"Rise for Branksome readilie!"
(Scott, Walter 1802: 85–86)

Reed comments that, as Jamie Telfer rides from place to place, repeating his cry for assistance, "slowly the band is gathering, knit by bonds of blood and neighbourliness" (Reed 1973: 106). Moral superiority in this and other Border ballads is based on *loyalty*, compared to the personal *honesty* so integral to Robin Hood narratives.[17]

The ballad form's adaptability to circumstances is aptly illustrated by "Jamie Telfer of the Fair Dodhead". Another documented variant attributes the rescue to the Elliots, a completely different family who in the Scott version refuse to help recover the stolen cattle.[18] Evidence of yet another variant may be found in a letter to Walter Scott from James Hogg (30 June [1802]), who had provided ballads for the *Minstrelsy*, in which he writes, "I am surprized to find that the songs in your collection differ so widely from my mothers [...] 'Jamie Telfer' differs in many particulars" (Hogg 2004: 15). The sense of these narratives belonging to families has contributed to their longevity through transmission and their continued relevance to tradition; and local circumstances figure prominently in public support for an outlaw-hero.

Another rescue narrative, "Kinmont Willie" (186), describes a daring raid to retrieve the notorious thief William Armstrong of Kynmonth from his imprisonment by the English in Carlisle Castle in 1596. In a contemporary history of the Church of Scotland, John Spottiswood attests that the historical Armstrong was being held "for many wrongs he had committed, as he was indeed a notorious thief"

---

[17] Passing through oral tradition, this ballad retained the conjunction of alliance and defiance. See the fragment of this ballad sung by Willie Scott in a recording collected by Hamish Henderson for the University of Edinburgh's School of Scottish Studies (Scott, Willie 1992). The text appears in a compilation of Scott's songs (Scott, Willie 2006: 65, 151).

[18] For this variant, see Child 1965: 249.

(Child 1965: 3: 469; Scott, Walter 1802: 1: 112). Though based on historical events, the ballad alters facts to enhance the sense of drama and immediacy by making the prisoner about to be executed. Further suspense is built by detailing the difficulties encountered by the troop of kinsmen called to rescue him from the other side of the border: a storm, high water, a lead wall, and great opposition from the English. Undaunted, defiant, they persevere and, using ladders, retrieve Kinmont Willie from his cell; their alliance makes their defiance possible:

> They thought King James and a' his men
> Had won the house wi' bow and speir;
> It was but twenty Scots and ten,
> That put a thousand in sic a stear!

The Border ballads privilege such bold action, and this quality provides another point of comparison between Scottish and American narratives. Meyer describes the American outlaw-hero as "character-ized by the audacity, daring and sheer stupendousness of his exploits" (Meyer 1980: 105). This feature may clearly be discerned in the audacious rescues of the Border reivers and in Wallace's single-handed slaying of thirty English soldiers. The American outlaw-hero ballads share the Scottish Border ballads' exuberant appreciation for a defiance that obscures, overrides, or even obliterates the morality of the outlaw's actions. A ballad about the Confederate bushwhacker William Clarke Quantrill, collected from oral tradition by John A. and Alan Lomax, captures in heroic language and relentless rhythm the boldness of the Quantrill Raiders' attack on the unsuspecting town of Lawrence, Kansas, across the Missouri-Kansas line:

> Come all ye bold robbers and open your ears,
> Of Quantrell the lion-heart you quickly shall hear,
> With his band of bold raiders in double-quick time
> They came to burn Lawrence just over the line.

> *Chorus:*
> All routing and shouting and giving the yell,
> Like so many demons just raised up from Hell,
> The boys they were drunken with powder and wine,
> And came to burn Lawrence just over the line.

> They came to burn Lawrence, they came not to stay,

They rode in one morning at breaking of day,
Their guns were a-waving and horses a-foam,
And Quantrell a-riding his famous big roan.

They came to burn Lawrence, they came not to stay.
Jim Lane he was up at the break of the day;
He saw them a-coming and got in a fright,
Then crawled in a corncrib to get out of sight.

Oh, Quantrell's a fighter, a bold-hearted boy,
A brave man or woman he'll never annoy,
He'd take from the wealthy and give to the poor,
For brave men there's never a bolt to his door.
(Lomax and Lomax [1934] 1989: 132–33)

Of note is the outlaw-hero's courtesy ("A brave man or woman he'll never annoy") and the rich-poor motif. From another perspective, however, the burning of Lawrence by Quantrill and company was a horrific act; indeed, many innocents were killed. As Seal observes, "the facts of Quantrill's life do not appear to be of a kind deserving or attracting celebration", but during the violent confusion of the Civil War "it was quite possible for Quantrill to appear as a Confederate hero of some stature" (Seal 1996: 86).

As in the Scottish narratives, American outlaw-heroes' defiance is made possible by alliance. Meyer notes that during the career of the outlaw-hero, he is "helped, supported and admired by his people" (Meyer 1980: 107). Jesse James and his fellow outlaws, for example, were able to attack the representatives of economic power – the banks, railroads, express companies, and mercenary security forces (the Pinkertons) – with little condemnation from the farmers. Seal observes that "the extent of support and sympathy for the James-Younger gang in and around their native regions has been well documented". Kinship ties were critical: "they provided the outlaws with a sustaining network of informers, providers of food, ammunition, shelter and transport" (Seal 1996: 96). Community loyalties and obligations meant that the outlaws could rely on a wide network of people, extending to the ex-Confederate wing of the Democrats in Missouri, which allowed their defiance of authority to continue for some seventeen years after the Civil War. This relationship is deeply encoded in folklore. Alliance is at the core of the ballad of Jesse James, as demonstrated by the following three stanzas:

Jesse had a wife to mourn for his life,
Three children, they were brave,
But that dirty little coward that shot Mister Howard,
Has laid Jesse James in his grave.

It was Robert Ford, that dirty little coward,
I wonder how he does feel,
For he ate of Jesse's bread and he slept in Jesse's bed,
Then he laid Jesse James in his grave.

Jesse was a man, a friend to the poor.
He'd never see a man suffer pain,
And with his brother Frank he robbed the Chicago bank,
And stopped the Glendale train. (Larkin 1931; Botkin 1944: 108)

Even the legendary Billy the Kid has allies. Key to his outlaw-hero
credentials is alliance with, and defence of, an underdog faction that
"had the sympathy of the smaller landholders and workers, including
Mexican-Americans" (Seal 1996: 103–4). In balladry this alliance
surfaces in lines such as these from "Song of Billy the Kid": "Fair
Mexican maidens play guitars and sing / A song about Billy, their boy
bandit king" (Lomax and Lomax [1934] 1989: 138):

As in the Border ballads, when things go wrong in American
outlaw-hero ballads it is usually the result of betrayal by a close tie.
The outlaw's death, or some other tragedy, results when the bonds of
alliance are broken, either by the outlaw or a kinsman. Billy tells his
"friends" he is going to shoot Pat Garrett, "who once was his friend",
but Billy himself dies in that encounter. Jesse James is betrayed by
someone closely associated with his gang, "that dirty little coward"
Robert Ford. In concise, juxtaposed declarations, the ballad foregrounds the killer's violation of the outlaw's hospitality: Jesse had
provided Ford with food and shelter, but in return the traitor "laid
Jesse James in his grave". Violation of the laws of hospitality as an
unforgivable offence is deeply rooted in Scottish tradition, for
example in re-tellings of the Glencoe Massacre of 1692, in which
thirty-eight members of Clan MacDonald were killed by guests acting
on behalf of the crown, after enjoying the MacDonalds' hospitality.

Though outlaw-hero ballads do not dwell on the outlaw's guilt or
innocence, they do gesture towards justification of the crime, an
element that renders the outlaw's actions more supportable in the
public's eyes. Often this involves a mention, however brief, of the
"provocation theme"; the American outlaw's first "crime" is "brought

about through extreme provocation or persecution by agents of the oppressive system" (Meyer 1980: 100, 99). Evidence may be found in various legends concerning Jesse James of factors summarised here by Steckmesser:

Jesse and Frank James return from Confederate guerilla service in the Civil War to find their home state of Missouri overrun with carpetbaggers, Radicals and other vindictive Unionists. In the folklore version these persecutors attack Jesse's father, put his mother in jail, and savagely beat him with rope ends. The law itself has become a weapon of the Yankee oppressors. To secure justice for himself and his friends, Jesse must live outside the law. (Steckmesser 1966; Seal 1996: 95)

This motif may also be found in the Wallace legend, which presents the murder of Wallace's wife by English invaders under Edward I as the catalyst for his resistance to English authority.

In "Archie o Cawfield" (188A),[19] the reiver Archie Hall is held prisoner in a castle in Dumfries, set to be executed the following day. Like the James-Younger gang of the American ballads, historically the Hall family raiders who rescued their kinsman were no innocents; the family was the subject of legal complaints for "reif and away-taking of ky, oxen, etc." in 1579 (Child 1965: 3: 485). The ballad opens not with Archie's crime and capture, but with his two remaining brothers bemoaning Archie's fate. A rescue party is raised, consisting of the brothers and ten kinsmen. They manage to sneak into the castle, whereupon Archie's brother Dicky calls to the prisoner: "What is thy crime, Archie, my billy? / What is the crime they lay to thee?". Archie answers, "I brake a spear i the warden's breast, / For saving my master's land". It's enough for Dicky; he tells his brother,

"If that be a' the crime they lay to thee, Archie, my billy,
If that be the crime they lay to thee,
Work thou within, and me without,
And thro good strength I'll borrow thee."

The ballad is far less concerned with how Archie got into this mess than with how his kinsmen will exercise all their skill and ingenuity, in defiance of his captors, to get him out of it. "Archie o Cawfield" illustrates a dynamic common in the Border ballads which associates

---

[19] Variant A was communicated to Thomas Percy in 1780 (Child 1965: 3: 487).

family loyalty with justified actions undertaken to protect or promote the common interest.

Arthur L. Campa observes that the heroic legend "begins with an actual happening", which "in the transmission process is embellished and reinforced to such as extent that it is taken as fact" (Campa 1965: 4). Writing about the American outlaw-hero tradition, Meyer finds that underpinning the romance of the legends is a "surprisingly sparse and singularly unromantic core of verifiable historical fact against which one may balance the embellishment and selectivity of the folk imagination" (Meyer 1980: 95). This is a feature of all outlaw-hero texts. But as Kay McAlpine argues regarding the Border ballads, embellishment reflects the audience's engagement with the actual happening. Though history as reflected in records has been manipulated, the "emotional history" survives: the "urgent, reckless and intrepid nature" of the ballad narratives has been retained by the communities to which they belong (McAlpine 2000: 91).

What Knight has traced in the "process of localization" of myths and the "hybridization of borrowed features with local elements" (Knight 2008: 103, 104) is useful for considering how outlaw legends have adapted in their new American contexts. Scottish and American outlaw-hero ballads share much in their dependence on the motifs of alliance and defiance, enacted in dramatic narratives and staged in debatable lands that have national or quasi-national importance. While the moniker of "friend to the poor" originated with Robin Hood, the American outlaw-hero ballad seems to have gained considerable substance from its Scottish ancestors along the way. This legacy is encoded in the emotional history of stories still being told.

Bibliography

Borland, R. 1910. *Border Raids and Reivers*. Dalbeattie: Thomas Fraser; Glasgow: Fraser, Asher, & Co. Ltd.

Botkin, Benjamin A. 1944. *A Treasury of American Folklore*. New York: Crown Publishers.

Butterss, Philip. 1989. "Bold Jack Donahue and the Irish Outlaw Tradition" in *Australian Folklore* 3: 39.

Campa, Arthur L. 1965. "Folklore and History" in *Western Folklore* 24: 1–5.

Child, Francis J. [1882–98] 1965. *The English and Scottish Popular Ballads*. 5 vols. New York: Dover.

Coffin, Tristram P. 1950. *The British Traditional Ballad in North America*. Philadelphia: The American Folklore Society.

Cowan, Edward J. 2003. "Birth of the Clans" in *The Greatest Clans, part 1*, a supplement to *The Sunday Herald* [Glasgow] (7 September 2003). 4–7.

Devine, T.M. 1994. *Clanship to Crofters' War: The social transformation of the Scottish Highlands*. Manchester and New York: Manchester University Press.

Fletcher, Andrew of Saltoun. 1744. *Political Works*. Glasgow.

Guha, Ranajit. 1988. "On Some Aspects of the Historiography of Colonial India" [1982] in Guha, Ranajit and Gayatri Chakravorty Spivak (eds) *Selected Subaltern Studies*. New York: Oxford University Press. 3744.

Hanawalt, Barbara A. 1992. "Ballads and Bandits: Fourteenth-Century Outlaws and the Robin Hood Poems" in Hanawalt, Barbara A. (ed.) *Chaucer's England: Literature in Historical Context*. Minneapolis: University of Minnesota Press. 154–57.

Hobsbawm, Eric. [1969] 2000. *Bandits*. London: Weidenfeld & Nicolson.

Hogg, James. 2004. *The Collected Letters of James Hogg: Volume 1, 1800–1819* (ed. Gillian Hughes, with Douglas S. Mack, Robin MacLachlan, and Elaine Perie). Edinburgh: Edinburgh University Press.

Knight, Stephen. 1994. *Robin Hood: A Complete Study of the English Outlaw*. Oxford: Blackwell Publishers.

—. 2008. "Rabbie Hood: The Development of the English Outlaw Myth in Scotland" in Phillips, Helen (ed.) *Bandit Territories: British Outlaws and their Traditions*. Cardiff: University of Wales Press. 99–118.

Larkin, Margaret, ed. 1931. *Singing Cowboy: A Book of Western Songs*. New York: A.A. Knopf.

Laws, Jr., G. Malcolm. 1957. *American Balladry from British Broadsides*. Philadelphia: The American Folklore Society.

Lockhart, John Gibson. 1839. *Memoirs of the Life of Walter Scott*. 10 vols. Edinburgh and London: Robert Cadell, John Murray and Whittaker & Co.

Lomax, John A. and Alan Lomax (eds). [1934] 1989. *American Ballads & Folk Songs*. New York: Dover.

Lundgren, Tim. 1996. "The Robin Hood Ballads and the English Outlaw Tradition" in *Southern Folklore* 53(3): 225–47.

McAlpine, Kay. 2000. "Proude Armstrongs and Border Rogues: History in 'Kinmont Willie', 'Jock o the Side', and 'Archie o Cawfield'" in Cowan, Edward J. (ed.) *The Ballad in Scottish History*. East Lothian: Tuckwell Press.

MacDonald Fraser, George. 1995. *The Steel Bonnets: The Story of the Anglo-Scottish Border Reivers*. London: HarperCollins.

Mack, Douglas S. 2006. *Scottish Fiction and the British Empire*. Edinburgh: Edinburgh University Press.

Meyer, Richard E. 1980. "The Outlaw: A Distinctive American Folktype" in *Journal of the Folklore Institute* 17: 94–124.

Phillips, Helen. 2008. *Bandit Territories: British Outlaws and their Traditions*. Cardiff: University of Wales Press.

Prideaux, W.F. 1986. "Who Was Robin Hood?" in *Notes & Queries*, 7th series 2: 421–24.

Reed, James. 1973. *The Border Ballads*, University of London: The Athlone Press.

Roberts, J.W. 1981. "'Railroad Bill' and the American Outlaw Tradition" in *Western Folklore* 40: 315–28.

Scott, Walter 1802. *The Minstrelsy of the Scottish Border*. 2 vols. Kelso: printed by James Ballantyne for Cadell and Davies, London.

Scott, Willie. 2006. *Herd Laddie o the Glen: Songs of a Border Shepherd* (ed. Alison McMorland). Selkirk: Scottish Borders Council.

—. "Jamie Telfer o the Fair Dodheid" in *The Muckle Sangs: Classic Scots Ballads*. Edinburgh: School of Scottish Studies, University of Edinburgh; London: Greentrax Records.

Seal, Graham. 1996. *The Outlaw Legend: A Cultural Tradition in Britain, America and Australia*. Cambridge: Cambridge University Press.

Simeone, W.E. 1958. "Robin Hood and Some Other American Outlaws" in *Journal of American Folklore* 71: 27–33.

Spence, Lewis. 1928. "Robin Hood in Scotland" in *Chambers Journal* 18: 4–96.

Steckmesser, Kent L. 1966. "Robin Hood and the American Outlaw" in *Journal of American Folklore* 79: 348–55.

Watson, Godfrey. 1974. *The Border Reivers*. London: Robert Hale & Co.

Wurzbach, Natascha and Simone Salz. 1995. *Motif Index of the Child Corpus: The English and Scottish Popular Ballad* (tr. Gayna Walls). Berlin and New York: Walter de Gruyter.

Lateral Literary Biography: Robert Fergusson, Herman Melville and "Bartleby"

Susan Manning

Herman Melville's short story, "Bartleby the Scrivener" is suggestive of the drudging life of eighteenth-century Scots poet Robert Fergusson as a copyist clerk. Melville knew the life and work of Fergusson, but even without insisting on direct influence here, a comparative perspective on Melville's short story and Fergusson's biography is suggestive of complex debates about the moral purpose of humanity as we move through the Enlightenment and Romantic periods. A comparative reading of "Bartleby" and Fergusson's life is suggestive of new directions in the study of narrative upon which Transatlantic (especially American and Scottish studies) might capitalise.
Keywords: Robert Fergusson; Herman Melville; "Bartleby the Scrivener"; Gilles Deleuze; Adam Smith; Theory of Moral Sentiments; Scottish Enlightenment; Robert Burns; life writing; narratology; transatlantic studies.

The narrator of Herman Melville's short story "Bartleby the Scrivener" (1853) has in his legal line of business known "very many [...] law-copyists, or scriveners", and might, should he choose, "relate diverse histories" of this "somewhat singular set of men", stories "at which good-natured gentlemen might smile and sentimental souls might weep". Renouncing such consolatory narratives at the outset of his story, he almost perversely "waive[s] the biographies of all other scriveners for a few passages in the life of Bartleby", because

> While, of other law-copyists, I might write the complete life, of Bartleby nothing of that sort can be done. I believe that no materials exist, for a full and satisfactory biography of this man. It is an irreparable loss to literature. Bartleby was one of those beings of whom nothing is ascertainable except from the original sources, and, in his case, those are very small. (Melville 1987b: 13)

Two different models of biography are in play in this first paragraph: the exemplary, typifying tale whose aim is to educate the moral sentiments of a sympathetic reader; and the quasi-archaeological discovery of "original sources" from which a unique interior self may be construed through a traceable process of maturation and development. The shaping presence of the biographer is as important as the subject in both stories ("I" occurs over 500 times in the narrator's tale, compared with just over 100 occurrences of "Bartleby").

This chapter addresses certain problems in literary biography, and certain issues in comparative literary history, that emerge from tantalising transatlantic connections between "Bartleby" and the posthumous reconstruction of the life and poetry of the eighteenth-century Scottish poet Robert Fergusson by *his* biographers. I begin by recapitulating the stages of this celebrated American story first published in *Putnam's Monthly Magazine* in 1853. Then, addressing the question of whether Fergusson was a direct source for one of the nineteenth-century American tales, I retrace what I know about what Melville knew about Fergusson, as a prelude to asking what the singular combination of opacity and interpretability in "Bartleby" may alert us to in the work and the "story" of Fergusson. Finally, I will consider the significance of the transatlantic nature of this comparison, in terms of the relation between biographical methodology and comparative cultural politics in the late eighteenth and early nineteenth centuries.

1 Bartleby

"Bartleby the Scrivener" was part of Melville's bid (following reviewers' rejection of *Moby-Dick* and *Pierre*) to win a readership through short fiction and periodical publication. The story of the "unaccountable" clerk is told by his employer, a highly accountable, benevolent and complacent lawyer, by his own reckoning doing "snug business among rich men's bonds, and mortgages, and title deeds. All who know me consider me an eminently *safe* man" (Melville [1853] 1987b: 14). Bartleby appears in answer to advertisement for a copyist in a law office whose view, the narrator admits, is "deficient in what the landscape painters call 'life'" (14). He embraces the task assiduously:

At first, Bartleby did an extraordinary quantity of writing. As if long famishing for something to copy, he seemed to gorge himself on my documents. There was no pause for digestion [...] he wrote on silently, palely, mechanically. (19–20)

Copying is, the narrator fears, "a very dull, wearisome, and lethargic affair", inimical to creativity:

to some sanguine temperaments, it would be altogether intolerable. For example, I cannot credit that the mettlesome poet Byron would have contentedly sat down with Bartleby to examine a law document of, say five hundred pages, closely written in a crimpy hand. (20)

Bartleby writes impassively on, but when asked to verify the accuracy of his copy, he announces that he "would prefer not to" (20). For this refusal he gives no reason, merely reiterating his negative preference to the increasingly anxious interrogatories of the narrator. There is, as I'm not the first to point out – though we shall need to return to it – a grammatical ambivalence between transitive and intransitive in this curious formulation: "I prefer not to ..." (with the object implied rather than stated), or/and, "In general, what I prefer is not to" (intransitive) (Deleuze 1998: 68–91). As time goes on, Bartleby prefers to do less and less, never, apparently, leaving the office to eat or even to sleep. Preferring "to be stationary" (Melville [1853] 1987b: 41), he increasingly resists all efforts at relationship and exchange. The narrator struggles to assimilate this indigestible behaviour to his benevolent world view:

Nothing so aggravates an earnest person as a passive resistance. If the individual so resisted be of a not inhumane temper, and the resisting one perfectly harmless in his passivity; then, in the better moods of the former, he will endeavor charitably to construe to his imagination what proves impossible to be solved by his judgment. (23)

The capacity to formulate a deserving other rapidly hits a limit. The narrator's "fraternal melancholy" (28) draws him to contemplate with sympathy the copyist's appalling solitude amid the urban bustle of New York: "but just in proportion as the forlornness of Bartleby grew and grew to my imagination, did that same melancholy merge into fear, that pity into repulsion" (29). The psychology revealed in this movement is a near-exact exemplification of Adam Smith's theory of moral sentiments, in which the imagination's sympathetic identification with the sufferings of another must be tempered by prudence in order for the observer to arrive at a just (ethical) assessment of the situation. Such – surely? – would be the appropriate stance of a judicious biographer. And so the narrator presents himself. The texture of his account betrays this assurance.

Returning to his office on a Sunday morning, the narrator finds it locked from the inside, and hears the voice of Bartleby: "I am occupied". Intransigence is caught in the now unambiguous intransitivity of the scrivener's verbal construction. Further, the scene allegorises the problem of the narrator-biographer, who, excluded from the inner life of his subject, conjures a surrogate fabricated from projection and inference. Acknowledging, while resisting, the "wondrous ascendancy" of the copyist over him and finally unable to rid himself of this "intolerable incubus" (38), he changes his offices, leaving his successor to take responsibility for the disposal of Bartleby, who is "removed to the Tombs as a vagrant".[1]

The return of control renews the narrator's benevolence; he visits and tries to arrange good prison fare for Bartleby, but the scrivener with an insatiable appetite for copy now "prefers not to dine", and turns to face the wall. On a second visit the lawyer finds him in the courtyard, "strangely huddled at the base of the wall, his knees drawn up, and lying on his side, his head touching the cold stones" (44). (A single page of an earlier manuscript version survives, in which the lawyer finds Bartleby dead not in the yard, but in his cell, leaning on a tombstone that is written out of the published version of the tale. I'll return to this.)

When sympathetic imagination fails the biographer, he turns to "original sources" to supplement the deficit. The only explanation – if indeed it can be called that – for Bartleby's decline, is occasioned by almost the sole "biographical fact" (actually, only a posthumous "vague report") offered in relation to Bartleby's past – and as such seized upon by the narrator as the opportunity for a consolatory maxim at the end of his tale: that prior to his presentation as a scrivener he had been employed in the Dead Letter Office.[2] At once the narrator has a handle both on his subject's character and the trajectory of his story:

---

[1] The Central Prison of New York City, built in 1839, was styled after an Egyptian tomb, and named accordingly. Monroe Edwards, the "gentleman forger" to whom Bartleby is likened by the gaoler near the end of the tale, was confined in the Tombs.

[2] The origins of the Dead Letter Office went back to the 1770s, when Congress authorised Ebenezer Hazard to open undelivered letters that might assist in the prosecution of the Revolutionary War of Independence. In 1792, a Post Office Act in America prohibited post offices from opening letters, unless they had proved impossible to deliver. In this case, they were returned to the "Dead Letter Office", opened and either returned to sender or destroyed. The annual burning of dead letters became a public occasion in Washington.

Conceive a man by nature and misfortune prone to a pallid hopelessness, can any business seem more fitted to heighten it than that of continually handling these dead letters, and assorting them for the flames? For by the cart-load they are annually burned. Sometimes from out the folded paper the pale clerk takes a ring: – the finger it was meant for, perhaps, moulders in the grave; a bank-note sent in swiftest charity: – he whom it would relieve, nor eats nor hungers any more; pardon for those who died despairing; hope for those who died unhoping; good tidings for those who died stifled by unrelieved calamities. On errands of life, these letters speed to death.

 Ah Bartleby! Ah humanity! (44)

A satisfying coda seems to have emerged from the unsatisfying and unsatisfied story of the mysterious scrivener. It tells the reader nothing about Bartleby's sensibility; a great deal about the narrator's. At every stage, the blankness of Bartleby's life to scrutiny has thrown the focus back on the biographer's shifting responses to his subject's failure to compose itself into a story. It has become, in short, an autobiographical tale, the coherence and self-projection of whose first-person voice is the product of its author's rhetorical control. At this point, tense and voice shift from the historical narration that has attempted to account for the unaccountable by offering the sequence of events that have connected biographer and his subject, towards a frankly imaginative reconstruction in a vocative mode that implicates the reader in the story-telling project. This concluding demonstration of Smithian sympathy allows the narrator a brief moment of satisfaction as the pieces of his subject finally appear to cohere. That story – exemplary, biblically sanctioned, and appropriate to the narrator's range of reference – is a negative parable of redemption: in the image of Bartleby's despair, the narrator is able at last to appropriate the subject who has eluded his narration, assimilating Bartleby's death in a comforting biblical epitaph: "Asleep […] with kings and counselors" (45).

2 Melville's knowledge of Fergusson

The narrator's allusion is oddly displaced: he ventriloquises the voice of Job wishing *he* had never been born, a sentiment that (the reader must assume) the narrator attributes to Bartleby in *his* abandonment. The dislocation raises uncomfortable echoes around an otherwise seamless moment of closure. The same phrase occurs in Robert

Fergusson's posthumously published "Job, Chap. III Paraphrased", a poetic rendering of Job's magnificent curse on the day of his birth:

Why have I not from mother's womb expir'd?
My life resign'd when life was first requir'd?
[...]
For now my soul with quiet had been blest,
With Kings and counsellors of earth at rest

A certain kind of literary historical explanation for the parallelism readily offers itself in the Authorised Version's translation of Job 3: 13–14, where Job wishes that he had died before birth:

For now should I have lain still and been quiet, I should have slept: then had I been at rest,
With kings and counselors of the earth.

It looks like coincidence: influence by a prior source known independently to both writers: a minimally interesting footnote in transatlantic literary history.

Early accounts of Fergusson's life and fate suggest other forms of connection that complicate the issue. Born in Edinburgh in 1750, he died there in 1774, aged just 24, having achieved modest fame as a poet in English and Scots.[3] By the turn of the century, Fergusson was respectfully enough remembered to be the subject of a Memoir by David Irving, a new edition of the poems, and a supplemental essay in the *Encyclopaedia Britannica*. In 1800, Irving gave a particular spin to what was already the received version of Fergusson's brief professional career in Edinburgh:

he was employed in the Commissary Clerk's Office, but being unable to submit to the tyranny of the deputy, he soon relinquished his situation [...]. There is surely a very material distinction betwixt studying Law, and transcribing Law-papers, at so much a page [...] Poetry and Law, are things too heterogeneous in their nature, ever to unite in the same individual. (Irving 1800: 8)

In 1851 (two years before the publication of "Bartleby") Alexander Grosart accentuated the pathos:

---

[3] One of the few contemporary reviews of his 1773 *Poems* described his "muse" as appearing "in the different characters of a Lady of Quality and a Scotch Moggy" (*Monthly Review: or Literary Journal*, LI (December 1774): 483).

This situation was miserably inferior to his talents and acquirements, but his straitened circumstances – his utter want – compelled him to accept it. [...] he spent in this lowly, machine-like employment, the remainder of his too, too brief and ill-fated life. (Grosart 1851: lxxii)

The Commissary Court in Scots Law appointed and confirmed executors of deceased persons leaving property in Scotland – the clerks, figuratively, handled the possessions of the dead; they also dealt with matters of probate and divorce. Fergusson's first duty is said to have been to transcribe all testaments dating from 1767 – truly an exercise in dead letters (McDiarmid 1954: 1: 23). Twentieth-century biographies follow this line: Allan MacLaine, for example, describes Fergusson's occupation as "one of the most drudging and utterly dispiriting occupations imaginable – the endless copying of endless documents" (MacLaine 1965: 20).

Fergusson's earliest recorded period of despair appeared in the second half of 1773: a posthumously-published verse letter carries the sobering postscript, "Yours, in the horrors, R. Fergusson" (McDiarmid 1954: 1: 68). By the end of that year he was forced to abandon his copying at the Commissary Office; the final document in his hand is a testament dated 30 December. "Despairing of life and salvation he burned his manuscripts and ceased to write; latterly he refused food and drink", as the modern historian Rab Houston has it in a study of "the social context of insanity in eighteenth-century Scotland" (Houston 1999: 138). Fergusson's death on 17 October 1774 was reported starkly in a Charity Workhouse minute-book as "Mr Ferguson [sic], in the Cels" (cited from Goodsir Smith 1952: 29). The biographies read his committal to the madhouse as a sorrowful, knowing betrayal on the part of friends who felt they had no other option – similar to the uneasy self-justification of the narrator whose actions indirectly consign Bartleby to the Tombs. From the beginning, then, Fergusson's "Life" has been construed as a paradigmatic tale of doomed poetic talent destined for despair and premature death.

This poet was not altogether unknown in America: selections from his poetry were first printed in 1788, by J. & A. McLean in New York, as an appendage to "Poems, chiefly in the Scottish dialect / by Robert Burns". Imitative poems in Scots (often by emigrants) occur in American periodicals from early in the nineteenth century, and frequently invoke Fergusson's name along with those of Burns and Ramsay, prompting American literary visitors to Edinburgh like

George Ticknor in 1819 to ask to see the home of the poet (Hook
1975: 135, 140, 195). A Philadelphia volume of 1815, *Poems of
Robert Fergusson: in two parts. To which is prefixed, the life of the
Author, and a sketch of his writings; with a copious glossary
attached*", was the first edition prepared specifically for an American
readership. It contained a brief, anonymous, introduction to the poet's
life which incorporates verbatim phrases both from David Irving's
1800 account and from George Gleig's entry on Fergusson in his
Supplement to the Third Edition of the *Encyclopaedia Britannica.*[4]
The "final episode" of Fergusson's incarceration – central to
"Bartleby" – is not mentioned by Gleig or in the Philadelphia edition,
though it gains emphatic pathos in David Irving's 1800 version of the
life, an edition which seems to find many verbal echoes in "Bartleby".
It is possible that Melville knew this edition; but I am unable to show
that he did. It is also possible that prior to the composition of
"Bartleby", Melville could have come across Alexander Grosart's
1851 "Life of Fergusson", which takes strong issue with Gleig.
Grosart's Preface notes his "special gratitude" to "America's favourite
poets, W.C. Bryant, Esq., and Professor W.H. Longfellow", for their
assistance (Grosart 1851: viii).[5] He described Fergusson as

an object of profoundest sympathy to all who feel the "frailty" of humanity. Your
"honest, fair, worthy, square, good-looking, well-meaning, regular, uniform, straightforward, clock-work, clear-headed, one-like-another, salubrious, upright kind of
people", as the author of Salmagundi calls them, have no materials in their nature for
charity. (xcii)[6]

---

[4] Gleig's *Supplement* first appeared in 1801, and with the main Encyclopaedia was a
widely used information source in America as in Britain. Charles Brockden Brown for
example, probably drew on the 1798 EB entry on "Ventriloquism" in the composition
of *Wieland* (1798).

[5] Grosart's Introduction requests American readers of his edition to let him know
details of any early American editions of the works of Ramsay, Fergusson or Burns,
and his "Essay on the Genius and Poems of Fergusson", appended to his biographical
memoir notes, "Very recently, on an occasion which assembled in Boston the learned
and the eloquent and the gifted of our daughter-land, with the peerless Bryant at the
head, I read a Scottish Memory-Toast which places the name of Fergusson foremost,
– 'The four Roberts.' Robert Fergusson, – Robert Burns, – Robert Tannahill, – Robert
Nicoll: and touching, and graceful, and heartfelt was the fourfold tribute: but
especially that to Fergusson" (Grosart 1851: cxxxii).

[6] *Salmagundi* was a collection of early American satirical periodical essays produced
by Washington Irving, his brother and their friend James Kirke Paulding.

So did Melville have Fergusson in mind when he composed the melancholy fiction of "Bartleby"? Textual parallels and verbal echoes apart, some tantalising but inconclusive pieces of evidence (postdating, for the most part, the publication of the story) indicate the American writer's interest in a relatively obscure Scots poet. Most tangibly, he acquired, on 17 February 1862 – as his own literary career was turning definitively away from prose towards poetry, much of which would remain unpublished in his lifetime – *The Works of Robert Fergusson, ed. by A.B. G[rosart]* (London, 1857), and marked his copy (Sealts 1966: 60). I have not been able to find evidence that he read any of the earlier editions with their memoirs. So we are driven, like thwarted biographers, to ask what else, prior to 1862, Melville might have known of Fergusson's poetry, and of the unhappy figure conjured by the poetic biographies.

Further frustration awaits: Melville spent about five days in Edinburgh at the end of October and beginning of November 1856, en route from New York to the Holy Land, but his sole journal record of this visit is a laundry memorandum (Leyda 1969: 2: 527). A long letter to his brother Allan written from Liverpool, which is otherwise more informative about Melville's brief Scottish tour, says nothing more of the Edinburgh days than that he "was much pleased there" (Melville 1993: 302). He makes no reference to any books bought there, or to people he met. We can only conjecture, much in the manner of the narrator of "Bartleby", that his habitual visiting of graveyards in places he travelled to would have taken him to both Greyfriars and Canongate kirkyards, and to Fergusson's grave, with Burns's inscription. Spending only one day in Glasgow immediately beforehand, for example, he noted "tombs, defaced inscriptions – thers worn in flagging – some letters traced in moss" at the "old cathedral" (Melville 1989: 49).[7]

The origins of Melville's interest in Fergusson remain mysterious, therefore, but his acquisition of Grosart's edition of the *Works* is

---

[7] Nathaniel Hawthorne, serving as American Consul in Liverpool, noted a visit from Melville in the days following 20 November 1856, when the latter was fresh from, in Hawthorne's words, "seeing Edinburgh and other interesting places". Hawthorne describes a walk they took together on the Liverpool Sands, during which Melville announced that he had "pretty much made up his mind to be annihilated" (Hawthorne 1997: 162, 163). The image of utter negation in Melville's life is abiding in the years before and after "Bartleby"; fear of its consequences led his family to urge the pilgrimage to the Holy Land which took him to Europe (Leyda 1969: 2: 521, 529).

worth remark, given that his library was not notably extensive, and, apart from a copy of Burns with Gilfillan's memoir, Scottish literature is sparsely represented in both his library borrowings and the books he possessed. Neither was Fergusson's poetry a casual acquisition: in his copy Melville scored the following passage from Grosart's "Memoir":

Go, – moralist, light of heart and jovial in intercourse, living at ease, quiet and happy, writing as a recreation in thy study, surrounded with all the delicacies, and comforts, and securities of life, on thy gilt-edged, prim-folded sheet, – shut up the kingly eagle in the stancheoned cage of thy court-yard, and bid him "fly", *because* his native hills are before him. (Grosart 1851: lxxvi)

The passage occurs immediately after Grosart's exclamation against the appalling drudgery of the copyist's life:

Why, the study of the law, had it even been as dry as the withered heart that could dictate such a calumny, [that Fergusson was "utterly destitute" of "mental vigour"], would have been absolutely a daily delight of the highest kind, compared to the monotonous duties of perpetual transcription. (Grosart 1851: lxxv)

The "moralist" with "dry and withered heart" is Fergusson's earlier biographer Gleig, author of the *Supplement* to the *Encyclopaedia Britannica*, Doctor of Divinity, Fellow of the Royal Society of Edinburgh; he seems to share strong affinities with "Bartleby's biographer". So too does Mr Abercromby, Fergusson's "employer in the Commissary Office", whom Grosart describes as

a worthy, precise, leal-hearted, fidgetty, fretful, per-nickety old gentleman: remarkable for hard-working assiduity in his profession: loveable for his patient, father-like "challenges and advices", which he gave the mercurial poet: and to be remembered in that he was not a-wanting in the evil day. (Grosart 1851: lxxvii)

This combination of decency and limitation, embodied in the narrator of "Bartleby", too, characterises the stance of "Moral Sense" derived from the Scottish Enlightenment, which became the "genteel tradition" in nineteenth-century America. So in nearly all nineteenth-century versions of Fergusson's "Life" there is a productive "lawyer" figure able to tell the story of the thwarted copyist-poet doomed to unproductive labour.[8]

3 Bartleby and construing a biography of Fergusson

That is about as far as I have been able to go with documentary connection that might support a mapping of story, life, and "life" onto one another. Materials appear not to exist for a "full and satisfactory account" of this transatlantic conjunction. Changing tack, then, and working against the grain of historical priority, I want to consider what the story can alert us to in the "life" (meaning the posthumous biographical construction of Fergusson), and what further bearing these might have on the poetry. Matthew McDiarmid sensibly warns against reading Fergusson's employment in the Commissary Office "in the spirit of a post-mortem investigation, as if it were a direct cause of the dreadful circumstances in which his life closed" (McDiarmid 1954: 1: 23). It is worth asking why this has, since Burns, been the approach of almost all Fergusson's commentators and biographers:

Fergusson! thy glorious parts
Ill suited law's dry, musty arts!
My curse upon your whunstane hearts,
Ye E'nbrugh gentry!
The tythe o' what ye waste at cartes
Wad stow'd his pantry! (Burns 1968: 1: 59)

The "E'nbrugh gentry" are the Enlightened Establishment: Hugh Blair and Henry Mackenzie, the lawyers, divines and doctors, themselves antecedents of Melville's well-meaning but essentially obtuse lawyer-narrator. "Fergusson the Scrivener", Bartleby-figure to the Scottish Enlightenment, is the shadow self of sociability and sentiment, whose narrative, resistant to the Whig project of Enlightenment, can only be

---

[8] Andrew Knighton makes a cogent case for reading Bartleby's unproductivity and subsequent death from despair and starvation through Weber's association in *The Protestant Ethic and the Spirit of Capitalism* of Calvinist-capitalist interpretations of the value of labour (Knighton 2007: 185–215). This may suggest another kind of common ground between the Scottish biography of Fergusson and the "American" tale of "Bartleby" (see Manning 1990: 102–5).

told negatively by that voice and by its descendants. Both figures
embody something like the rhetorical figure of *occupatio* – that which
being denied or negated, retains its trace in the reader's consciousness.

Fergusson's nineteenth-century poetic reputation, was condi-
tioned both in Britain and America by Robert Burns's genealogical
invocation:

Thou! my elder brother in misfortune;
By far my elder brother in the muse! (Burns 1968: 1: 323)[9]

Burns's Fergusson is the product of his own suspicion and distrust of
the real comprehensiveness of the "E'nbrugh gentry's" benevolence;
the mad, dissipated Fergusson was a manifest of anxiety about the
negation of the promise of Moderatism and Enlightenment betrayed
by his poetry. The sheer depth of his desolation rebuked the facility of
their optimistic project. There is, therefore, both a complicity and an
antagonism between Burns's neglected genius and the flawed genius
handed down to biographers by his contemporaries. Both figures are
characterised by their resistance – negation, nay-saying or "preferring
not to" – "copy" the approved practices of their culture; and for both
the inevitable outcome is failure of words (letters) to reach their
destination in an appreciative audience, and a miserable, untimely
death. But the source, and the significance, of that fatal resistance are
differently attributed: Burns blamed the "gentry's" neglect of poetic
genius; the "moralists" would lay it at the door of Fergusson's own
dissipation.

From another perspective, dissipation might look more like
simple conviviality. What we know of Fergusson's Edinburgh life
from Robert Chambers's account of the Cape and Poker Clubs in the
Traditions of Edinburgh, till the dark days of religious delusion at the
end (to which I'll come), suggests high-spirited conviviality, good talk
and good fellowship, rather than the dissipation and blackguardism
hinted at by Henry Mackenzie's *Anecdotes and Egotisms*. Fergusson
was the first Scots urban poet, celebrant of city streets and the
multifarious, anarchic, amoral life they support; the poems' comic
vitality sparks against the gathering gentility of polite Edinburgh

---

[9] Robert Burns, "Apostrophe to Fergusson, Inscribed Above and Below his Portrait".
Burns wrote these lines in a copy of *Poems on various subjects, by Robert Fergusson.
In two parts*, 1782.

society. They refuse to dwell in conscious pathos that might arouse the sympathetic feelings of its Enlightened readers: the physical frailty of the poet, his poverty, the hardness of his lot are all written out of the gleeful exuberance of verse that allows the life of the city to flow, like drink, uncensored through it. Burns, by comparison, is a much more "personal" poet. This may, in fact, have been one of the grounds of the Mackenzie circle's suspicion of the poet: a tavern existence, as described by Fergusson's early biographers, was a measure of urban implication at odds with the domestic focus of Sensibility and the Common Sense philosophy propounded in the *Mirror* and *Lounger* papers, in Hugh Blair's sermons, and the conduct books of James Fordyce.[10]

Fergusson appears as a man without a "home" to go to, whose life wore away not at the sanctioned sociable convivialities of the tea-table, but (so the reading goes) in low and dubious haunts, in excess and indiscipline rather than moderation and prudence. So we may suspect, at the least, a tacit tactic of accommodation at work in retrospective biographical summaries like Henry Grey Graham's *The Social Life of Scotland in the Eighteenth Century*, whose single mention of Fergusson is in a mode of conscious pathos that sets the idleness of the poet against the bustling social milieu of Blair, Hume, Boswell and Kames:

none of these aristocrats of literary society cast any regard on the poor, shabbily-dressed copying clerk that threaded his way through the High Street crowd with his law papers, who for but two years was to write Scots poems and songs of the truest ring, before Burns wrote them surpassingly, and after too fond carouses o' nights, was to die in 1774 on the straw of a madhouse, at the age of twenty-four, when ended the short pathetic career of Robert Fergusson. (Graham 1969: 116–17)

For American and Modernist literary critics "Bartleby" is a classic fiction of urban alienation: the narrator notes that his office – which becomes Bartleby's home as well as his workplace, is in "a building entirely unhallowed by humanizing domestic associations" (Melville [1853] 1987b: 36).

In February 1826 *The Mirror of Literature, Amusement and Instruction* published a "Monument to Robert Fergusson the Poet"

---

[10] Certainly, a poem like "The Sow of Feeling" can have done nothing to endear Fergusson to a literary Establishment which in the 1770s and 1780s advocated domestic sensibility as a guide to moral life, individual and social.

(the title in Gothic Script appropriate to an epitaph or headstone). The brief article is prefaced by just such a tombstone, semi-obscured, bearing Fergusson's name and (inaccurate) dates. The only poetry quoted is Burns's epitaph, and the information conveyed is drawn fairly directly from Currie's *Life of Burns*. There is also the greater monument to Burns himself behind it with the inscription in verse, which is quoted at length. This comes as a last word to the matter of Fergusson's tomb, pointing out not Burns's homage, but his superiority. The last (second) stanza runs: "Go to your sculptur'd tombs, ye great / in a' the tinsel trash of state! / But by the honest turf I'll wait, / thou man of worth! / And weep the sweetest poet's fate / E'er lived on earth". The biography of one poet is the "original source" for posthumous commemoration of another; for Currie, Burns's erection of the material memorial in the Canongate was an occasion to demonstrate the superior sensibility of his subject, who becomes "lawyer" to Fergusson's Bartleby:

> In relating the incidents or our poet's life in Edinburgh, we ought to have mentioned the sentiments of respect and sympathy with which he traced out the grave of his predecessor Fergusson, over whose ashes he obtained leave to erect a humble monument, which will be viewed by reflecting minds with no common interest, and which will awake in the bosom of kindred genius many a high emotion. (cited in *The Mirror of Literature, Amusement and Instruction* 7: 182, 89)

Currie's proleptic association is sanctioned by the verse Burns wrote for inscription on this large, otherwise blank stone – a strikingly odd epitaph, from one comic poet skilled in mock-elegy to another:

> No sculptur'd Marble here, nor pompous Lay
> No storied Urn, nor animated Bust
> This simple Stone directs pale Scotia's way
> To pour her Sorrows o'er her Poet's Dust. (Burns 1968: 1: 322)

The immediate oddity of this verse is its grammar of remembrance: Fergusson's life is commemorated in negation. And that negation is couched in an impeccably plausible imitation of English neo-classical funerary verse, what D.H. Lawrence might have called a "post mortem effect" (Lawrence 2003: 148). This, surely, is not the Fergusson of Burns's admiration, the Fergusson whose mock elegies gave a new stretch to the poetic repertoire of Scots:

DEATH, what's ado? the de'il be licket,
Or wi' your *stang,* you ne'er had pricket,
Or our AULD ALMA MATER tricket,
      O' poor John Hogg,
And trail'd him ben thro' your mark wicket,
        As dead's a log. (McDiarmid 1954: 1: 191)

Burns's nugatory epitaph tells the story of Fergusson's genius as one of pathos and neglect; the figure it commemorates is "Fergusson the Scrivener", and its biographic purpose is about equally to demonstrate the refinement of Burns's own moral sentiments and to reproach the unfeelingness of Edinburgh's self-appointed ethical élite.[11] There is a clear element of poetic self-identification. According to John Richmond (himself a clerk to an Edinburgh WS) with whom Burns stayed in Edinburgh, the poet's initial visit to the unmarked grave took place during the early days when Burns wandered the city in a state of great depression.[12] In 1796 he would rather self-consciously re-inscribe two lines of Fergusson's "Job, Chap. III Paraphrased" in a letter which points the parallel between the unhappy circumstances of both poets, and (to our triangulated view) connects them to the fate of Bartleby:

say wherefore has an all indulgent Heaven
Light to the comfortless & wretched given? (Burns 1985: 2: 378)[13]

---

[11] In his petition to the Bailies of the Canongate for permission to erect the headstone. Burns describes Fergusson's bones as lying "among the ignoble Dead, unnoticed and unknown"; "the simple stone" he proposes to erect will "remain an unalienable property to his deathless fame" (6 February 1787; Burns 1985: I: 90).

[12] In April 1787, Burns wrote a *Prologue* for the actor William Woods (earlier Fergusson's friend and supporter) in which he was careful to allude flatteringly to the works of Mackenzie and John Home, a local piety of which his poetic predecessor had perhaps been too neglectful for his own good (Mackay 1992: 279).

[13] Successive layers of poetic appropriation appear on the Canongate memorial: at the foot of the grave a notice erected by the Saltire Society declares Robert Louis Stevenson's intention (thwarted in the event by his death), to renovate the tomb and add his own mark of poetic filiation. Stevenson's "poor, white-faced, drunken, vicious boy that raved himself to death in the Edinburgh madhouse" is not, in the consensus of contemporary criticism, Fergusson the high-spirited celebrant of "Auld Reekie" and defender of Scots practices, but it is part of the legend, and the biographical figure Stevenson identified with: "both sickly, both pestered, one nearly to madness, one to the madhouse with a damnatory creed" (Caird 1952: 112).

Nonetheless, the retrospective projection of melancholy does not seem wholly without foundation in Fergusson's own self-conception. He reputedly found particularly congenial during his late illness Hervey's "Meditations Among the Tombs". An unsurprising gesture – and source of solace – for an ailing man of sensibility in the early 1770s (think, for example, of Henry Mackenzie's Harley in *The Man of Feeling*, whose grave opens *The Man of Feeling*, and is revisited in Mackenzie's second novel *The Man of the World*). Religious despair does appear to have engulfed him at the end. For a biographer not committed either to ethical exemplum or the Romantic story of neglected genius, nothing is more puzzling about Fergusson's life than his descent into religious mania. Unlike Burns's poems, in which religion and the long arm of the Kirk are a constant presence, there is, in John MacQueen's words, "virtually no hint of the religious and theological obsession of seventeenth and eighteenth century rural Scotland" in Fergusson's poems (MacQueen 1982: 1: 120). Did Fergusson consciously silence the force that finally claimed him? Did he "prefer not" to speak out about the religious terrors which resisted all the taming efforts of Moderatism, or was he simply ignorant of their power over his own soul until too late? A Melvillian reading of Fergusson's biography might see his end as the terrified psyche's refusal to align itself with the anodyne comforts offered by Whiggish Enlightenment and a Moderate theology.

However we deconstruct the implicit motives of successive biographers, they all gesture towards the poetry's irreducible figure of Fergusson the Scrivener. "Possessing [...] almost unrivalled talents for mimicry", like many poets he served a poetic apprenticeship as the copyist of English elegiac, sentimental, and mock-heroic modes (Gleig 1801: 1: 648). Imitation appears to endorse the primacy of its models, but it characteristically sets a wedge between manner and matter. Mimicry, like copying, is sterile, an avenue which seems to promise possibilities that in the end, like dead letters, cannot be delivered. (We know, if Gleig is to be trusted on this point, that Fergusson was sensitive about the imputation of copying: as a student he apparently composed two acts of a tragedy on Wallace, only to abandon it on encountering a similar work on the subject, "because {said he to a friend} whatever I publish shall be original, and this tragedy might be considered as a copy" (Gleig 1801: 1: 647). The relationship between copying and resistance is close; there is perhaps a sense in which the imitator also always "prefers not to", in which respectful homage to the dead letters of the past is also an aggressive gesture of appropriation which nullifies original content in borrowed manner. In preferring not to (copy insatiably, without measure), Bartleby learns prudence; arguably, it kills him. And his epitaph must be that he sleeps with kings and counsellors.

The parallel in "Bartleby" alerts us to a kind of death-wish at the heart of Fergusson's celebration of life, as in:

Health is attendant in thy radiant train,
Round her the whispering zephyrs gently play,
Behold her gladly tripping o'er the plain,
Bedeck'd with rural sweets and garlands gay. (McDiarmid 1954: 1: 78)

With nullifying inevitability, the zephyrs "whisper", the garlands are "gay", and Hope "trips gladly": only a hair's-breadth of intention separates this from the parodic mode of a poem such as "Playhouse in Ruins".[14] Imitation and parody are never far apart.

Christopher Whyte has recently suggested, following Northrop Frye, that "literary imitation [...] may be a form of creative misunderstanding, which draws its meaning from the extent to which an original model is left behind, betrayed or superseded" (Whyte 2000: 47). The puzzling thing about the verse Fergusson wrote as a "copyist" of English poetic tradition (which leads his commentators, almost universally, to abandon it in embarrassment or disgust) is how *little* it seems to "leave behind, betray or supersede" its models.[15] "Apprentice-work" is the usual explanation: Fergusson after all was only about nineteen at the time. Alluding, perhaps, to this, in the biographers' reconstructions of both Fergusson and Bartleby description of the copyist's occupation is heavily burdened with two separate though related strains of imagery: first, prisons, cages, and tombs; second, nourishment and digestion (or their absence).

Contrary to the received wisdom that Scots wrote better in Scots because it came naturally to them while English was an alien idiom

---

[14] Fergusson's English poems deal, by and large, in abstractions: "Hope", "Pity", "Conscience" – what George Santayana, referring to the "Genteel Tradition" in nineteenth-century American writing, would call "digestions of vacancy" (Santayana 1967: 44).

[15] "Worthless", "pedestrian", "vitiated", "pretty bad", "artificial" are some of the kinder adjectives used by critics (MacLaine 1965: 28; Goodsir Smith 1952: 18).

acquired by laborious study, the example of Fergusson suggests that
as far as poetic diction is concerned the assumption should be
reversed: having been educated in the study and imitation of classical
and neo-classical models, his initial attempts at composition readily
framed themselves in Augustan English; it was not until he began to
experiment with Scots forms that the intractability of form and idiom
slowed up his facility sufficiently to allow the creative misprision
which permanently expanded the poetic possibilities of the language.
In other words, it's not the copying that's the problem, but the
copyist's digestion. Elaborating the metaphor, we might say that the
need to chew on an idiom which presented itself, poetically at least, in
a less pre-digested form, to work out his own resources of rhyme,
rhythm and image, enabled Fergusson to re-connect and absorb the
concrete particulars of the moment, not to pass to quickly over them
on the way to a general reflection, as tends to happen in his English
verse.[16] In Scots, Fergusson is not only an urban poet, he is a poet of
the alimentary *process*, whose idiom returns expression to the body
and its appetites: "[…] round they gar the bicker roll, / To weet their
mouth" (McDiarmid 1954: 2: 33).

    Shortly before he composed "Bartleby", Melville identified
Hawthorne's literary achievement in strongly national terms: "We
want no American Goldsmiths, nay, we want no American Miltons".
Declaring that "it is better to fail in originality, than to succeed in
imitation", he acclaimed Hawthorne's capacity to say "No, in
thunder" to genteel optimism, and to express the "blackness of
darkness" at the heart of experience (Melville [1850] 1987a: 248, 247,
243). The story of Bartleby and the stories of Fergusson suggest rather
that in Romantic biography the power of digestion as much as the
power of darkness may be what truly differentiates national,
independent, poet from scrivener. Bartleby writes as if famished,
"gorg[ing]" himself on documents with no pause for digestion

---

[16] In the days of desolation, Fergusson seems to have reverted to English as a poetic
medium. The paraphrase of "Job, Chap. III" is of course a kind of copy – Cowper and
Smart "imitated" Biblical and Classical texts to keep their expression disciplined on
the near side of sanity. But though the verbal echoes of the King James Version are
pervasive, this is not "Fergusson the Scrivener", blandly rendering the facile surface
of a borrowed diction. "Paraphrase" it may be, but the strong Biblical rhetoric is
"digested", transformed and tempered in the forge of Fergusson's own despair. There
are signs in these final poems that he might have become if not a great poet in
English, at least a considerable one, as Burns also could be on occasion.

(Melville [1853] 1987b: 19); the *matter* of his work passes, as it were, straight through him, with no alteration in manner consequent on interaction with the copyist's self. Passing it "mechanically" from eye to hand at once sustains his existence and protects it from the threat of change or uncertainty. To "verify the accuracy" of his copy, as the narrator requests, would simply confirm the nullity of his own creative life. This Bartleby prefers not to do. Excess and idleness are equally opposed to prudent productivity. It was the implications of *this* observation that his fictional biographer, like Fergusson's historical ones, found hard to swallow.

4 Influence, intertextuality – or what? The transatlantic perspective

The material simply does not exist for a "full and satisfactory life" that might supply the inwardness absent from the poetry. In the end, silence is only silence; nothing, as Bartleby's narrator discovers, can be made of negation. Similarly, evidence of a historical connection between Melville and Fergusson is inconclusive. Conventional literary history does not offer very much purchase on this intriguing parallel. It is not even obvious that we should be greatly advanced if we knew that Melville had (or had not) visited Fergusson's grave, or could "prove" that he had the Job poem in his mind when he composed "Bartleby". The absence of the confirming "literary relation" imposes explanatory restrictions that may send us back into methodological reflection. A pilgrimage to the grave would be a fact of cultural history; the implications of the textual conjunction emerge not from the fact itself (or its absence). If some complex intertextuality is at work, it seems to operate retrospectively as much as prospectively, in ways that mutually implicate both the fictional character and the biographical subject. A series of homologies connects the symbolic elaboration of Fergusson's profession as a law-copyist with Bartleby's: the poet's lonely death in a madhouse is strikingly recapitulated in Bartleby's increasing alienation from life and eventual fate. Burns's Fergusson reflects his disenchantment with the Edinburgh "gentry" who took him up only on their terms, as Melville's Bartleby may project the author's own increasing alienation from the milieu which welcomed his early nautical tales. In both cases, self-representation is overwhelmed by the representations of others, and the failure of the substituted representation to produce a coherent narrative. And so on.

For Melville's contemporary Ralph Waldo Emerson the perception of "Correspondences" constituted a legitimate conferral of connection and unity on disparate manifestations. Discovery of primal correspondences, driven by a desire to "find out connections", informed Emerson's epiphanic experience in the Jardin des Plantes in Paris, for example. The *locus classicus* of the relation between words and things is Blair's *Lectures on Rhetoric and Belles Lettres* (1783), which Emerson studied at Harvard; it left pervasive traces in his writing:

> throughout the radical words of all Languages, there may be traced some degree of correspondence with the object signified. With regard to moral and intellectual ideas, [...] in every Language, the terms significant of them, are derived from the names of sensible objects to which they are conceived to be analogous. (Blair 1783: 1: 103)[17]

Melville's narrator, who links Bartleby's ceasing to "copy" (to replicate language) with a possible failure of sight (perhaps equating to Emersonian vision), employs metaphors as dead as Bartleby's letters; seeking to assimilate the passive scrivener into a sympathetic universe, he fails to ask *why* Bartleby's passive resistance to correspondence is intolerable. Bartleby's "I would prefer not to" – what Deleuze calls his "formula" – drops all "correspondent" use of language into a black hole (Deleuze 1998: 73). His language is as starved as his life. It refuses both sympathy and transference, offers no metaphors or figures, is shorn even of the tonal inflections of irony.

Something (historical) has "happened" in the narrator's encounter with the scrivener, but the textually mediated nature of the reader's encounter with that presumed event resists appropriation absolutely. The contradictions in the tale's very precisely indicated internal chronology make it yet clearer that its "meaning" is not going to become available through recovery of a consistent sequence of events (Swann 1985: 357–58; Meindl 1996: 63–103). So let us return to the conjunction of "Bartleby" and "Fergusson", and ask a different

---

[17] The punning possibilities of correspondence is the starting point for the ubiquitous presence of letters – dead, purloined, and Scarlet – in psychoanalytic and deconstructive readings of American literature's status as the first postmodern writing.

question. How may critics and literary historians deal with manifest transatlantic "correspondences" in the absence of evidence of influence? Job's futile but emotionally potent retrospective desire to have died before he was born offers some support for the possibility that chronology, translated transatlantically, may, for literary criticism, be as illuminating viewed retrospectively as prospectively. If, rather than pursuing an "original source" for the verbal coincidence, we attend to the tense changes across the iterations from the pluperfect subjunctive (Job) to the imperfect subjunctive (Fergusson) to the present indicative (he *is* asleep "with kings and counsellors") in "Bartleby", and the transferred imputation from a first-person experiential (Job) to a third-person attributive voice (Bartleby's narrator), a different sequence of association unfolds, suggesting that what we might call the "lateral" connections of grammar and rhetoric may offer some heuristic potential to the comparison. With each iteration and each shift in context the phrase becomes more definite and present in tense, as it becomes more distant in attribution: Job's curse is appropriated as a wished-for state by Fergusson's narrator, then re-appropriated as a description of the actual condition of Bartleby by his well-meaning narrator. It "advances" grammatically as it "recedes" deictically. The temporal sequence becomes part of a matrix of different kinds of relation. Sequence and chronology, that is, themselves emerge as functions of representation; textual presence and historical process are mutually modifying in the transatlantic literary relation so construed.

In this frame appropriation is signalled by textual disruption. The "Authorised Version" is a translation of a presumed "original", and Fergusson's poem is entitled "Job, Chap. III, Paraphrased". Translation, as Walter Benjamin puts it in a famous phrase, "issues from its original – not so much from its life as from its afterlife" (Benjamin 1992: 72). The aspect of belatedness, the "afterlife", might seem to return us to the chronology of traditional "history", but the multiplicity of possible translations does away with origins and finitudes of meaning (such as, for example, those instantiated in narratives of national origin). For Benjamin, translation "seems to be the only conceivable reason for saying 'the same thing' repeatedly" (Benjamin 1992: 70). This, if anything, sums up Bartleby's life: it is, after all, what he does for a living.

A repeated concern through the different contexts of this chapter has been the relationship between transitivity and intransigence:

between the things that will "cross" or transmit – of a life, of a literature, of a culture – and those that will not. Bartleby's major characteristic seems to be that he is completely alone, without connection of any kind; he is compared by the narrator to "A bit of wreck in the mid Atlantic" (Melville [1853] 1987b: 32). The writing that defines this miserable being's existence has no point of origin, either in America, or Britain. Leaving aside the complex political discussions around "representation" in nineteenth-century America, we note also that the copyist has no copyright; he cannot control subsequent appropriation or impersonation by others.[18] The copyist's activities alienate thought from its production in writing, which furnishes the rationale for strong Marxist readings of "Bartleby". My emphasis here is slightly different, though continuous with such attempts to read the story – and the biographical dilemmas it points towards – contextually. Imitation appears to endorse the primacy of its models, but it characteristically divorces manner from matter. As Derrida made clear, iteration (and this is where it is anathema to Romantic transcendence and national literary history alike) does not transform or contextualise singularity; in "Bartleby" it instantiates it as the sequential, non-progressive mode that governs the passing of time. Its relationship to resistance is close; there is a sense in which the imitator also always "prefers not to", in which his respectful homage to the dead letters of the past is also an aggressive gesture of appropriation which nullifies the copyright of the original. A whole approach to literary history, with its rationale for evolutionary progression, is advanced, and rejected, here. One point that "Bartleby" would seem to make very forcibly for American literature – and in which Fergusson criticism has concurred in Scottish literary history – is that there is no "future" for an idiom which simply "copies" the output of inherited expression; more than merely stifling poetic creativity, it may reduce all of culture to the ashes of "dead letters", so many pious words inscribed on a tombstone. Iteration halts the teleological march of History.

---

[18] In mid-nineteenth-century Anglo-American cultural politics the absence of reciprocal international copyright agreement determined Melville's publication strategies and preoccupied Dickens, who makes a displaced metonymic appearance in "Bartleby" in the pastiche characters Nippers, Ginger Nut and Turkey, and whose face "blazed like a grate of Christmas coals" (Melville 1987b: 15).

This returns us to the subversive-subservient nature of mimicry. The more "perfect" the copy, the more it throws into question the status of an "original" or the purposive narrative that might issue from such a sequence. As Borges's Pierre Menard and his Don Quixote project imply, a "perfect" copy, like a good translation, would undo the relation of priority between the two manifestations, and therefore the categories "original" and "copy" that are presumed to relate them. Bartleby's passive intransigence is equally intransitive: his life cannot be made to mean, even by the well-meaning narrator. The story constructed around this "irreparable loss to literature" (Melville [1853] 1987b: 13) is supplementary (in Derrida's sense) to the point of being *de trop*. But it is in keeping. For Bartleby's narrator it is the *singularity* of the scrivener which requires the biographical attempt to assimilate the unaccountable "fact" of Bartleby to a textual genealogy of suffering that may lean, finally, on the authority of a Biblical original. It is not necessary to reach for a "higher" explanation in (say) Melville's subversive intentions towards Transcendental optimism, to find the verbal coincidence helpful in exerting some leverage on how the Romantic biography of Fergusson seems to have been developed against the grain of the (very limited) evidence on which it was construed, and on the cultural hegemony it was designed to support.

To elucidate this transatlantic comparison in terms of simple analogy – the narrator of "Bartleby" is like Fergusson's biographers, as "Bartleby" is like Fergusson the poet – seems unsatisfactory. The next question then has to be simply: why? If we're unable to adduce traditional comparative literary history's preferred term of influence, where do we turn? I spoke earlier about the dilemma of the narrator-biographer of "Bartleby" who, finding himself excluded from the inner life of his subject, conjures a surrogate subject fabricated from projection and inference. Developing a model for "circumatlantic performance", Joseph Roach has recently described how "improvised narratives of authenticity and priority" (such, we might posit, as the narrator's finding explanations for his subject's singularity in his life story) solidify into "full blown myths of legitimacy and origin" in response to anxieties provoked by surrogation or substitution in the processes of cultural continuity. "The key", he writes,

to understanding how performances worked *within* a culture [...] is to illuminate the process of surrogation as it operated *between* the participating cultures. The key, in other words, is to understand how circum-Atlantic societies, confronted with

revolutionary circumstances for which few precedents existed, have invented
themselves by performing their pasts in the presence of others. (Roach 1996: 5)

Faced with the spectre of their own obsolescence, cultures – like
individuals – attempt to reify their position in the accepted terms of
their milieu. Their resistance comes through as negation, an
occupation whose traces remain to trouble overt acquiescence. This
seems accurately to describe both the strategies of Melville's narrator
and Fergusson's biographers, and the effects of their stories.

Perhaps even more to the point, copying itself, like mimicry, is a
kind of surrogacy, a transposition or translation of the "content" of an
"original" into the manner of imitation. But (to return to Pierre
Menard) the more exact the copy or mimic is, the closer it may come
to undoing the priority, perhaps even the existence, of an "original".
The result is a kind of reciprocal haunting whereby "original" and
"copy" bear the textual traces of one another. As Roach makes clear,
however, these mutually-defining performances of difference must
always be understood *in relation* to the conditions of an earlier
performance: historical context is conceived appositionally rather in
terms of origins. Reframing transatlantic relationships in terms of
surrogation, I suggest, opens new possibilities for critical comparison
relieved from dependency on implied narratives of priority or
influence.

Bibliography

Arsic, Branca. 2007. *Passive Constitutions or 7 ½ Times Bartleby.* Stanford, CA: Stanford University Press.
Benjamin, Walter. 1992. "The Task of the Translator" in *Illuminations* (tr. Harry Zohn). London: Fontana.
Blair, Hugh. 1783. *Lectures on Rhetoric and Belles Lettres.* 2 vols. London: Strachan and Cadell.
Brockden Brown, Charles. [1793] 1991. *Wieland.* London: Penguin.
Burns, Robert. 1968. *The Poems and Songs of Robert Burns* (ed. James Kinsley). 3 vols. Oxford: Oxford University Press.
—. 1985. *The Letters of Robert Burns* (eds J. De Lancey Ferguson and G. Ross Roy). 2 vols. Oxford: Oxford University Press.
Caird, James B. "Fergusson and Stevenson" in Goodsir Smith, Sidney (ed.) *Robert Fergusson, 1750–74: Essays by Various Hands to Commemorate the Bicentenary of his Birth.* Edinburgh and London: Thomas Nelson & Sons Ltd. 112–22.
Chambers, Robert. 1980. *Traditions of Edinburgh.* Edinburgh: Constable.
Deleuze, Gilles. 1998. "Bartleby; or, The Formula" in Smith, Daniel and Michael Greco (eds) *Essays Critical and Clinical.* London: Verso. 68–91.
Gleig, George. 1801. "Robert Fergusson" in *The Supplement to the Third Edition of the Encyclopaedia Britannica.* Vol. 1. 2 vols. Edinburgh, Bonar.
Goodsir Smith, Sidney (ed.) 1952. *Robert Fergusson, 1750–74: Essays by Various Hands to Commemorate the Bicentenary of his Birth.* Edinburgh & London: Thomas Nelson & Sons Ltd.
Graham, Henry Grey. [1899] 1969. *The Social Life of Scotland in the Eighteenth Century.* London: Adam & Charles Black.
Grosart, A.B. (ed.) 1851. *The Works of Robert Fergusson. Edited, with Life of the Author and an Essay on his Genius and Writings.* London, Edinburgh, and Dublin: A. Fullarton & Co.
Hawthorne, Nathaniel. 1997. *The English Notebooks, 1850–1860* in Woodson, Thomas and Bill Ellis (eds) *The Centenary Edition of the Works of Nathaniel Hawthorne.* Vol. 22. Columbus, Ohio: Ohio State University Press.
Hook, Andrew. 1975. *Scotland and America 1750–1835.* Glasgow and London: Blackie.
Houston, Rab. 1999. "Madness, Morality, and Creativity: Robert Fergusson and the Social Context of Insanity in Eighteenth-Century Scotland" in *British Journal for Eighteenth-Century Studies* 22(2): 133–54.
Irving, David (ed.) 1800. *The Poetical Works of Robert Fergusson, with the Life of the Author.* Glasgow: Chapman & Lang.
Knighton, Andrew. 2007. "The Bartleby Industry and Bartleby's Idleness" in *ESQ* 53(2): 185–215.
Lawrence, D.H. [1923] 2003. *Studies in Classic American Literature* (ed. Ezra Greenspan et al). Cambridge: Cambridge University Press.
Leyda, Jay. 1969. *The Melville Log. A Documentary Life of Herman Melville 1819–1891.* 2 vols. New York: Gordian Press.
Mackay, James. 1992. *Burns. A Biography of Robert Burns.* Darvel: Alloway Publishing.

Mackenzie, Henry. 1996. *The Anecdotes and Egotisms of Henry Mackenzie, 1745–1831*. Bristol: Thoemmes.

MacLaine, Alan (ed.) 1965. *Robert Fergusson.* New York: Twayne Publishers.

MacQueen, John. 1982. *The Enlightenment and Scottish Literature.* 2 vols. Edinburgh: Scottish Academic Press.

Manning, Susan. 1990. *The Puritan-Provincial Vision: Scottish and American Literature in the Nineteenth Century.* Cambridge: Cambridge University Press.

McDiarmid, Matthew P. (ed.) 1954. *The Poems of Robert Fergusson.* 2 vols. Edinburgh: Scottish Texts Society.

Meindl, Dieter. 1996. *American Fiction and the Metaphysics of the Grotesque.* Columbia: University of Missouri Press.

Melville, Herman. [1850] 1987a. "Hawthorne and His Mosses" in *The Writings of Herman Melville, Volume 9: The Piazza Tales and Other Prose Pieces 1839–1860.* Evanston and Chicago: Northwestern University Press and the Newberry Library. 239–53.

—. [1853] 1987b. "Bartleby the Scrivener" in Hayford, Harrison, Alma A. MacDougall and G. Thomas Tanselle (eds) *The Writings of Herman Melville, Volume 9: The Piazza Tales and Other Prose Pieces 1839–1860.* Evanston and Chicago: Northwestern University Press and the Newberry Library. 13–45.

—. 1989. "Journal, 1856–57" in Horsford, Howard C. and Lynn Horth (eds) *Journals. The Writings of Herman Melville.* Vol. 15. Evanston and Chicago: Northwestern University Press and the Newberry Library.

—. 1993. "Correspondence" in Horth, Lynn (ed.) *The Writings of Herman Melville.* Vol. 14. Evanston and Chicago: Northwestern University Press and the Newberry Library.

Monthly Review: or Literary Journal. 51 (December 1774)

Roach, Joseph. 1996. *Cities of the Dead Circum-Atlantic Performance.* New York: Columbia University Press.

Santayana, George. 1967. *The Genteel Tradition. Nine Essays by George Santayana* (ed. Douglas L. Wilson). Cambridge, MA: Harvard University Press.

Sealts Jr., Merton M. 1966. *Melville's Reading. A Checklist of Books Owned and Borrowed.* Madison: The University of Wisconsin Press.

Swann, Charles. 1985. "Dating the Action of Bartleby" in *Notes and Queries* 32(3): 357–58.

The Holy Bible. New international version. London: Hodder & Stoughton, 1985.

The Mirror of Literature, Amusement and Instruction. 1826 (February). 7(182).

Whyte, Christopher. 2000. "Competing Idylls: Fergusson and Burns" in *Scottish Studies Review* 1(1): 47–62.

The Military Kailyard: The Iconography of the Nineteenth-Century Soldier

Trevor Royle

From the mid-nineteenth century a powerful iconography of the Scottish soldier is projected in the periodical press, especially *Blackwood's Magazine*, and elsewhere. Strong Scottish pride in the martial image is reflected not only on and through the regular Scottish regiments of the British army, but in volunteer militia units. This martial mythology is a powerful repository of Scottish identity through the nineteenth century, but complicated international conflicts such as the Indian Mutiny and the Crimean War ensure that this ultimately must reside within the context of British identity. The military Kailyard fiction of James Grant is exemplary of this trajectory.
Keywords: The Scottish martial myth; Scottish regiments in the British army; John Blackwood; *Blackwood's Magazine*; Crimean War; Indian Mutiny; Laurence Oliphant; Laurence Lockhart; Volunteer militia; James Grant; Kailyard.

At the end of the Crimean War in 1856 the Edinburgh publisher John Blackwood decided to form what he called an informal "military staff" of writers from army backgrounds to produce material for *Blackwood's Magazine*. The intention was to enter the debate about the much-needed reforms of the army in the wake of the widespread and well-publicised mismanagement which had been revealed during the conflict, but Blackwood was also keen to benefit from the accompanying interest in military literature that had blossomed in the middle of Queen Victoria's reign. He was well placed to make this move because among his stable of regular contributors were some of the best known military writers of the mid-Victorian period and, being a shrewd publisher, Blackwood also understood that military literature, fiction as well as non-fiction, sold well. Although Blackwood considered himself to be a British publisher in that his firm had offices in Edinburgh and London and his list included a wide range of authors, including the novelists George Eliot and R.D. Blackmore, there were a number of Scots amongst his "military staff". Among the most notable were Sir Archibald Alison, the soldier son of the historian; G.R. Gleig, the author of *The Subaltern* (1826), one of the most entertaining fictional accounts of life in Wellington's army; James Hope Grant, a general turned military historian; Laurence Lockhart, nephew of Walter Scott's biographer John Gibson Lockhart;

and Laurence Oliphant, who had written about the fighting in Circassia for *The Times* during the Crimean War. Along with writers such as A.W. Kinglake, George Chesney, Edward and William Hamley they kept *Blackwood's Magazine* and the publishing house of William Blackwood at the forefront of contemporary military writing for most of the nineteenth century.

John Blackwood was one of the most successful entrepreneurial publishers of his day. Not only did he possess business acumen, but from an early age he demonstrated editorial flair and he had the happy knack of being able to spot literary talent, but also to develop it to his own and the author's benefit. In addition to Eliot and Blackmore, he fostered the work of a large number of mid- and late-Victorian writers, many of whom became personal friends and lifelong associates of his publishing house. Amongst them were William Edmonstoune Aytoun, Elizabeth Barrett Browning, Edward Bulwer-Lytton, Charles Lever, Charles Reade, Thomas Hardy, Margaret Oliphant, George Henry Lewes and Anthony Trollope. He also understood the need to produce good narrative fiction and, in addition to his military writers, he encouraged the publication of work by explorers and adventurers, men such as Richard Burton, who had visited the forbidden city of Mecca in disguise, and James Augustus Grant and John Hanning Speke, who had both been involved in expeditions to discover the source of the River Nile. Later, by the twentieth century, the publishing house of Blackwood became – to its great detriment – over-dependent on this kind of writing, but under John Blackwood it seemed to have captured the spirit of the age with its interest in exploration and warfare. In 1871, at the conclusion of the Franco-Prussian war in 1871 he wrote to Bulwer-Lytton's son, expressing his contentment that "the old ship, I am happy to say, holds on her course satisfactorily" (Tredrey 1954: 138).

Blackwood was born in 1818, one of the seven sons of William Blackwood, the firm's founder, who had established himself as a bookseller at 64 South Bridge in Edinburgh in 1804, before cautiously entering the world of publishing. In 1816 he moved his business premises to 17 Princes Street in the newly built New Town and the following year he began publication of *Blackwood's Magazine*, which quickly established itself as the rival to Francis Jeffrey's Whiggish *Edinburgh Review*. *Blackwood's Magazine* was initially an insipid publication, and William Blackwood sacked its editors after six issues and employed two young advocates, John Wilson and John Gibson Lockhart to produce the seventh issue in October 1817. The result was the publication of the "Chaldee Manuscript", a scurrilous attack on Scotland's leading Whigs and all those associated with the *Edinburgh Review*, which was written in the language of the Old Testament and purported to be the "Translation from an ancient Chaldee Manuscript, recently discovered in the Bibliothèque Nationale in Paris". As a result, the magazine became a *succès de scandale* overnight and the editors followed up their initiative with virulent critical broadsides aimed at "the Cockney School of Poetry", work written by John Keats, Leigh Hunt and William Hazlitt; together with the editors' aggressively pro-Tory stance, this earned *Blackwood's Magazine* a notorious reputation in its early years. Hunt was castigated for his "low birth and low habits" and the magazine marked Keats's early death in 1821 with the remark that he had "left a decent calling [pharmacy] for the melancholy trade of Cockney-poetry" (Mason 2006: 6: 96).

By the time that John Blackwood took over the firm in 1852 both Wilson and Lockhart were dead and the editorial line had become less raucous, a leading article claiming that "impetuosity has given place to a calm, where no breeze breaks the mirrored images", but the magazine and publishing house still upheld Conservative and traditional values ("North and the Noctes" 1855: 395). Under John Blackwood's direction Margaret Oliphant became a regular contributor to the magazine and her novels also appeared under the Blackwood imprint. Blackwood also persuaded George Eliot (Marian Evans) to write for him, and all but one of her novels (*Romola*) were published by him, first in serial form in the magazine and then as complete volumes. By 1860 her work was so popular that she persuaded Blackwood to publish *The Mill on the Floss* in book form without prior publication in the magazine. During this period Blackwood expanded his lists to include books on exploration and adventure and this interest was also reflected in the magazine. He was also fascinated by the two great military near-disasters of the 1850s – the Crimean War and the Indian Mutiny of 1857. During the latter part of the decade the magazine carried articles on such subjects as "The State of the Army", "Military Education", "Fleets and Navies", "Ironclad Ships of the War", "Medicine and Surgery in the Army", all written by naval and military experts. Partly this leaning reflected

Blackwood's own interests – one of his brothers was an officer in the Indian Army – but another factor was his close friendship with John Delane, the editor of *The Times*, whom he had met and come to admire while working in the firm's London office.

Both men were closely involved in the problems exposed by the British military deployment in the Black Sea in 1854 to prevent Russian expansionism in the Black Sea area. The oft-told tale of the Crimean War has a curiously British ring, of an enterprise begun badly and ending tolerably; of initial bumbling, ineptitude and, above all, disavowal giving way to something approaching hope. It created a heroic myth out of the Charge of the Light Brigade, in Florence Nightingale it produced one of history's great heroines, it was the first conflict to be covered by the press and it pointed the way to what warfare would become in the twentieth century. That it received so much attention owed everything to Delane, who decided at an early stage that his newspaper's resources should be used to cover the conflict faithfully and accurately. On 12 October 1854 he published a revealing account of the revolting conditions faced by the sick and wounded at the British Military Hospital at Scutari, which stood on the opposite side of the Bosphorus from Constantinople. Written by Thomas Chenery, an Etonian barrister who acted as the local correspondent for *The Times*, the story caused an uproar. Following the euphoria of the recent victory on the River Alma, the newspaper's 40,000 readers were treated to the harsh reality of the aftermath of battle and the suffering of the British soldiers. Suddenly Delane had a campaign on his hands and *The Times* became a focus for fund-raising to ease the suffering of the British soldiers. Another initiative of Delane's was to bear fruit – the despatch of William Howard Russell to "the seat of war" as the first officially-recognised war correspondent. Derided by the Prince Regent as "that miserable scribbler" and generally loathed by the British high command, Russell stuck to his task as an impartial reporter and was not afraid to reveal the "unpleasantness" he witnessed in the British camp throughout the war.

At the same time Blackwood showed that he was also unafraid to cover the war in a disinterested way. In October 1854 he started publishing first-hand accounts of the fighting from a young artillery officer, Edward Hamley, one of three brothers who were to become regular contributors. Published in the magazine under the title "The Story of the Crimea" and in book form as *The Campaign of*

Sebastopol, the despatches painted a realistic and "not particularly sanguine" picture of the frontline fighting and the problems facing the soldiers of the British Army. After the war Hamley returned to Britain and was posted to Leith, where he quickly became a member of the "military staff".

Laurence Oliphant was another journalist-cum-historian who was associated with both *The Times* and *Blackwood's Magazine*. He was born in Cape Town in 1829, where his father was attorney-general; his family had deep roots in Scottish society, his father being the third son of Ebenezer Oliphant of Condie and Newton, Perthshire, and his mother Mary, daughter of Sir William Stirling of Ardoch. As a child, Laurence Oliphant had spent time in Scotland at the family home at Condie and throughout his life he had a maudlin attachment to Scotland and all things Scottish. Described by the *Oxford Dictionary of National Biography* as a "diplomatist, traveller and mystic", Oliphant had been sent by Delane to accompany the Turkish forces in the campaign in Circassia that ended with the fall of Kars and his experiences were published in 1856 in *The Trans-Caucasian Campaign under Omar Pasha: A Personal Narrative*. Leslie Stephen called Oliphant one of the most brilliant writers of his generation (Stephen 1907) and his first novel *Piccadilly* (1870) showed that he possessed both narrative flair and a gift for satire. Despite a glittering diplomatic and political career he was undone by falling under the influence of Thomas Lake Harris, a spurious self-proclaimed prophet who had established a community in New York State called the Brotherhood of New Life. So completely did Oliphant fall under its spell in 1867 that he surrendered all his money and property to Harris.

Supported by a small allowance, Oliphant was allowed to continue writing for Blackwood and quickly established himself as a regular contributor to the magazine, writing on a wide variety of subjects. Despite his curious subornment to the Brotherhood, which also cost him his marriage, he remained as interested as ever before in events in the outside world – in 1870 he covered the Franco-Prussian War for *The Times* – and showed himself to be a shrewd and disinterested observer of international affairs. He was also a talented financier and in that role undertook several successful transactions for the Brotherhood and, according to Stephen, he learned the secrets of "commercial jugglery". His novel *Piccadilly* showed that he was more than capable of delineating the venal side of London social life or, as

Blackwood put it, describing "the unaccountable, general bubble-spawned, fellows who keep an establishment in London, and entertain everyone of note for a season or two, and then burst with some disclosure or bankruptcy or fraud" (Tredrey 1954: 132). The novel was serialised in *Blackwood's Magazine*, then published with illustrations by the artist Richard Doyle, and was counted a great success with the contemporary reading public.

Oliphant's near contemporary Laurence Lockhart had a similar, if less exciting career as public figure and writer. Born at Inchinnan in Renfrewshire in 1831, the third son of the Revd Laurence Lockhart of Milton Lockhart, Lanarkshire, and his wife, Louisa, daughter of David Blair, an East India merchant of Glasgow, he was educated privately and at Glasgow University and Gonville and Caius College, Cambridge. After graduating in 1855 Lockhart received a commission as an ensign in the 92nd (Gordon) Highlanders and served with them as part of the Highland Brigade in the Crimean War. Following a number of regimental appointments in England and Scotland, he served with the 92nd in India before retiring from the army with the rank of captain in 1865. In his retirement he became a regular contributor to *Blackwood's Magazine*, writing authoritative articles on military reforms in addition to short stories with a Scottish background and Scottish themes. It was perhaps not surprising that these fell into the category of sentimental exploitation so beloved of many of the writers associated with the Blackwood group. In common with work by Wilson who wrote under the pen name of "Christopher North", Lockhart produced a number of anecdotal humorous stories that gave a distorted view of Scottish rural life and character far removed from everyday reality. His first novel *Doubles and Quits*, a light-hearted comedy of errors set in the army, was published in 1869: its only claims to any merit are Lockhart's ear for dialogue and his comic talent for describing ridiculous situations.

Lockhart was also deeply interested in the volunteer movement which came into being at the end of the 1850s as a result of a number of invasion scares instigated by the hostile attitude of Napoleon III. With a large number of the regular army committed to imperial policing duties, particularly in India, the security of the British homeland was deemed to be in danger and there were regular calls for the creation of part-time rifle volunteers to be raised and trained for home defence. In 1859 the government passed the necessary legislation and the resultant volunteer rifle corps proved to be exceptionally popular: it involved little more than some gentle shooting practice and drills and, best of all, dressing up in turkey-cock uniforms. In Scotland the recruitment figures for the Volunteer units were twice the UK average, a figure which was undoubtedly assisted by the creation of units with Highland affiliations, most of them in the Central Belt. With their panoply of kilts, tartan trews, ostrich feathers, ornate sporrans and pipe bands, they were an irresistible attraction and everywhere men rushed to join. From being a feared figure, no better than a savage in the badlands north of the Highland Line, the Highlander was reborn as an entirely admirable character and his dress, a much despised dull checked cloth, was transformed into confections based on a colourful and carefully codified set of tartans, most of them created with unhistorical abandon. The craze was particularly popular in the Lowlands where volunteer corps members dressed in their own contrived tartans and added further adornments, buckles and badges to produce a military fashion that would have been unrecognisable to any soldier who had fought under Jacobite leaders such as Montrose and Alasdair MacColla or Charles Edward Stewart and Lord George Murray. Most of these outlandish uniforms owed nothing to tradition, but were invented by local colonels and they came to represent self-conscious nationalism or what the military historian John Keegan has described as "a force for resistance against the creeping anglicisation of Scottish urban life" (Keegan 1982: 168).

Nostalgia for a half-forgotten romantic past was a factor, as was the existing iconography of the Scottish soldier ("a lion in the field, a lamb in the house"), which found its apotheosis in Roger Fenton's Crimean War photographs of the sternly bearded Highland soldiers of Queen Victoria's army. Memories of the Royal Visit to Edinburgh in 1822 were also still strong. This was the first to be made by a British monarch since 1651 when Charles II left the country with his Scottish army to try to win back his throne in return for imposing Protestantism on his three kingdoms. In the intervening 171 years no British monarch had troubled to visit Scotland and perhaps with good reason; in that time the Stewarts made two attempts to retrieve their thrones from the House of Hanover and the parliament of Scotland was united with that of England in 1707. As if to make good the lost years, Edinburgh went tartan-mad during the ten days that George IV graced the capital: under the direction of Sir Walter Scott, who acted as pageant-master, an invented mythology of Highland customs, replete with clan gatherings and balls, was represented as solid historical fact. Most were utterly bogus, drawing on instant traditions which allowed those attending the various gatherings to dress up in tartan fancy-dress, dance reels and strathspeys, drink copious amounts of whisky and make sentimental toasts to the grandeur of dear old Scotia.

Innocuous in itself – the Duke of Atholl dismissed Scott's "great gathering of the Gael" as a fortnight of play-acting – the visit left a hangover from which Scotland never fully recovered. It cemented the kilt as the national dress and created a bogus tartan caricature that became the accepted and increasingly acceptable face of Scotland. The Royal Family became part of the myth and, after George's porcine figure had appeared swathed in tartan, successive kings and princes have lost no opportunity to don the kilt when in Scotland. For a country whose identity was increasingly bound up with its English neighbour at a time of encroaching anglicisation of Scottish life, tartan kilts and an imagined Highland past became a means of satisfying a deep emotional need. From being a "bare-arsed bandit", the scourge of the Lowlands and a figure who provoked fear and mockery in equal measure, the Highlander was transformed utterly into a manly, colourful, patriotic figure who managed to be both respected and respectable. And in no other part of Scottish life did this put down deeper roots than in its regiments. Once derided, the figure of the Scottish soldier became an admired exemplar, stern in his kilts and plaids and ostrich feathers and unbending in his patriotic duty to country and empire. By the century's end, even the Lowland regiments were sporting tartan trews and Highland doublets, while their officers carried basket-hilted claymores, a transformation which bemused military historians: "They lacked only the kilt and feather bonnet to resemble the sort of figure whose ancestors their ancestors had despised, feared and slaughtered but who, by 1881, had come to personify Scotland" (Wood 1987: 76). In his kilt and sporran, his feathered bonnet and white spats, the Scottish soldier became a colourful yet utterly respectable figure; marching in serried ranks behind the pipes and drums against the dramatic backcloth of Edinburgh or Stirling castle, he is as familiarly Caledonian as the bonnie banks of Loch Lomond or the heather-covered Road to the Isles.

However, there was more to soldiering than putting on fancy dress. Being a part-time soldier meant following an honourable calling: it was companionable, offered self-respect and produced steadiness of character, all important moral virtues in Presbyterian Scotland. For retired army officers the Volunteers offered the chance to maintain links with the army and to provide professional skills as local commanders and Lockhart took full advantage of the opportunity, becoming associated with the corps in Lanarkshire. The experience also gave him the background for his story "A Night with the Volunteers of Strathkinahan", which appeared in *Blackwood's Magazine* in September 1869, shortly before Lockhart re-entered the army as a major in the 2nd Royal Lanarkshire Militia. Like his first novel the style is conversational and told from the first person, for, as he told Blackwood, the story was based on a real incident when he inspected a formation of Volunteers at Dalmally in Inverness-shire; the ambience is intimate, as if trying to make the reader feel at home. ("One autumn day, a good many years ago, I was taking mine ease in mine inn in Edinburgh, when it was announced to me that a visitor, by the name of Captain Cumming, was waiting below.") From the outset, too, the tone is set so that the reader is in no doubt about the backgrounds of the two main protagonists: the narrator and Tom Cumming are old army friends, the latter having changed his name on marriage to inherit a Highland estate, but who now finds himself in difficulties in his role as adjutant of the 2nd Administrative Battalion of the (imaginary) Keltshire Volunteers. And the reader of *Blackwood's* is left in no doubt that the narrator and Cumming are from the upper classes, both enjoying military and landed backgrounds and a shared experience in the same hussar regiment. When Cumming invites the narrator to stay with him the underlying assumption is that the reader will know perfectly well the kind of world both men inhabit:

Couldn't you make a run down with me, and then come on for a few days to my place and try your hand at grouse-driving? It's a glorious district – splendid scenery, and all that – and I'm sure the natives will amuse you; and then your diplomatic talents might be of immense assistance in helping an old friend out of a difficulty. ("A Night with the Volunteers of Strathkinahan" 1869: 106: 647: 324–45)

This is a Scotland blessed with magnificent scenery made for hunting, shooting and fishing and inhabited by quaint rustics, a rural arcadia where all know their place and are happy with their lot. The officer classes are at the apex of local society and below them the Volunteers are a collection of local worthies, some better than others, but all distinctly below the salt. In that sense Captain Cummings' Strathkinahan bears all the marks of the Kailyard: here was a well-defined arcadia of rural sentimentality peopled by characters who represent solid virtues: the minister or the village worthies who voice pastoral morality, the industrious son who rises by dint of hard work and his own endeavours, the honest tenant farmers who give of their best for no other reward than their families' improvement, and sickly virginal heroines who are not long for this world. Behind them are stock rapacious landlords, self-satisfied incomers and the ever-present figures of death and disease. The city only appears as a distant rumour, a place to be avoided; instead the virtues of village life are emphasised and in this case membership of the Volunteers plays an important part in maintaining local cohesion and creating pride in country.

Not everything, however, is blooming in the Kailyard. The locals of Strathkinahan have rebelled against the appointment of an unpopular landowner as their captain because he is a "temperance man", and it is left to the narrator and Cumming to sort out the matter by appealing to their sense of duty, an important consideration in the creation of the Volunteer movement. The plot is flimsy and absurd, involving the narrator's subterfuge as a senior officer to impress the Volunteers, but that is secondary to Lockhart's purpose. The narrator and Cumming represent military tradition and social stability from a strictly unionist point of view. (Asked by a Volunteer if Queen Victoria speaks any word of Gaelic, Cumming retorts: "Not a single one, she'd be ashamed to do it.") On the other hand the Volunteers are all stock local characters – a bibulous sheep farmer with an incomplete command of English, a tremulous doctor and a variety of peasant-like worthies, all in need of some military discipline. The narrator's description of the entry of one of the Volunteers makes clear two aspects of Lockhart's thinking: first, he is adopting an attitude of superiority, which he expected his readers to share; and second, the inference is that his distorted and debased image of Scottish rural life can only be rectified by military discipline and the commonsense methods of the Volunteer system.

His English was broken and almost unintelligible, and every sentence was preceded, accompanied, and followed by a series of sputterings and hootings which, with the working of his face, I could refer to no mental emotion whatsoever. Mephistopheles, the Black Dwarf, the Gorilla, Waterton's Nondescript, the laughing hyena, the horned screech-owl, and the vampire, were a few of the ideas instantly suggested by the contemplation of this Highlandman. "Well, Mr M'Tavish," said Tom, "so you got my letter all right; I suppose you warned the corps, and I hope we shall have a good meeting, and get through our business?" "Shess, captain – that's adjutant, shess, sir. Letter? shess, Corps come? shess. Business? Tit, tit, tit! no business." Then after a pause, and with an insinuating assortment of puckers playing all over his face. "Bheil Gaelig a'gad?" "What?" said Tom."Spoke Gaelic? tit hish!'"No," said Tom."No spokes? ach tit! no spoke Gaelic?" "But we *have* business, Mr M'Tavish, and very important business too." ("A Night with the Volunteers" 1869: 330)

This attempt at humour is very much within the Blackwood tradition. At the time of the magazine's foundation Wilson and John Gibson Lockhart waged their literary war against the "Cockney School" not so much on account of its alleged lack of literary values, but because they believed that, unlike them, the practitioners were not "men of some rank", but rather middle-class scribblers. Reviewing Hunt's *The Story of Rimini*, a long poem based on Dante's story of Paolo and Francesca, the *Blackwood's* reviewer (probably Lockhart) castigated it for its "glittering and rancid obscenities" and likened it to the experience of

a man of fashion, when he is invited to enter, for a second time, the gilded drawing room of a little mincing boarding-school mistress, who would fain have an *At Home* in her house. Everything is pretence, affectation, finery and gaudiness. (Mason 2006: Vol 5, 58)

In describing the Volunteers of Strathkinahan in similarly conde-scending terms, Laurence Lockhart demonstrated that he had lost none of his uncle's capacity for mocking the aspirations of those he believed were not his social equals. Lockhart and Wilson attacked the Cockney School with a snobbishness even their own critics considered "naked and unashamed", the later equivalent of sneering at suburban values "where lofty cultural judgements shade into everyday class prejudice" (Gross 1969: 15). Half a century later the same social animus was present in Laurence Lockhart's jaundiced view of the Volunteers – the Highlander as whisky-soaked imbeciles – but there is a difference. While the men are all portrayed as drunks or half-wits whose native cunning makes them difficult to control, the saving grace is that they are members of the Volunteers and possess the ability to accept military discipline.

Lockhart died in 1882, Oliphant in 1888, his last scheme being a plan to create a Jewish settlement at Haifa in Palestine, and their passing broke up the "military staff" of John Blackwood, who had predeceased them in 1879. Not that the firm changed direction. Under William Blackwood III both the publishing house and the magazine continued to produce work from senior generals and admirals – among the contributors were Wolseley and Kitchener, both leading late Victorian generals – but the writing became more realistic and factual. George Warrington Steevens of the *Daily Mail* wrote an account of Kitchener's campaign in the Sudan, *With Kitchener to Khartoum*, which sold 100,000 copies when it was published in 1899 and Blackwood's also published the work of Charles à Court Repington, the distinguished military correspondent of *The Times* who wrote about his experiences in the Boer War. As a result the writing in *Blackwood's Magazine* became less Scottish and more bound up with the imperial ethos; in time John Buchan would become a leading contributor, a writer who managed to retain his inner sense of Scottishness while adopting the persona of a British imperialist.

Ironically the last flowering of the military Kailyard in Scotland was perhaps the most successful. In the hands of James Grant it reached its apotheosis with the publication of the author's many novels based on military and historical subjects and an equally large number of popular and readable historical narratives including *Memoirs of Montrose* (1851), *British Battles on Land and Sea* (1873), *Cassell's Illustrated History of India* (1876), and his best book, the three volumes of *Old and New Edinburgh* (1880). Grant was a prolific author and it comes as no surprise that he was related to Sir Walter Scott on his mother's side of the family. He was born on 1 August 1822, the eldest son of an officer in the 92nd (Gordon) Highlanders who had served with distinction in the Peninsular Wars and who was appointed to the garrison in Newfoundland in 1833. Grant followed his father into the army in 1840, being commissioned into the 62nd (Wiltshire) Foot, but he resigned three years later to join a firm of architects in Edinburgh. Once back in his native city he turned to writing and published his first novel *The Romance of War* in 1845. Published in four volumes it tells the story of the Scottish regiments which fought against Napoleon's forces in Egypt and the Peninsula, many of the episodes based on stories told to him by his father. With its breathless style and high romance it presented a heroic view of battle and, as Grant explained in his preface, he was keen to capture the sense of Scottish nationhood which he had experienced in the Scottish regiments:

It is impossible for a writer to speak of his own production without exposing himself to imputations either of egotism or affected modesty; the Author therefore will merely add that he trusts most readers may discover something to attract in these volumes which depict from the life the stirring events and all the romance of warfare, with its various lights and shades of military service, the principal characters being members of one of the brave regiments which from their national garb, national feelings, romantic attachments and esprit de corps, are essentially different from the generality of our troops of the line. (Grant 1845: I: viii)

As he was to do in later novels, Grant managed to marry his pride in being a Scot and a member of a martial nation with his understanding that the action was taking place within a British context. *The Romance of War* attracted an enthusiastic readership and he followed it up with a sequel, *The Highlanders in Belgium* (1846). Grant was now on a well-worn and increasingly lucrative track and by the middle of the century he had emerged as one of the most successful writers of his generation. His total output in forty years of writing was 61 novels and 12 narrative histories, but although this brought him fame and, in time, considerable wealth, not all of his contemporaries were impressed: "These figures may be impressive as evidence of energy, ingenuity and mental power, but are deplorable from an artistic point of view," wrote Stewart M. Ellis in one of the first surveys of Victorian writers. "No man has it in him to write twelve or more superlative books" (Ellis 1925: 110). In fact most of Grant's best fiction was written in mid-life and Thomas Hardy admitted that *The Scottish Cavalier* was an influence on his own early writing. Other fictional works worthy of mention are *Jane Seton*; *Bothwell or the Days of Mary Queen of Scots*; *The Yellow Frigate*; *Philip Rollo*; *Frank Hilton*; *Legends of the Black Watch*.

Grant was an enthusiastic Volunteer and was one of the main supporters for introducing uniforms which were identifiably Scottish. In that capacity he advised the War Office on questions regarding uniforms, especially facings, and was much in demand as an expert on military matters. He was also associated with another mid-Victorian enthusiasm in Scotland, the emergence of a nationalist sentiment and the creation of a movement to regenerate many aspects of Scottish life. There were calls for a greater Scottish political involvement at

Westminster and objections to the lack of parliamentary time for Scottish affairs. While these arguments came mainly from the fringe, they did add to a belief that, in the words of one of the activists, the Rev James Begg, Scotland was "sinking in our national position every year, and simply living on the credit of the past" (Begg 1850: 35). Grant entered the fray in 1852 when he started producing a series of letters and articles listing Scottish grievances since the Act of Union of 1707, which attempted to demonstrate that the highest rates of public expenditure had been devoted to England. In particular he pointed out that there were fewer government offices in Edinburgh, naval expenditure was concentrated on English shipyards and that as result of lack of investment Scottish talent was being attracted to London. Grant's solution was to restore Scottish institutions and to increase Scottish representation at Westminster.

At the same time he and his brother John Grant, who acted as Marchmont Herald, appealed to the Lord Lyon King of Arms, asking him to suppress various irregularly quartered arms used by flags on public buildings such as Edinburgh castle (as well as on the new florin coin), on the grounds that they contravened laws of heraldry and the Act of Union. The heraldic grievance became a popular issue and was supported by the Convention of Royal Burghs, demonstrating that it was possible to whip up popular support on a nationalist issue. As a result, the National Association for the Vindication of Scottish Rights was founded a year later under the chairmanship of the Earl of Eglinton, a prominent Tory, and attracted a broad level of support in its campaign to uphold Scottish rights. On the left it was backed by Begg and the Edinburgh reformer Duncan McLaren, while on the right it received the support of leading contributors to *Blackwood's Magazine*, including Alison and Aytoun, both committed Tories. Public meetings were held and pamphlets published and for the next three years the association and Grant received a good deal of publicity. Among their demands was the restitution of the post of Scottish Secretary of State with a seat in the Cabinet and a greater Scottish representation at Westminster. A recent historian of the period has claimed that these demands saw the emergence of "the first effective nationalist movement" (Hanham 1969: 77), but at the time not everyone was impressed. The association and its promoters were attacked by *The Scotsman*, which called the campaign "ludicrously lame" ("Scotland and the Union" 1853: 2), and later by *The Times*, which published a vicious leading article leaving its readers in no doubt that the Scots were the authors of their own misfortunes and that by fretting over emblematic devices they were simply living in the past.

We south of the Tweed have risen to the conception of a United Kingdom; nay, more, of a British Empire, and every subject of the Queen finds here a career in which he may advance without fear of jealousy or prejudice. But in Edinburgh the cry, or at least the feeling, still is, Scotland for the Scotch. Yet, the more Scotland has striven to be a nation, the more she has sunk to be a province. (*The Times* 4 December 1856: 6)

The problems thrown up by the Crimean War and the Indian Mutiny put paid to any of the association's ambitions being acted upon and gradually nationalist sentiment was transferred to a campaign to build a monument on the Abbey Craig near Stirling to commemorate Sir William Wallace and his victory over the English army in 1297 during the Wars of Independence. Funded by public subscription, it was eventually completed in 1869. By then the National Association for the Vindication of Scottish Rights had disappeared and by then, too, Grant seems to have taken the decision to leave Scotland. The following year he left Edinburgh to live in London, where he quickly became forgotten and died in obscurity in 1882, leaving his first biographer to lament: "In Edinburgh he was a notable personality and had hosts of friends. In London he was no one in particular, and seemingly unknown in literary or social circles, for his name does not appear in any memoirs of the period" (Ellis 1925: 112).

In his heyday Grant was a popular and best-selling author, but after his death his military novels and histories were quickly forgotten. However, a clue to his thinking can be found in his promotion of the National Association for the Vindication of Scottish Rights. At its core was a demand "to obtain for Scotland the benefit of local administration in all matters which are exclusively Scottish", although behind that seemingly nationalist statement of intent there was an equally strong desire "to place the Scottish nation on a footing of full and permanent equality with the English nation" (Burns 1854).

In other words, although the association was involved in a nationalist discourse, it was doing so within the framework of the union and its supporters were at pains to argue that they were not interested in secession, but "wanted to maintain the power of the Scottish local state and civil society within the Union and the Imperial

Parliament" (Bültmann 2005: 65). The same thing might be said about Grant and his fascination with the military aspects of Scottish history. With their kilts and tartans the soldiers and regiments he wrote about so lovingly were expressions of Scottish identity, but they served in a British army and the wars they fought were imperial wars in pursuit of British power and authority. That understanding also lay at the heart of the military Kailyard: its literature was a manifestation of Scottish identity, but it was created within a solidly British framework.

Bibliography

"A Night with the Volunteers of Strathkinahan" in *Blackwoood's Edinburgh Magazine* (September 1869): 106: 647.

Begg, James. 1850. *National Education for Scotland practically considered.* Edinburgh: Johnstone & Hunter.

Bültmann, Tanya. 2005. *Scottish Rights Vindicated: Identity and Nationalism in Mid-Nineteenth Century Scotland.* Bielefeld: Fakultät für Linguistick und Literaturwissenschaft.

Burns, William. 1854. *National Association for the Vindication of Scottish Rights, Tract Number One.* Edinburgh: Mould & Tod.

Ellis, Stewart M. 1925. *Mainly Victorian.* London: Hutchinson.

Grant, James. 1845. *The Romance of War.* 4 vols. London: Henry Colburn.

Gross, John. 1969. *The Rise and Fall of the Man of Letters.* London: Weidenfeld & Nicolson.

Hanham, J.H. 1969. *Scottish Nationalism.* London: Faber.

Keegan, John. 1982. *Six Armies in Normandy.* London: Cape.

Lockhart, John Gibson ["Z"]. 1817. "On the Cockney School of Poetry" in *Blackwood's Magazine* 2, 7 (October): 38–41.

Mason, Nicholas (ed.) 2006. *Blackwook's Magazine, 1817–25: Selections from Maga's Infancy.* 6 vols. London: Pickering & Chatto.

'North and the Noctes' in *Blackwood's Edinburgh Magazine* (October 1855). 78: 480.

"Scotland and the Union" in *The Scotsman* (20 July 1853). 2.

Stephen, Leslie. 1907. "Laurence Oliphant" in *Dictionary of National Biography.* Vol 14. London: Smith Elder: 1027–31.

Tredrey, F.D. 1954. *The House of Blackwood* 1804–1954. Edinburgh and London: William Blackwood.

Wood, Stephen. 1987. *The Scottish Soldier.* Manchester: Archive Publications, in association with the National Museums of Scotland.

"The Key to their Hearts": Scottish Orientalism

Michael Fry

Alongside British imperial interventions in the "East", in India, China and the Arabian Peninsula, Scottish orientalists propelled in the first instance by the ideas of the Scottish Enlightenment sought to make sense of "oriental" culture in its stages of developmental study with recourse to language and anthropological study in the first instance. These enquiries also traversed the fields of religion and science as Scottish orientalists sought to find proving grounds in the East for their theories of universalism. Although not entirely successful in their endeavours, Scottish orientalists ought not to be seen simply as naked imperialists. Their story is only glimpsed in imaginative Scottish literature of the period and features more strongly elsewhere in memoirs, texts of what today we would call social science, and the periodical press.
Keywords: Orientalism; Oriental Languages; Scottish Enlightenment; Gilbert Elliot (Lord Minto); India; Walter Scott; *The Surgeon's Daughter*; Charles Grant; James Mill; Alexander Duff; John Wilson; Missionary orientalism; John Muir; China; James Legge; Arabian peninsula; William Robertson Smith.

The twenty-first century has opened with clashes between East and West so brutal that it is easy to forget past times when for both sides dialogue proved not just possible, but fruitful. Even intellectual rationalisations of what is going on today tend to take a short and sombre view. Many are indebted to Edward Said's *Orientalism* (1978). Said himself condemned an earlier phase of violence, while showing it had deep origins not only in politics but also in culture – for example, in the traditional literary representations of the East by the West. A major reason for the disjunction in the late twentieth century was, in Said's view, too much uncritical application of western categories to eastern civilisation. He showed how concepts of the orient had become habitually distorted.

Today, when western discourse dominates global culture and looks set if anything to grow yet more dominant, the East finds it can scarcely speak for itself, not at least with any hope of being understood. Nor will it accept that the West might speak for it: hence the resort to more direct and drastic means of making its mind known. Still the West sees no problem, or only one of international law and order. Yet, in previous phases of the relationship between East and West, mutual sympathy and comprehension was not beyond the reach of either side. To this exchange the Scottish Enlightenment and its sequels in the nineteenth century made a contribution. The Scots had been among the small European nations following, or trying to follow, the great powers eastwards in the age of discoveries. One aim of the notorious Darien Company, set up in 1698, was to foster trade with the East; it did send a couple of ships there before meeting its doom in the West. After the Union of 1707, needy but mobile Scots filled up an English East India Company now open to them through common British citizenship. By the late eighteenth century, half its employees came from Scotland. Some were just Scotsmen on the make, but others took the intellectual interests of their homeland with them to the orient (McGilvary 1989; Fry 1992). Those interests would already have been stimulated by the range of disciplines from history to philosophy routinely taught to students at the Scottish universities. A central tenet of higher education in Scotland was that history could be regarded as a philosophical subject because it was the product of general laws, analogous to the laws of natural science. Once understood, they might reveal the interplay of diverse causes in gradual change. The sort of history written from this point of view, supplying a framework of speculation and interpretation even where direct evidence was lacking, went by the name of conjectural history.

One prime text of the Enlightenment offered that sort of history in an oriental context. It was the last published work from the hand of no less a personage than the principal of the University of Edinburgh, William Robertson. Robertson's *Historical Disquisition concerning the Knowledge which the Ancients had of India* (1791) was typical of conjectural history in showing how the sub-continent had passed through successive stages of civilisation marked by different kinds of economic activity and social structure. But the problem with India – and doubtless what attracted him to the theme – was that here stadial history seemed to have stalled, or even to have gone into reverse. An ancient civilisation was now in decay, at least in European eyes: not what a theory of progress would lead the observer to expect. It had to be explained, or explained away. Robertson saw behind the decay the same malign influences of superstition and priestcraft as during his previous studies he had uncovered in the history of Europe and of the Americas, not to speak of Scotland.

In India the effects imposed themselves through the immemorial caste system, which governed everyday life despite its bizarre or even horrible aspects. At its base, however, lay a corpus of scripture, the

Sanskrit *Vedas*, which in the earliest times, before the Christian era, had set forth moral principles that all civilised people could recognise and share. In this way, India might be fitted into the great narrative of humanity. The one thing now was for commerce, brought by the British, to give a fresh impetus to the social and economic progress that such morality might underpin. Though Robertson never went east himself, his philosophical confidence stopped short of mere pontification. He could, after all, check what he wanted to say against the testimony of Scots home again after making their fortunes in the orient. Often they had also been seduced by the easy-going way of life there: if, as in certain cases, they prospered enough to set up an Indian household complete with harem (British memsahibs being as yet rare), then a whole exotic culture stood open to them, from its pleasures to its intrigues. Some Scots hobnobbed with rajahs or sultans and rode round on elephants. Others preferred to sit at the feet of the brahmans, the men of holiness and learning who preserved the ancient Hindu wisdom. Scots cultivating such interests were said themselves to be "brahmanised" – in effect to have joined this highest caste.

At the turn of the nineteenth century one of them, Alexander Hamilton, counted among the leading western scholars of Sanskrit. He had begun his career as a soldier for the East India Company but retired to devote himself to linguistic studies. These he followed for some years in Calcutta before returning with his native wife to settle down in Scotland and, among other pursuits, write for the *Edinburgh Review* as its resident expert on everything oriental.[1] After the Peace of Amiens in 1801 he visited Paris to inspect the Indian materials held in archives there, only to be stranded by the early renewal of war between Britain and France. Luckily for him, French intellectuals had come to hold him in such high regard that he was not, like other enemy aliens, interned. It was arranged for him to live with two German exiles, Friedrich and August Wilhelm Schlegel, to whom he taught Sanskrit. The brothers' work, *Über die Sprache und Weisheit der Indier* [On the Language and Wisdom of the Indians, 1808] inaugurated their own nation's formidable orientalism.

The Scots community in India was meanwhile being refreshed under a new governor-general, Gilbert Elliot, Lord Minto, a Whig politician, son of the Gilbert Elliot who had been a friend of the

---

[1] Hamilton's only published book was *A Key to the Chronology of the Hindus* (Hamilton 1820).

philosopher David Hume. At the outset of his career the younger Elliot sought the hardly less brilliant company of Edmund Burke, to whom he acted as aide in the impeachment of Warren Hastings for alleged crimes in the East. Elliot had been a pupil at Edinburgh of Dugald Stewart, professor of moral philosophy, who in turn had been a pupil of Adam Smith. This gave Elliot direct access to Scottish theories of historical development. And when he sailed out in 1807 to Calcutta, he took with him a shipload of classmates, including John Leyden, the poet, and William Erskine, who was to become the historian of the early Moghul Empire (Erskine 1854). Erskine would marry the daughter of Jonathan Duncan, the British resident at Benares whose long service at this the centre of Hindu learning had turned him into the model of the brahmanised Scot (Shakespear 1873). Awaiting the shipload at the other end was Sir James Mackintosh, recorder of Bombay, who in his spare time from his official duties had made himself an expert in Indian linguistics. The first thing Mackintosh did after Minto arrived was write a dispatch urging him to bestow official patronage on study of the sub-continent's languages (Minto Papers, NLS MS 11726, 10, based on Mackintosh 1806).

Scottish orientalism soon branched out from this philological basis. Minto's papers document how with his encouragement a Sanskrit press was set up in Calcutta to publish dictionaries of Indian languages, together with canonical texts of history, philosophy, law, religion and literature. These included the whole of the *Ramayana*, which Minto took to be the Indian equivalent of the *Iliad* and *Odyssey*. Since all these works had previously existed only in manuscript, his efforts marked a huge step forward for oriental scholarship. Minto sought to stimulate Calcutta's intellectual life in another and specifically Scottish way by patronising the *Moofussul Magazine* as a local equivalent of the *Edinburgh Review*. "Moofussul" was the Anglo-Indian term for "up-country", so this cultural organ evidently had the aim of helping officers of the Company to pass the long hours in remote out-stations. It seems to have run for only six issues, but they contained translations of both eastern and western poetry, including George Buchanan's Latin epigrams, together with accounts of traditions of the Moghul Emperors (Minto Papers, NLS MSS 11734–9).

Official patronage began to be used to promote men sympathetic to native culture, so the British administration could put behind it the rapacity and brutality that Burke had condemned in Hastings. For example, Minto appointed another Scot, Colin Mackenzie, surveyor-general of India. In travelling round the sub-continent, this son of Stornoway assembled an immense collection of manuscripts and books in Sanskrit, Arabic, Persian, Burmese and the Javanese language (today called Bahasa Indonesia). He had besides in the course of his professional duties, for the purpose of measuring land, to become an expert in Indian mathematics. That led him on to Indian astronomy. He went to be instructed in these subjects by pandits at the college of Madura in the Carnatic. And he started to transmit his knowledge home: papers on the astronomy of the brahmans were read to the Royal Society of Edinburgh ("Biographical sketch" 1835; "Index" 1890).

Of the Scots patronised by Minto in India, Leyden showed the greatest accomplishments. His contemporary reputation rested partly on the fact that Sir Walter Scott had discovered and encouraged him. Leyden, the son of a shepherd, supplied versions of ballads for *The Minstrelsy of the Scottish Border* (1802), together with some imitations by himself. But this did not earn him a living. He had had a medical education and decided to go east as a surgeon. He took to the exotic life, language and literature with such zest that soon he became professor of Hindustani [Hindi] at the College of Fort William, Calcutta's institution of higher learning. Minto wrote:

Leyden's oriental learning is stupendous, and he is also a very universal scholar. His knowledge, extensive and minute as it is, is always in his pocket, at his finger ends and on the tip of his tongue. He has made it completely his own, and it is all ready money.

According to Minto, then, it was peculiar that,

he has never learnt to speak English, either in pronunciation or idiom. In both respects he is [...] faithful to the scenes of infancy as if he had never quitted [...]. It is not merely Scotch, but the proper dialect of Tweeddale. (Minto Papers, NLS MS 1106, 45)

In 1811 Minto led a naval expedition to seize Java and put a stop to Napoleonic designs on that strategic and profitable island. He took with him another shipload of Scots, including Leyden, whom he dubbed a "perfect Malay" for the knowledge he had in advance acquired of the local culture. Leyden felt elated at the prospect of getting into the archives of Batavia [Jakarta], capital of the Dutch East Indies, but he perished of a sudden fever within a day or two of landing (see also Leyden 1821; Leyden 1826; Leyden 1886). The news, reaching Scott a year later, deeply grieved him. He and Leyden had remained correspondents, and what Scott learned from their exchanges may well have contributed to his own tentative excursion into orientalism in *The Surgeon's Daughter* (1826). In its way this book is built on the intellectual structure of conjectural history too, for like others among the Waverley Novels it shows human progress in action and the practical results that follow. Only here again, India presents puzzling contradictions.

The story is in part set towards the end of the eighteenth century, when the Moslem sultanate of Mysore had been the most formidable native foe of the British. It attained that position under Hyder Ali who, though a despot, yet appears in the novel endowed with some admirable qualities:

[he] certainly was one of the wisest that Hindostan could boast; and amidst great crimes, perpetrated to satisfy his ambition, displayed many instances of princely generosity, and, what was a little more surprising, of even-handed justice". (Scott [1826] 1891: 412)

It need hardly be said that we cannot otherwise expect from Scott much by way of political correctness – from time to time he unblushingly exhibits the prejudices of his age. For example, the narrator of the novel comments that Hyder may be a just man by nature and by calculation,

but by temperament, his blood is as unruly as ever beat under a black skin, and if you do not find him in the vein of judging, he is likely enough to be in that of killing. Stakes and bowstrings are as frequently in his head as the adjustment of the scales of justice. (Scott [1826] 1891: 447)

And it is hardly possible to see in his successor, his son Tippoo, any kind of historical progression: "Tippoo has the cunning of his father and his military talents, but he lacks his cautious wisdom" (Scott [1826] 1891: 442).

Where conjectural history does put in a slightly spectral appearance is among the Scottish characters. At the outset Scott reflects on his muse: "Send her to India to be sure [...]. That is the true place for a Scot to thrive in" (Scott [1826] 1891: 248). Still, here he records historical progression among his countrymen not with the delighted astonishment of his preface to *Waverley* (1814), when he recalled that "'tis but sixty years since" Scotland had been a scene of savagery. In *The Surgeon's Daughter* the time-span from the events narrated to the actual narration is shorter. Yet progression is there. After Scott's typical sort of insipid hero arrives in India about 1780 he writes "conveying the welcome intelligence of his having taken possession of his new station in a large frontier town of the Company's dominions, and that great emoluments were attached to the situation" (Scott [1826] 1891: 230). The author later remarks, to nobody in particular:

If you want rogues, as they are so much in fashion with you, you have that gallant caste of adventurers, who laid down their consciences at the Cape of Good Hope as they went out to India, and forgot to take them up again when they returned.

But by the time of writing, all that lies in the past: "It is scarce necessary to say, that such things could only be acted in the earlier period of our Indian settlements, when the check of the Directors [of the Company] was imperfect, and that of the Crown did not exist" (Scott [1826] 1891: 440). These are just asides, though, and we find little else in a rather thin novel of that entwining of historical and personal destinies which mark Scott's greatest works.

The achievement of Scottish orientalism in the first third of the century had been to construct a general hypothesis about the history of India out of the riches of her literature. The conjectural approach allowed this, indeed required it, for the corpus of Sanskrit writings was maddeningly inexact on matters of fact. What it did do was reveal a cultural continuum from antiquity to the present. In this sense the Scots took seriously the idea of an Indian classicism. They supposed Sanskrit bore the same relation to its culture as Greek and Latin did to the West's, and brahmans the same relation to their society as philosophers and poets of ancient Athens and Rome had to theirs. But it was to the credit of the Scottish intellect that it could modify and in the end discard a convenient hypothesis, and do so by drawing on other, equally unconventional historical evidence as it became available. As early as 1816 Alexander Campbell raised an awkward question over the hypothesis when he published a grammar of Telugu, the vernacular of the present Indian state of Andhra Pradesh (Campbell 1816). He showed how utterly it diverged from both ancient Sanskrit and modern Hindi: here was not just a separate language, but one as different from them as English is from Chinese. Further definition of linguistic boundaries came from John Stevenson, sent to Bombay by the Scottish Missionary Society in 1823. Though expected to combat idolatry, he became brahmanised too. He stayed in India for over 30 years, served as president of the Asiatic Society of Bombay and made himself an accomplished Sanskritist with his editions of Vedic texts. His most original contribution to learning came as a grammarian of Marathi, the language of Bombay's hinterland, which he proved to be Indo-European, though spoken in the same latitude as Telugu (Stevenson 1843: 84–91).

The Indo-European family's southern geographical boundary (except for the insular Sinhala of today's Sri Lanka) had now been set. What lay beyond it? The answer eventually came from the missionary Robert Caldwell, who learned many vernaculars as tools of his trade. He mastered the main tongues of southern India and traced their relationships, navigating the daunting divergences among them. In 1856 he proposed the name of Dravidian for the whole family (Caldwell 1856). To all intents and purposes his work established the modern consensus on Indian linguistics. Now it could not be doubted that Sanskrit and the Dravidian tongues arose from distinct origins. And since it had loaned words to them, rather than the other way round, this was most likely the result of an irruption by ancient Aryan culture over a yet older substratum of civilisation that had existed long before recorded history. In other words, the Dravidian linguistic stock had preceded the Indo-European. With this Caldwell shattered the idea that Sanskrit could have been the classical language of the whole sub-continent.

1

Meanwhile, the enlightened orientalist assumptions about Indian history were subverted in a different way. Scottish attitudes in the East had not always been so benevolent. In fact there emerged an opposite streak of hostility to native cultures that reckoned them to be degenerate. In this view, such cultures did not deserve to be preserved and cherished, but ought to be reformed and westernised. This current of thinking was in large part Christian, though not entirely so. Just before the turn of the nineteenth century it had taken its impetus from the writings of Charles Grant. He was the son of a Jacobite soldier at the Battle of Culloden who had died in exile in Jamaica; as in many such cases, the family made sure the next generation would be free of all taint of treason. Young Charles was shipped to Calcutta and apprenticed to a merchant there. He made himself rich, but in ten years also ran up gambling debts of £20,000. Then his two infant daughters died of smallpox. He overcame this personal crisis by turning to "vital religion", constantly searching his conscience and exhibiting his piety in public duty.

In 1792 Grant published *Observations on the State of Society among the Asiatic Subjects of Great Britain, particularly with respect to morals, and the means of improving it*. These morals he judged to be low, while the means of improving the state of society was to convert it to Christianity, if need be by the agency of its British rulers. After his return home he served as chairman of the East India Company and was elected MP for Inverness-shire, spending his spare time in the company of William Wilberforce and the Clapham Sect. When the charter of the Company came up before Parliament for renewal in 1813 he forced through a clause ordering its territories to be opened to Christian missions, which had previously been banned so as to avoid antagonising pious Hindus or Moslems. Grant's damning estimate of eastern civilisation found wide support. The first big Scottish book of the nineteenth century on an imperial theme rejected the conjectural history of India as it had been elaborated up to that point. The author was James Mill, who as a student had forsaken the high road to a career in the Church of Scotland for the low road to Grub Street and journalism in London. He turned aside from that, too, for an administrative billet in the East India Company. He never went to the orient: as with others, this did not shake the confidence of his conviction about its cultures. In fact his life was more deeply shaped by Jeremy Bentham, father of utilitarianism, a doctrine that aspired to apply scientific analysis to society as a means for reforming it. Bentham was a bit of a dreamer while Mill had a more practical bent. He wrote a stream of publications to hammer home the utilitarian message. The six volumes of Mill's *The History of British India* (1817) were the first complete treatment of the subject in English. In one way this too represented the Scottish tradition of a philosophical approach to the past, setting out general laws and detailed evidence for different stages of development defined by mode of subsistence. But, unlike Robertson, Mill thought India remained stuck at a primitive stage, far behind either modern or ancient Europe. What was more, India had shown no progress – which rendered redundant Robertson's surprise at the present state of the country. For example, the usual Indian form of government was despotism, which in the ancient world represented the crudest level of political organisation. Even now the East had not gone beyond it, so there should be no silly, sentimental fawning on rajahs and sultans. The sole relief from these comparisons to India's relentless disadvantage came in an implicit, tendentious line of argument drawing on a second aspect of conjectural history. It sought a deeper understanding of the advanced stages of development by inquiring what had survived in them from the less advanced. To Mill the conditions in India and Britain, outwardly so different, illuminated each other. The British still had traditional elites and social exclusions too, as the merest comparison of life among the aristocracy and the people showed. Britain had to reform herself before she could sensibly reform India. In both cases Mill posited that all the defects of the past could be swept away by mechanical application of the universally valid principles, revealed by utilitarianism, on which modern civilisation was advancing. He depicted Indians as labouring under burdens of superstition, privilege, tyranny and caste, which kept their government, religion, learning and law backward. A better future beckoned for them in westernisation, in reforms like those sought by the philosophical radicals at home. Britain would then reap the true benefit of her oriental links. These lay not in domination or exploitation, which were unnecessary, but in opening up India to free trade and to capitalist enterprise.

Similar thoughts occurred to Scots who did have personal experience of the sub-continent, and who a generation earlier would have turned into orientalists. John Crawford had been one of Minto's bright young men, but came to different conclusions from the rest after being sent to survey commercial openings in Southeast Asia on behalf of the East India Company. As he reflected on the region's economic prospects he convinced himself that westernisation offered the best way forward. What impressed Crawford was the ever wider disparity between low levels of technology in traditional economies and the much higher levels being attained in the West. Nobody before had made this sort of comparison: Adam Smith condemned the government of Bengal, yet thought the province otherwise possessed all it needed to prosper. But by now westerners entertained no doubt of the superiority of their outlook and methods. According to Crawford, India's commercial backwardness was the root of every other problem. He proposed to reform the currency and monetary system, to lower taxes and inject funds from Britain, together with the skills of her entrepreneurs. The way to do all this might be not only by "unlimited and unshackled application of British capital and intelligence", but also by "free settlement", or white colonisation of India. He denied this could take her the way of the United States in 1776, towards independence, because of the character of the people: "the Indians know not what freedom is: they are for the most part, a timid, often an effeminate, and, as a nation, a feeble race of semi-barbarians" (Crawford 1828: 27, 47–48; see also Crawford 1820; Crawford 1830). Crawford would win his greatest influence after his return to Britain. In 1841 he became president of the Ethnological Society of London, which propagated theories of scientific racism. The ideal of a universal Enlightenment was being lost from view: now it would be for each race to develop its full potential, if necessary at the expense of others.

As science wandered down such new and deviant paths, so too did religion. The Church of Scotland had been slow to respond when India was first opened to missions, but in 1830 it sent out a pair of its rising stars to embark on the evangelisation of the sub-continent. One, Alexander Duff, went to Calcutta. He arrived amid the continuing ferment originally set off by the orientalism of Minto. Duff sought to divert it into Christian channels. The Kirk charged him with bringing the blessings of Scottish education to India, and he began classes at what became known as the General Assembly's Institution (today the Scottish Church College) immediately on his arrival.

Duff met an eager response, for the urban elite of India was eager to absorb western learning. He had 200 boys enrolled in no time. He recorded: "It was our studied endeavour to court the society of those natives belonging to the more wealthy, influential and learned classes, who had already received a liberal education". He knew that his pupils came to him not for Christian dogmatics, but for subjects of practical use. Yet to him this was a distinction without a difference. He reported to the General Assembly of 1835:

Every branch of sound general knowledge which you inculcate becomes the destroyer of some corresponding part of the Hindu system. It is this that gives to the dissemination of mere human knowledge, in the present state of India, such awful importance.

If in Scottish terms Duff was a typical Evangelical tub-thumper, in Indian terms he was a moderniser and rationalist (Duff 1840: 518–19; Smith 1879: 93).

Pupils were taught a broad western curriculum of science, history and political economy, all of which Duff thought he could reconcile with Christianity: he held, for example, that the economic laws of Adam Smith were divine laws. He taught in English, while other missionaries used Bengali. Duff, a native of Gaelic Perthshire, had been brought up speaking Gaelic. English had long been the medium of Protestantism and social advance there, so he could readily associate it with the western culture he meant to impart to his pupils in Calcutta, and through them to India. He compared them to the young Highlanders who completed their education at the English-speaking universities of Scotland. He wrote:

In the very act of acquiring English, the mind, in grasping the import of a new term, is perpetually brought into contact with the *new ideas,* the *new truths* [...] so that, by the time the language has been mastered, the student must be *tenfold less* the child of pantheism, idolatry and superstition than before. (Duff 1840: 207)

While conversion to Christianity was Duff's ultimate goal, progress there remained frustratingly slow. But by 1848 he was able to form a Bengali congregation out of former pupils and others. They were mainly well-born intellectuals: lawyers, doctors, journalists, one who even went the length of becoming an ordained Presbyterian minister. That was just what Duff wanted: through education the replacement of the old Moghul ruling class with a new elite ready to reform Indian society by diffusion of Christianity and of western learning among the masses. He could not foresee how this new elite, once the Indian Mutiny of 1857 destroyed the old Moghul ruling class, would turn rather to nationalism.

Duff was only one side of the Presbyterian mission in India; the second minister sent out with him in 1830 represented another. John Wilson went to Bombay and stayed there the rest of his life. He saw it rise from backwater to metropolis, enriched by the ethnic mix of the population and by the vibrant intellectual life it stimulated. He took to linguistic scholarship himself. Soon fluent in several vernaculars, he sought not to be "too frequently inclined to speak on the folly of idolatry, and to neglect the preaching of the unsearchable riches of Christ". He formed a native congregation and a school where Marathi was the language of instruction. He urged "general education of the natives *through the medium of their own tongues*, which form the readiest key to their hearts" (Wilson 1849: 31). He held public disputations with Hindu, Moslem, Parsee and Jewish scholars. As eventual president of the Literary Society of Bombay, he collected Sanskrit manuscripts. He sought to decipher the Edicts of Ashoka from the columns that still stood marking the boundaries of the ancient Gupta Empire. And he became the first European scholar of Zend, the liturgical language of the Parsees, of whose religion he published a study in 1841 (Wilson 1843). At the founding of the University of Bombay in 1857, Wilson was the obvious choice for its inaugural vice-chancellor. One reason for the city's rapid progress lay in an educational system owed in no small measure to him. A college founded in his memory, 14 years after his death in 1875, still shows off its saltires to the Arabian Sea. "What is it that Scotland intends to do by this college?" asked the Governor of Bombay and son of Sutherland, Donald Mackay, Lord Reay, on opening it. "The professors wish to ennoble your hearts by imparting that moral fibre which is the mainspring of the Scottish character" (Laird 1979: 346).

Missionary orientalism was also winning support in lay circles. A wealthy donor to Presbyterian initiatives was John Muir of the East India Company. Scholar as well as official, he wrote Christian tracts in Sanskrit verse. But in his deep respect for Indian culture, he tried in a pamphlet of 1849 to persuade missionaries that they could not reject some things that orthodox Hindus believed; on the contrary, "there is much in their learning which we can honestly admire and praise" (Smith, 1879: 1–20). He feared that the dissolution of the Company after 1857 and the imposition of direct imperial rule would spell the end not only of Scottish opportunity, but also of Scottish orientalism, because the grounding in native languages routinely given to cadets setting out eastwards would no longer be available. So, in 1862, Muir endowed the chair of Sanskrit at the University of Edinburgh, one of only three in Britain.[2] He set scholars a philological example in his own five volumes of *Original Sanskrit Texts* (1868–70). Among other

---

[2] A chair at Oxford had been founded in 1830 and at University College, London, in 1852; Cambridge followed only in 1868.

things, these sought to give chapter and verse for the new theory of Indian history elaborated by Scottish scholars.

Similar interests come through in the work of a second official, William Hunter. He published a *Statistical Account of Bengal* (1875–77), then set down for posterity, with greater affection, his *Annals of Rural Bengal* (1897). An excursion into fiction, *The Old Missionary* (1896), is a novel of disillusion at efforts to convert Indians to Christianity. Hunter had come to deplore such efforts, and his hero is an example of a man, originally an Evangelical, who during long decades in the East has been brahmanised. Now he dislikes attempts to seduce the natives into western ways, even into western religion if that entails, as is often the case, sectarian competition. In the plot Presbyterians fight with Catholics for the souls of the people, while the old missionary reads the Sanskrit scriptures and finally dies at peace with himself.

2

British imperialism became harsher from the mid-nineteenth century, not only in India, but also beyond. It is to the credit of the school of Scottish orientalists that, while they suffered setbacks from this trend, they did not meekly succumb to it. Their school retained some vigour up to the turn of the twentieth century, and arguably marked up its greatest achievement in a final phase.

As westerners prised China open with the blunt instrument of the Opium Wars in 1840–41 and 1857–60, not only trade followed the flag, but missions too. Their first move further east than India had been to Malacca, an emporium with a largely Chinese population in the present-day Malaysia, where the London Missionary Society set up a college to which it appointed a Scot as principal, James Legge. When the British took over Hong Kong in 1841, he moved the college there. It was now to be financed by Jardine Matheson, the greatest trading house in the orient. The fact that the partners made their fortunes from drug-running did worry some of them, good Scots Presbyterians to a man; but they, too, thought free trade part of the divine ordering of the world and so could square it with their consciences. Legge proved useful as economic enterprise merged into political domination, giving instruction not only to junior colonial officials from home, but also to trainee mandarins sent to him by the Manchu regime in Beijing for acquaintance with western ways (one or two he passed on to study at his own *alma mater*, the University of Aberdeen). Yet the experience turned Legge, too, into an orientalist scholar: "The idea that a man need spend no time in studying the native religions, but has only, as the phrase is, to *preach the gospel* is one which can only make missionaries and mission work contemptible and inefficient" (Latourette 1929: 246, see also 396, 665). Legge immersed himself in classical Chinese literature. It contained nothing like the mythology of other ancient peoples, let alone religion in a western sense. It was rather an agnostic civilisation's prose corpus of moral philosophy. Legge found in it no idea of sin or salvation. But he satisfied himself that a divine presence could be discerned here, too, if only in debased form; for example, in the ritual traditions of the imperial ruling house. So when Legge had to invent a term for the true God now obscured to the Chinese, he sought one that bore some meaning within their culture. He used *shang ti*, "supreme emperor". To missionary colleagues this seemed suspect: did it not concede divinity to the *ti*, the Emperor in Beijing? They grew more worried still as Legge in his copious writings drew further parallels between Confucianism and Christianity. After surveying all Confucius had to say about God, man's destiny and his moral or social duties, Legge found this ancient wisdom to be not wholly in error: the *Analects* contained material that could be turned to evangelical purposes. A paper on these lines, sent by him to be read at a missionary conference in Shanghai in 1877, so alarmed his critics that they had it excluded as heretical from the published proceedings. It made no odds to him: his work had taken him in 1873 to inaugurate the chair of Chinese at the University of Oxford, which he graced till his death in 1897 as the father of British sinology (Giradot 1997).

3

Scottish orientalism finally embraced a third great culture of Asia – that of the Semitic peoples in the Near East and the Arabian Peninsula. They were of special interest to pious Scots as "peoples of the book", Jews and Arabs who had received their own divine revelations. So their religions could not be written off as in themselves of little or no redemptive value, like Hinduism and Confucianism. The man who tackled the task of reconciling the theology of these peoples with modern scientific insights was William Robertson Smith, minister of the Free Church and professor of Hebrew at its college in Aberdeen. He was in one sense an enlightened Scot. He accepted the results of dispassionate inquiry into oriental religion. Others might put the vindication of Christianity above their scholarship, but not he. He still saw in the Christian God the absolute reality, to be apprehended by faith – not works – according to Calvinist doctrine. That absolute reality was then, by definition, incapable of being contradicted by scientific advance. If a problem emerged of harmonising the two, it had to be done with unorthodox, not to say revolutionary new thinking on the scholar's part, rather than by clinging to dogmas of the past. The divine revelation would by this means be constantly renewed. In particular, Scottish stadial theory allowed Christianity and science to move forward in tandem (as they had already done in the work of Principal Robertson a century before). For example, it was abundantly clear that out of the primitive world of the Old Testament a more civi- lised world of the New Testament had proceeded. From the time of Christ higher forms of belief and morality emerged and still continued to emerge. Christianity improved on Judaism, and Presbyterianism improved on Roman Catholicism. Among Presbyterians themselves improvement could continue through returning to the Bible armed with advancing scholarly technique.

   To Robertson Smith the process carried on right into the present age, into the Scottish Enlightenment and its sequels. For instance, Adam Smith had propagated those economic principles of Victorian society that, above all in Scotland, rested on an individualist rather than collectivist spirit. Now, in the late nineteenth century, things changed again. Robertson Smith himself questioned the Presbyterian, indeed Protestant, assumption that the vital relation was the one between the individual and God. He found that the group had been the primeval cradle of religion. In the ancient world members of the group, related by blood, included within it also their deities and the totemic animals from which they thought themselves descended. They accepted as a religious duty the performance of rites needed to sustain the order of things in their world, that is, to preserve the group and affirm their identity as its members. What they really worshipped, Robertson Smith concluded, was that order of things their own society idealised and deified. They gave it religious sanction just because it seemed to their uninstructed minds natural and inevitable, so divinely ordained. Thus the source of symbolic behaviour lay in the group. Beliefs had a social origin. Robertson Smith at the same time conceded how all religions had begun in superstition, magic and taboo, stained by demonic, polluting and irrational elements. These were lower forms of belief or morality only to be expected in lower stages of human development. They appeared in the Bible too: books of the Pentateuch are full of instructions for bloody rituals, beside the Ten Commandments and more edifying matters. Robertson Smith's greatest work, *The Religion of the Semites* (1889), analyses the many types of sacrifice mentioned in ancient records, biblical or non-biblical (see also Robertson Smith 1882; Robertson Smith 1885; Black and Chrystal 1912).

In the highest form of sacrifice, at important points of the year or in time of danger, members of the group killed their totemic animal, otherwise taboo to them, and devoured it as their brother-god. Robertson Smith's own unshakeable faith gave him the freedom to construct this startling hypothesis. But it is easy to see how his clerical brethren in the Free Church feared his ideas might appear in another light to people of weak faith or of none. Why should these regard the culmination of all religion that he found in Christ as symbolism qualitatively different from its primitive forms? Why should they not conclude that when Christians took communion they were acting out a modern survival of totemic bloodletting? Why should they not see this as just another product of primeval confusion and error? (Said 1978: 235). The fundamentalist doubts about Roberton Smith and the dogmatic strictures on his work brought him at length to a trial for heresy before the General Assembly of the Free Church, and to deposition from his chair in 1881. It was a Highland clique of diehard Calvinists that forced this harsh retribution through. Despite the sympathy he won among Scots at large, Robertson Smith opted to go into English exile at the University of Cambridge. There he served as editor of the ninth edition of *Encyclopaedia Britannica*, the "scholar's encyclopaedia", so called because it featured articles by the distinguished range of authorities that he commissioned. Dying young, he asked to be buried in his native Aberdeenshire; he had never worked in Scotland again.

In his homeland, Robertson Smith stands at the end of a tradition. It was an international community of scholars, not brother Scots, that carried his work forward. Enlightenment had had its day – in particular the Scottish Enlightenment in two of its most distinct aspects, its historical theories and its dialogue with Christianity. A final crowning achievement had come from Robertson Smith in placing history and religion on a common conceptual basis. But soon that did not in itself matter, as the conjectural theories were superseded and a dialogue of history and religion on such terms ceased to be necessary. Robertson Smith lives on rather through ideas about the psychological origins of religion (and everything else), in the works of figures as diverse as T.S. Eliot, Ezra Pound, James Joyce, D.H. Lawrence, Joseph Conrad and Ludwig Wittgenstein.

4

The orient and orientalism had played an interesting part in this cycle of the Enlightenment's history, albeit skewed in a peculiar manner. But Scottish culture of the nineteenth century was in general skewed. Like the other human raw material going into the scientific inquiry, the data from the East never generated that much by way of imaginative literature. To consider Scotland and the orient in a cultural context, we have had to cast our net beyond the shallow waters of the available fiction – as is more widely necessary for anyone wanting to savour the national culture of the nineteenth century. We have had instead to fish in that open sea of learned disciplines where enlightened Scots voyaged, pursuing far horizons which continued to beckon. Social science, to use the parlance of the present day, is the term that comes closest to covering them all.

Luckily works of this genre or these genres were not then always academic in the modern sense. Many were aimed at the general reader, mythical creature as he or she may seem today. The flourishing state of the reviews (the *Edinburgh Review* the grand-daddy of them all), the huge sales for books of popular science, the avid attendance at public lectures, the bated breath with which laymen followed debates on evolution and other novel theories, all indicate that we may with justice range them alongside novels or poetry when we try to reassemble the mental furniture of the cultivated person of that age.

The Scottish contribution then appears more impressive than if we consider imaginative literature alone.

Scots used the orient as a proving ground for their theories. Conversely, knowledge of faraway places modified their mental constructions. This fruitful exchange was a remarkable feature of the Scottish nineteenth century, and came out in some of its most significant works. "Orientalism" is a good name for the whole phenomenon, because it took exotic cultures on their own terms (with what success is a different question) and because it played a vital part in fulfilling the Enlightenment's aspirations to universality. In that case we have to think of some other name for the sort of orientalism condemned by Said, an imposition on the passive and suffering East by the hostile and intolerant West. Some Scots in the orient set themselves up as agents of such an imposition, yet it cannot in justice be said that most did so.

Bibliography

Black, J.S. and G. Chrystal, (eds). 1912. *Lectures and Essays of William Robertson Smith*. London: Adam & Charles Black.

Caldwell, Robert. 1856. *A Comparative Grammar of the Dravidian or South-Indian Family of Languages*. London: Harrison.

Campbell, Alexander D. 1816. *A Grammar of the Teloogoo Language* (Madras: College of Fort St. George Press).

Crawford, John. 1828. *View of the Present State and Future Prospects of the Free Trade and Colonisation of India*. London.

—. 1820. *History of the Indian Archipelago*. [Indonesia] Edinburgh: Constable.

—. 1830. *Journal of an Embassy from the Governor-general of India to the Courts of Siam and Cochin*. London: Henry Colburn.

Duff. Alexander. 1840. *India and India Missions*. Edinburgh: J. Johnstone.

Erskine, William. 1854. *A History of India under the first two Sovereigns of the House of Taimur, Baber and Humayun*. London: Longman, Brown, Green and Longmans.

Fry, Michael R.G. 1992. *The Dundas Despotism*. Edinburgh: Edinburgh University Press.

Giradot, Norman. 1997. "James Legge and the Strange Saga of Sinological Orientalism and the Comparative Science of Religions in the Nineteenth Century". Unpublished paper delivered at the University of Aberdeen.

Grant, Charles [1792] 1813. *Observations on the State of Society among the Asiatic Subjects of Great Britain*. London: The House of Commons.

Hamilton, Alexander. 1820. *A Key to the Chronology of the Hindus*. Cambridge: Rivington.

Hunter, William. 1875–77. *Statistical Account of Bengal*. London: Trübner & Co.

—. 1896. *The Old Missionary*. London: H. Frowde.

—. 1897. *Annals of Rural Bengal*. London: Smith, Elder & Co.

Laird, M.A. 1979. "John Wilson: aspects of his educational work" in *Colloques Internationaux du Centre de la Recherche Scientifique* 582: 346.

Latourette, Kenneth Scott. 1929. *A History of Christian Missions in China*. London: Society for Promoting Christian Knowledge.

Legge, James. 1867–76. *The Chinese Classics*. 3 vols. Hong Kong.

Leyden, John. 1821. *Malay Annals*. London.

—. 1826. *Memoirs of Babur, Emperor of Hindustan*. London.

—. 1886. *On the Languages and Literatures of the Indo-Chinese Nations*. Singapore.

Macintosh, J. 1806. *Plan of a Comparative Vocabulary of Indian Languages*. Bombay.

McGilvary, G.K. 1989. *East India Patronage and the Political Management of Scotland 1720–1774*. Unpublished Ph.D. thesis. Open University.

Mills, James. 1817. *The History of British India*. 6 vols. London: Baldwin, Cradock and Joy.

Minto Papers. National Library of Scotland [NLS], MS 11726.

— NLS MSS 11734–9

— NLS MS 11066.

Muir, John. 1869–70. *Original Sanskrit Texts on the Origin and History of the People of India*. London: Trübner & Co.

Said, Edward. 1978. *Orientalism*. London: Routledge & Kegan Paul.

Scott, Walter. 1891. *The Surgeon's Daughter*. [1826] London: J.C. Nimmo.

Shakespear, A. (ed.). 1873. *Selections from the Duncan Records*. Benares: Medical Hall Press.

Smith, George. 1879. *The Life of Alexander Duff*. London: Hodder & Stoughton.

Smith, Robertson. 1882. *Prophets of Israel and their Place in History*. Edinburgh: Adam & Charles Black.

—. 1885. *Kinship and Marriage in Early Arabia*. Cambridge: Cambridge University Press.

—. 1889. *The Religion of the Semites*. London: Adam & Charles Blade.

Stevenson, John. 1843. "Observations on the Marathi Language" in *Journal of the Royal Asiatic Society* 19: 84–91.

Wilson, John. 1843. *The Parsi Religion: Unfolded, Refuted and Contrasted with Christianity*. Bombay: American Mission Press.

—. 1849. *The Evangelisation of India*. Edinburgh: W. Whyte.

Exporting the Covenant: Scottish Missionary Tales and Africa, c.1870–c.1920

Richard Finlay

Nineteenth-century Scottish Presbyterian missionary narratives transferred certain Protestant aspirations to Africa, not least at a time when Scottish towns and cities represented stony ground for evangelisation. Sincere Scottish Presbyterian missionary activity became entangled with British imperial ambition, though not always operating entirely in consonance with it, providing particularly anti-Catholic and anti-Islamic accents to British activity in collision with Arab, Portugese and other European endeavour in Africa.
Keywords: Missionary Narratives; David Livingstone; Mary Slessor; Alexander Mackay; British imperialism in Africa; Calvinism; Islam; Anti-Catholicism; Slavery; British-Portugese relations; British Central African Protectorate.

In the late nineteenth-century, Scottish society began to venerate the activities of its overseas missions, especially in Africa.[1] As Henry Morton Stanley was to comment at the inaugural meeting of the Scottish Geographic Society in 1886, there was a strong connection between Scotland and the Dark Continent.[2] In the second half of the nineteenth-century, Scottish missionary endeavour increasingly focused on Africa, especially after the death of David Livingstone, when his call for further work was taken up with gusto as a tribute to a Christian martyr.[3] Apart from the fact that the continent was at the centre of European imperial ambitions, overseas missions in India were facing obstacles from imperial authorities following the Mutiny of 1857. The conversion of the Jews, which had been an important plank of all the Scottish churches' missionary endeavours, had to tackle a diverse range of geographical locations, many of which were politically inhospitable, and had limited success to show for its fairly

---

[1] For a general introduction to the history of missionaries and the British Empire see Breitenbach 2009, Porter 2004, Porter 2003, Ross 1971, and Ross 1996. For Scottish involvement in the London Missionary Society see Thorne 1999.
[2] Covered in the first issue of the *Scottish Geographic Magazine*, 1 (1886).
[3] For details of the of Livingstone's memorial in Edinburgh see Mackie 1888: 78. See also, John M. MacKenzie 1990: 24–33.

expensive efforts.[4] Also, the 1870s witnessed the growth of another burst of evangelical revivalism which put forward a fairly simple Christian message and avoided the pitfalls of theological disputation (Brown 2008: 278–84). A host of popular and populist publications celebrated the lives and achievements of intrepid adventurers who battled against the odds in Africa to bring Christianity to the far flung corners of the earth. The genre was especially popular as a form of instruction and guidance for children and a publishing industry was built on the achievements of these Scottish icons.[5] The topic is an important one because it sheds light on a number of aspects of late nineteenth-century Scottish society. Firstly, it provided an outlet for spreading the word that could be presented in more successful light than the seeming failures that dogged the inner cities where the godless masses clung on obstinately to heathenism. Also, it deflected attention from the mass of Catholic immigrants from Ireland where little effort was made at conversion. At a time when contemporaries were bemoaning the spread of godlessness in the inner cities, the missionary endeavour could be presented as a beacon of success. How could the problems of home, asked one churchman, John Campbell White, "compare with those of Darkest Africa with its 180 million, who no fault of their own, were sunk in misery and vice?" (McCracken 2008: 61). Indeed, it is worth noting that in terms of the literary genre, the popularity of reading about the darkness of the inner cities was increasingly transferred to Africa, presumably because there was a greater distance and more security.[6] Secondly, it was glamorous and exotic and with the advent of the "magic lantern" it was possible

---

[4] The Committees for the Conversion of the Jews were among the first reports received at the General Assemblies up to the 1870s. Missions in Central Europe, Constantinople, Amsterdam and elsewhere usually reported limited converts. See for example the volumes of the *The Home and Foreign Record of the Free Church* and *The Home and Foreign Missionary Record of the Church of Scotland* and Hunter 1873.

[5] For example, John Ritchie, Publisher of Christian Literature in Kilmarnock, the "Splendid Lives Series" published by the Sunday School Union, and a host of memoirs and hagiographers, perhaps the most important in a Scottish context being William P. Livingstone.

[6] It is worth pointing out that the social commentary of Shadow, *Social Photographs of Glasgow* (1847), the commentary of W.P. Alison in *Blackwood's Magazine* and most famously Owen Chadwick's *Report on the Sanitary Conditions of the Labouring Classes* (1837) had dried up at the same time as the appearance of the missionary tales in the second half of the nineteenth century, although the genre continued in England.

to bring to life exciting and intrepid stories which were altogether more epic, in the biblical sense, than the footslogging witnessed in domestic society. In terms of exciting the public imagination, the drunks and destitute of Glasgow and Dundee were no match for witch-doctors, lions and exotic climes. Each church could have its own missionary who would report back regularly and whose endeavours could connect the local with the broader missionary movement. It also had the advantage that the public had little means to substantiate or verify the claims of missionary success or otherwise. The war against slavery, devil worship, cannibalism and human sacrifice was much more significant than labouring among the ingrates of the inner cities who were increasingly presented as the authors of their own misfortunes, rather than the innocent and childlike African.[7] Thirdly, it was possible to present the missionary endeavour as a united Scottish venture, at a time when following the Disruption of 1843, ecclesiological disputes were something of a Scottish forte.[8] The cult of David Livingstone, for example, allowed all Scots to celebrate his achievements, even though he was sponsored by the London Missionary Society, and although there were disagreements concerning his legacy with both the Free and Established churches in Nyasaland (modern Malawi) claiming his inheritance at their missions in Livingstonia and Blantyre respectively, by and large overseas endeavours could deflect attention away from divisions at home (MacKenzie 1990). Finally, the escapism of missionary tales allowed the public, and the missionaries themselves, to distance themselves from some of the complex theological problems facing a modern urban and industrial society. The growth of secularism, the scientific challenges posed by Darwin and the fundamentals of Calvinism all posed particular challenges and the missionary story represented a sort of back-to-basics primitive form of Christian endeavour that could sidestep these issues. The "elect" could be seen to be instruments of God, where success was evidence of providence while death ensured martyrdom. The fallen also provided

---

[7] This was especially the case with the growth of Christian political economy and an emphasis on self-discipline and hard work. See Brown 1983, and for an English context, Mandler 1990: 81–103.

[8] This was the opinion of Hugh Miller who thought that the Disruption should not be carried out to Scottish Churches in the colonies. See Miller 1870: 221–31.

nineteenth-century Scottish society with martyrs to provide continuity
with their seventeenth-century Covenanting heroes.

It is the objective of this chapter to explore the insights that
missionary stories provide us about Scottish society through their
descriptions of African society. Although there were some serious
endeavours in what might be called anthropological and linguistic
studies of African society, European accounts are plagued by
misunderstandings, loaded assumptions and other problems that post-
colonialists have warned about.[9] That said, missionary accounts can
tell us much about who wrote them and there is no doubt that these
missionaries were sincere in their beliefs. By using missionary tales as
a mirror, we can see reflected what many Scots thought constituted the
essentials of the Christian mission, what they believed it contributed
to civilisation and what they feared were the worst elements of the
human condition and how these could be improved. Drunkenness,
immorality and other vices, although set in an African context, were
not unique to that place and more often than not, domestic sins were
simply projected onto a faraway place. The objectives of the
missionaries will be explored and the ways in which their success was
conveyed to Scottish society to show that it was a worthwhile
endeavour. Such examination also shines light into what missionaries
saw as the fundamentals of society; the establishment of schools and
medical centres were essential to this vision. Also, the idea of
legitimate trade and work was important as an alternative to slavery,
which loomed large in missionary accounts of Africa. The relationship
with capitalism, however, was not straightforward as missionaries
were often the severest critics of what they saw as western economic
exploitation (see Fields 1982; Fraser 1914: 303; Livingstone 1931:
128). This chapter will examine too the unique aspects of Scottish
identity that missionaries brought to their endeavours. Complex
echoes of Calvinism resound in missionary accounts amid the Scottish
engagement with the British Empire. Finally, the role of providential
British imperialism will be explored. As Jay Brown has recently
demonstrated, British churches were heavily influenced by the idea
that they had a global moral imperative to fulfil, and the ways in
which Scottish missionary endeavour was portrayed as part of a
contribution to a wider British imperial mission will be explored

---

[9] For a good example of an attempt by a missionary to subject Africans to a form of
anthropological study, though fundamentally flawed, see Elmslie 1899.

(Brown 2008: 195–206). There was also sometimes a sense of atonement; for instance, for its part in the slave trade, the United Free Church sent its mission to Calabar (Nigeria) following the Jamaican Massacres as it was that part of Africa that the slaves originally came from (Livingstone 1920: 13).

Conventional Scottish accounts of African society do not differ much from the popular European imagination of the "dark" continent. A key factor that may be suggested to explain the Scottish impetus to take an interest in Africa concerns the popular opposition to slavery. Duncan Rice has charted the activities of the Scottish abolitionist movement and in particular its involvement with North America (Rice 1981). A neglected aspect of the story, however, is that with the ending of the Civil War attention turned to the existence of slavery in African society and the belief that their the trade continued. Religion was a key factor, as the villains of the piece were Islamic society and the activities of Catholic Europeans, especially the Portuguese who, it was believed, were illicitly slaving to South America where slavery remained legal. As Anthony Ross has reminded us, a key aspect of Livingstone's exploration in Africa was to find suitable land and navigational routes for the establishment of cotton plantations. It was believed that African cotton grown by free labour would put the southern slave-owing states out of business and end the institution of slavery in North America (Ross 2002: 119). Although it would be hard to prove that the emotional, moral and organisational dynamic of the abolitionist cause in Scotland simply transferred itself to Africa, the link between the two cannot be discounted. It has to be emphasised that the issue of slavery in Africa failed to generate the same degree of public interest that existed in the first half of the nineteenth century. For some, however, the belief in the widespread existence of slavery in African society provided an immediacy for moral intervention. In the late 1880s, for example, freelancing anti-slavers held fund-raising campaigns to buy a Gatling gun to fight Arab slavers (Stevenson 1888). The independent activities of Scottish anti-slavers caused Lord Salisbury numerous headaches and Nyasaland became a British protectorate in 1894/5 largely because of a united campaign by the churches in Scotland who argued that surrendering the territory to the Portuguese would be a victory for Catholicism and slavery (Robinson et al 1970: 223, 245; Hanna 1956: 106–32). It is probably the only time that British foreign policy was determined solely by Scottish public opinion. Again it is worth stressing how popular Protestantism was quite adept at linking the issue of slavery with Catholicism, a parallel that required little elaboration among the Presbyterian community.[10] Elsewhere, concerning nefarious Islam, the biographer of Henry Drummond commented that his subject "saw the cruelty of the Slave Trade in its most ghastly features – the cruel Arab dealer, the track dotted with human bones, the stockades with human heads impaled upon them" (Smith 1903: 210). A key aspect of missionary activity in Nyasaland was the ambition to found plantations and establish trading stations as an alternative to slave trafficking. The biographer of Alexander Hetherwick of Blantyre illustrated the extent of the problem in the early days of the mission:

He also discovered how it was that hundreds of natives disappeared annually from his district. From the main slave caravans small companies broke off, remained in a village, and ingratiated themselves with the headman. When they left they carried with them twenty to thirty victims, usually useless dependents or offenders or strangers who had been exchanged for calico and powder. Others, encountered on the by paths, or in their gardens, were seized and placed in the slave sticks. No one had sufficient interest to protest against these outrages. Before the coast was reached the slaves were disposed of for rubber and wax, and the slavers remained undetected. (Livingstone 1931: 41–42)

The moral imperative against slavery was such that some took freelance intervention for granted and gave missionaries the excuse for violence. Alexander Mackay and a party of European missionaries chased slave caravans, fought them and where possible, set the victims free ([Melrose] 1894: 29). Other stories indicated the casualness of slavery within African society and the tendency for chiefs to make presents of slaves to missionaries, often children (*Two Missionary Pioneers* c.1900: 33). War and slavery went hand in hand. Another *leitmotiv* that runs through missionary accounts is the desire for guns and ammunition to make slaving more effective and to wage war to capture booty.[11] Given the opprobrium in which slavery was held in Scottish society, missionary activity could be presented in a positive light. Intervention was also presented as form of atonement for the

---

[10] See for example, Livingstone 1865, "Slavery" 1876, Jack 1900: 190–213, Swann 1910. Swann was from the North East of England. Fredrick Lugard accused the Portuguese of being "inveterate slavers", see Luggard 1893: 2: 15–16.
[11] By and large, this was blamed on Indians trading in Zanzibar who sold weapons that then made their way into the Centre of Africa (Lugard 1893: 2: 45–48).

British involvement in the slave trade. The establishment of the mission was presented as "the first step which she [the Church of Scotland] has taken to make some reparation to the African people for the unnumbered wrongs which our forerunners perpetuated upon them" (Macdonald 1882: 20).

Tales of immorality and vice were used to contrast the light that was brought by the missionary movement. A conventional technique used in the magic lantern shows was to show pictures of Africans before and after Christianity. The former picture showed cowering, naked and savage creatures, holding spears and weapons, while the latter presented smiling, clothed, upright and happy individuals holding baskets or tools. Such contrasting images would leave the viewer in no doubt of benefits from missionary endeavour. For many, the degraded state of the African and the absence of a work-ethic were critical in explaining the prevalence of slavery and the abundance of vice and immorality. In spite of the populist obsession with cannibalism, the vice that received a disproportionate amount of attention in Scottish accounts is drunkenness. According to one account, Africans "acted as too many people in Britain do when in a state of excitement; they drank large quantities of beer". As the biographer of Alexander Mackay elucidates, "over and over again in his journals, MacKay says that drink is the curse of Africa. So much did he see the evils of drink in Africa, that he became a teetotaller after starting on his journey" (Macdonald 1882: 45–46). In one account, drink was the only way the natives gave expression to their social instincts and "carousals" would last for many days while "children went neglected and unprovided with food" (Livingstone 1919: 74–75). Donald Fraser, likewise, claimed that alcohol was corrupting African society: "Young people and even children are now allowed to drink to intoxication, and practically the only abstainers are those who have come under the influence of the schools" (Fraser 1914: 185).[12] He elaborated in terms that would be familiar to those who campaigned against alcohol at home:

Against two firm habits of the people the wave of religious life broke continually, and with some disintegrating effect. The first is the beer habit. How productive of crime, how demoralizing to village life, how clogging to all progress this custom of the people is only those who have passed their years among them can tell. One knows that

[12] For a recent assessment of the work of Fraser see Thompson 1995.

their beer grain is a food, and that chiefs subsist on little else, and were it possible for them to use it in moderation one would have nothing to say against it. But indulgence is more congenial to the African than restraint [...]. All public events, funerals, dances, harvesting, hoeings, are carried through with drunken bouts. While beer is plentiful, the recruiting of labour is impossible. No attraction of money or cloth can compete with it. Out of these public carousals a crop of crimes, homicides, adulteries, and quarrels invariably is produced. Mothers neglect their children, or let them roll into the fire at night and get burned; men club one another to death; quarrels over nothing end in such furious hatred that villages are broken up and scattered. (Fraser 1914: 96)

The availability of alcohol and its corrupting effect is recounted in great detail and is presented as one instance of the corroding impact of contact with Europeans, though was usually blamed on other nationals or on the drink industry which had been thwarted at home by the temperance movement. In spite of one traveller's claim that missionaries exaggerated the impact of alcohol, the issue remained a potent one and during the Second World War, the Rev. James Barr MP sponsored a Bill against the drink trade in Western Africa.[13] When the African Lakes Trading Company was established in Glasgow in the 1880s, its founding charter proclaimed that it would trade in neither guns nor drink. The combination of drink and primitive society, it was claimed, was a lethal combination that brought out the worst in African society. Native rites and communal practices were described as drunken orgies. Alcohol was blamed for increasing war, violence, slavery and exacerbating the existing state of savagery. Irresponsible traders were another source of criticism who plied naïve Africans with drink as a means to secure favourable trading advantages (Livingstone 1920: 86). Parallels can be drawn with the domestic situation in which drink caused untold social damage and rotted the fabric of society and "it seems to be a reproach to have a beer drinking without a fight" (Macdonald 1882: 206).

To complement the picture, missionary tales highlighted the success of indigenous society once alcohol had been banned. According to Donald Fraser:

Beer, then, is one of greatest enemies to the economic and moral welfare of the land, and against it the native church has declared uncompromising war. Every catechumen and Church member is a total abstainer. One curious result of this is that the

---

[13] Lugard estimated that huge revenues were made on the import of alcohol to Africa (Lugard 1893: 2: 213). See also Kingsley [1897] 1965: 568–606, and Barr 1943.

Christians instead of providing beer for their neighbours who come to hoe their gardens, provide a good square meal. And today the native can be distinguished at once where gardens have been prepared and cleared by beer and where by food. Those who hoe for beer wasted their day, and scamped their work, so that the maize is dwarfed and weedy compared with that in the gardens of the Christians. (Fraser 1914: 97)

Although missionary reports exalted the benefits of teetotalism and its practical benefits, their work was cut out for them. The war on beer was a constant one and backsliding had to be stamped on. Alexander Heatherwick happened on a "perfect orgy" outside of Blantyre where the crowd fled and "[w]ithout a moment's hesitation Dr. Heatherwick went up to the pots and smashed them to pieces. It was a practical lesson in temperance which had so salutary an effect that beer ceased to be made in a wide area around" (Livingstone 1931: 103). The hard line on alcohol meant that "severer measures for maintaining the purity of the Church had been imposed than would have been adopted in Scotland – drunkenness, making beer for sale, and the presence of a member at a public beer drinking were matters for discipline" (Livingstone 1931: 147). The war on beer was part of a larger strategy to encourage permanent settlement based on agriculture and the cultivation of crops. The nomadic existence of African society militated against the fundamentals of what the missionaries were trying to achieve and the establishment of schools, medical centres and trading posts were all designed to hold the population to a fixed locality. Labour shortage and transience was always considered a problem and fixed cultivation of cash crops was one way of harnessing the population to the missionary outposts. Civilisation was static.

In addition to slavery and drink, polygamy was presented as an ever-present evil in African society. Polygamy was presented as evidence of the low esteem in which women were held and given the large number of female Scottish missionaries in Africa, it comes as no surprise to find that it looms large in many accounts. The treatment of women and children was taken as an indicator of civilisation, or the lack of it, and their treatment was viewed as a form of domestic slavery. Women and children were regarded as being the lynch-pin in the assault on heathenism, as the family was regarded as the fundamental building block of Christianity and civilisation. They were also regarded as the key means to spread the word among indigenous society. Polygamy challenged the Victorian conception of the family and contradicted the basic tenets of Christian marriage. Without marriage and conventional family life Christian civilisation could not be built. According to Donald Fraser:

Polygamy is another habit with which no compromise is made. I know that there are people who hold that polygamy is necessary for the African. But they provide for no rise in his civilized status, and so make no readjustments. I can say with confidence from some knowledge of thousands of Africans, that it is no more necessary for the African than for the European, who has any idea of home. Polygamy is necessitated by two things. The one is, the desire on the part of ambitious men for an adventitious respect and social standing which they think a plurality of wives will give them. The other is lust. So long as polygamy exists, there can be no family life, and the forces that bolster it are unchristian. (Fraser 1914: 97)

According to Mary Slessor, polygamy was part of a condition of African debasement. She dismissed the idea of the African as innocent and held the view that in the absence of Christianity, the human condition was degraded. Those who held otherwise, were told to spend a month in an African harem (Livingstone 1920: 74). The harem was blamed for making the condition of women worse than slaves. Women could be sold, beaten, killed or abused at will and this absence of western family life was, she believed, responsible for passing on the degraded nature of humanity to children (Livingstone 1920: 70–75).

In missionary tales the existence of ritualised infanticide, polygamy and witchcraft are given pride of place in lurid accounts in order to stress the magnitude of the difficulties that the missionaries faced. A conventional literary technique is to highlight the cruelties inflicted by warlike tribes on passive and simple Africans. The "wild Okoyong" were a tribe of terrorists who plagued the Ibibios and engaged in the worse form of "African devilry" (Livingstone 1920: 65–68). The "wild Ngoni" likewise inflicted a reign of terror on passive tribes in the Shire Highlands:

Terrible stories were related of their cruelty to the children they had taken in tribute: it was said that they had the obstreperous ones tied to branches and kindled fires beneath them; or placed them in earthen pots and boiled them with maize. Criminals were fastened to the ground and smeared with honey, and the red ants came and ate them alive. (Livingstone 1921: 191)

In South Africa the Xhosa of the Bantu or "Kaffirs" terrorised the peace-loving Fingoes (Livingstone 1919: 25–30). The superstition of African society is constantly highlighted and the witch doctor was presented as the arch-villain whom the missionaries had to engage in spiritual combat for African hearts and minds. The witch doctor was the epitome of African savagery and barbarism and numerous accounts wax lyrical on the prevalence of belief in magic and supernatural powers. Hair and nail clippings were buried to stop natives using them in magic rituals, body parts from the dead were used as medicine, trials by fire, poison and terror were used to determine innocence or guilt and orgiastic practices were common. Illness and natural misfortunes were blamed on evil magic and unfortunates were put to death on account of their witchcraft. Africa was presented as a violent place in which anarchy reigned and death through war was commonplace. The biographer of Mary Slessor regularly managed to squeeze all the horrors in one fell swoop:

It was strange, even for her, to pass from the trim, well-ordered life of Britain into the midst of West African heathenism to find waiting in her yard two refugees, who, being charged with witchcraft, were condemned to be sold and killed and preserved as food, to be interviewed by a slave women who had been bought by an Okoyong chief as one of his many wives, after having been the wife of two other men, one of whom had been disposed of to the cannibal tribe, whilst her boy had been carried to Calabar in bondage. (Livingstone 1920: 117–18)

In addition to the proclivities of the natives, the missionaries had to endure a harsh and unforgiving climate and the prospect of deadly disease. Swamps, marshes, inaccessible terrain, jungle and incessant heat made the missionary endeavour a test of forbearance and stamina. Nature also provided ferocious wild animals. This ever present danger added to the excitement of missionary stories and made the endeavour seem more biblical in scope in that it related to a primitive society and geographical climate that was closer to the land of the Bible than was the case at home. Such tales were often recounted in church through letters from missionaries and the following example of an account of the work of Christina Forsyth is replete with biblical imagery:

But I don't think you would sleep much at night. All the night through you would likely hear, from some of the huts nearer or farther away, great shouting and chanting of strange wild voices, and clapping of hands. You would hear too, on many a night, voices crying out in strife, and the loud rattle of sticks as the people fought. And you would wonder at a lady living alone, save for two little Kaffir girlies, among such wild scenes and sounds. You would be afraid, for often blood is shed, for often men are wounded and sometimes men are killed. And if you went visiting among these huts, you would sometimes be afraid too, for after these long nights of drinking and of dancing or of fighting, the men and women are often sulky and cross and often there are fierce dogs at the huts. Only a short time ago, while this lady was going from hut to hut, trying to tell the people about Christ, a dog sprang out at her and bit her in the face. But nothing will keep her from going. And she has long rough ways to walk, steep and stony, and the African sun burns like fire. A lonely place and a wild people and hard, hard work [...]. She would tell you of the love that sends Him to seek the lost, over stony ways, and through hunger and thirst and under burning suns. And she would tell you how that love burned in her heart until she felt compelled to rise up and follow him to the huts and steep paths of the Xolobe Valley in heathen Africa. (Livingstone 1919: 153–54)

The role of suffering and persecution was an important link to early Christianity and, arguably, the foreign missions had an appeal over the domestic ones in that the overseas endeavours were closer to the experience of the early founders of the Church.

Success was a key element of the missionary tale and this was enhanced by emphasising the overcoming of impossible odds. It also added to the dramatic effect. Stories emphasised the negativity of government officials and local natives and the hopelessness of the initial situation. Not only did this make the success seem all the more astounding, but it demonstrated the key importance of faith and the role of providence. A key element of the missionary story is the idea that faith and charity could accomplish more than those of force of arms and commerce, and there are clear echoes of the early founders of the church wandering into the wilderness alone to build the house of God. The mission station as a harbinger of civilisation occupies pride of place in these stories. Rude and primitive, it was the base from which operations commenced and civilisation slowly spread outwards. The creation of accompanying schools and medical centres illustrated the practical benefits of civilisation and were useful tools for juxtaposing against traditional African society. For example, the medical care of missionaries was used to contrast the African use of witch doctors and a tendency towards fatalism and belief in spells and magic: "Every cure, too, was like a nail in the coffin of superstition and witchcraft. Patients went back to their homes cured, taking with them the praises of the white man's skill and kindness, and, better still, carrying in their hearts some message of the Gospel of God's grace" (Jack 1900: 130). In a number of cases, it was the practical demonstration of medical expertise that won over converts who plainly saw the superiority of western knowledge. The following extract is fairly typical:

They knew nothing of tools and implements, and were deeply astonished at the sight of them. Saws, planes and similar instruments were marvels to them. The spirit level was an extraordinary novelty: they thought it possessed supernatural powers, as there was a small drop of water in it, they said, that always ran uphill! [...] considering their lifelong degradation, they made rapid headway. Some became carpenters, some sawyers, some gardeners and agriculturalists, some brick makers, some builders, some blacksmiths, and some sailors and stokers. They helped to erect the houses, the schools, the storehouse and the workshop, and to make the sawpit, the boathouse, the dispensing counter and other things. (Jack 1900: 123)

Donald Fraser contrasted the Christian work ethic and use of reason with that of the heathen to highlight the success of missionary endeavour:

I have seen the beggarly shelter in which some poor old widows were housed in the rainy season, open to rain and cold and comfortless and filthy. They had no power to erect a decent hut, and their heathen friends had no use for them. And I have seen the Christian boys spending days, while they were still busy with their own houses, building a goodly dwelling for some poor widow [...] I have known men and women whose lives were drunken, whose conversation was filthy, and whose passions were demonical, changed to sober-living, clean-talking, kindly and compassionate people. I have seen dull eyes that looked about with a listless lack of intelligence lighting up with a new knowledge that sweetened the face and smoothed out its coarse lines when the knowledge of Christ dawned upon them. And I have been in villages where churlish inhospitality and stupid fear made one's visit a painful memory, and again returned to find their atmosphere changed to frank and cheerful hospitality and an easy friendliness when the Gospel had been proclaimed and taught there. And I know men whose hands were red with the blood of the slain, and whose kraals were stocked with what they had robbed, becoming peaceable citizens of the kingdom and fervid evangelists of the message of peace. (Fraser 1914: 268–69)

Likewise, the stalwarts of heathen African traditions did everything in their power to prevent the education of children and a number of stories focus on this crucial battle for the hearts and minds of the future. Mary Slessor cured a chief from an abscess and prevented the sacrifice of numerous innocents accused of witchcraft by the witch doctors (Livingstone 1920: 79–80). Children were prevented from attending, schools were attacked and pupils intimidated:

Periods of persecution recurred, during which the school had to be closed. Atten-
dances often mysteriously dwindled, puzzling the teacher until she noticed that the
following away always happened after some girl or boy had expressed a desire to
become a Christian. The first lad converted was handed over to the tender mercies of
the witch doctor and forced to renounce his faith. When four scholars made an open
confession that they had accepted Christ, every "red" child was taken away on some
pretext or other. (Livingstone 1919: 83–84)

In the biography of Christina Forsyth, her "greatest enemy", Loqina,
the witch doctor, was struck blind after an excessive drinking bout and
lost his followers. Forsyth showed the man kindness and he was to die
praying, while his wife, after buying some clothes, became a regular
attender at church (Livingstone 1919: 97–99). The story of triumph
after a period of persecution and suffering by native Christians chimed
in with the experience of missionaries.

   Missionary tales were able to build on a theme of persecution
that had been growing in evangelical British culture. The massacres of
Christians in the Bulgarian atrocities in the 1860s and the reports of
persecution of the Armenians in the 1890s added to the sense that that
faith was under threat from Islamic forces (Brown 2008: 294–98,
363–67; Shannon 1975). In Africa, this was a constant theme which
built on a growing sense of anti-Islamic sentiment following the war
in Egypt and the Sudan when the British press painted a lurid picture
of Arab fundamentalism. This intensity increased following the death
of General Gordon who was portrayed as a Christian martyr
("Excellent Supplement" 1885). With increased anti-Arab and anti-
Islamic sentiment among the Scottish population, it was easy to
present the colonisation of Africa as advancing civilisation against the
forces of Arab darkness. H.M. Stanley advanced the notion that the
influence of Islam was fundamental to the existence of slavery.[14] Anti
Arabic sentiment reached a peak in 1888 when it was reported that the
Scottish missions were under attack in Nyasaland from Arab slavers
who were trying to disrupt the legitimate trade of the African Lakes
Company. In reality, however, the slavers were Swahili. In emotive
language, it was reported that trading posts were attacked, converts
enslaved and massacred and the missions assaulted with the intention
of driving them out of the area ("Arab Attack" 1888; "More Details"
1888). The Free Church reported that there was butchery on Lake

---

[14] Speech at the Edinburgh Literary Institute, quoted in the *Glasgow Herald*, 5
December 1884.

Nyasa and that "captured women were bound and speared" (*Scottish Leader* February 1893). An anti-slavery and defence fund was launched and raised over £3,000 to fund a private war by the African Lakes Company against slavers (*Glasgow Herald* 13 November 1890). The rising was presented in terms that claimed that the Arabs were so dependent on slavery that their efforts were driven by a desire to wipe out legitimate commerce and reduce the area to its former barbarity. Given that the essence of the missionary story was that commerce and Christianity went hand in hand, there could not be one without the other. The building of a legitimate trading and plantation economy in Lake Nyasa (Malawi) region had been the key focus of Scottish missionary enterprise and the attack was presented as an assault on the foundations of civilisation. The construction of the Stevenson road, the establishment of plantations and the growth of trading posts along the Lake that were supplied and cargoed by steamships, were presented as the successful economic alternative to slavery that was now bringing peace and prosperity. It was far too rosy a picture. As John McCracken has pointed out, slavery was the response to economic problems in the region and not the cause, and the initial expectations of the African Lakes Company had been widely optimistic, as had assessment of the agricultural quality of the land (McCracken 2008: 36–45). In many ways, the rising acted as an opportunity to reinvent what was essentially a failed economic project as a successful humanitarian mission in which the elevation of African society was presented as the primary object, rather than making money. Attention focused, particularly, on the personal investment made by the directors of the company in a humanitarian venture. Not entirely in harmony with this tincture, the key protagonists tended to recite the story as a form of "Boys Own" adventure story (Moir 1923; Fotheringham 1891). As Andrew Porter has claimed, the phrase "Christianity and Commerce" went into decline after the 1870s and the experience of Scots in the Lake Malawi region would endorse such a view (Porter 1985).

As Esther Breitenbach has recently argued, Scottish missionary endeavour was an important factor in the creation of a Scottish imperial identity in which the specific contribution of the Scottish missions and its relationship with the expansion of British imperialism was highlighted and celebrated at home as being a specific Scottish contribution to a wider imperial endeavour. In spite of religious divisions at home, missions, "not only brought the Empire home to the Scottish people, but it gave them a new sense of themselves" (Breitenbach 2009: 186). The Presbyterian and Scottish character of the missions is something that was constantly emphasised in missionary accounts. The singing of Scottish songs to Scottish tunes and transplanting of Scottish customs and traditions is one that is constantly referenced in missionary accounts. The traveller on the Niger who was greeted by Scottish Sunday School songs, or the Scotticisms picked up by Africans speaking English or the recreation of the Scottish Sabbath in the Shire Highlands were frequent reference points to remind the reader of the essentially Scottish nature of the missionary enterprise. The gifts from back home and the domestic speaking tours, likewise, emphasised the Scottish nature of the project. Missionaries iterated a home from home such as "plates of cakes and scones that could make a Scots-fed man smile with appetite and satisfaction" and forget "all the ramshackle untidiness of Africa" (Fraser 1914: 22). The missionaries were not just Scottish and British, but also a cause for celebration in the local, regional press. "Ma" Slessor was very much the Dundonian matriarch transferred to Africa where she ran a tight ship and kept her "bairns" safe and was not afraid to administer her rough justice of a swift clout on the ear to any transgressor, including burly Africans. She conducted her palavers with African chiefs while knitting and was not afraid to get her hands dirty with manual labour. Similarly, Christina Forsyth represented the best of Scottish womanhood with a strong matriarchal tendency, her qualities here being celebrated by the Greenock Ladies Missionary Association. Female missionaries were often surrogate mothers for orphans and Mary Slessor adopted five African children. Missionary tales very much reinforced the idea of Africans as children. Slessor refused to speak in public with men present in Scotland, but found no difficulty in bossing African chiefs about. Also, no-one batted an eye about female missionaries wandering around naked men, nor their embroilment in societies that were portrayed as sexually deviant.

The issue of Scottishness, however, is not clear cut. In the early phases of missionary endeavour, there was a tendency for Scots to represent themselves as Scots who belonged to the "English" nation. Livingstone, for example, referred to himself as English and it was to the English prime minister, the English state and the English people that he addressed his pleas for a more active engagement in Africa to suppress the slave trade (Livingstone 1865). Likewise, early accounts used the term "English" as the national category of the settlements. John Buchanan, who was an original settler at the Blantyre mission, but became a plantation owner and vice counsel, wrote a short work in 1885 to inform the Scottish public about the Nyasa area and "take a still greater interest in what is undoubtedly an excellent country with a bright future". He went on to argue for the establishment of a British protectorate in the following terms: "For the Shire Highlands and Lake Nyassa one may well claim that England should assume the protectorate. The lake was discovered by an Englishman and English money, and the sum total of English capital invested in the country at the present is not small" (Buchanan 1885: 2: 52–53). Likewise, the Rev. Duff Macdonald, the first leader of the Blantyre mission claimed that "No Arab gangs will come near an Englishman if they can help it. With them the English name is synonymous with the destroyer of slavery" (Macdonald 1882: 27). When the Rev. Horace Waller was asked by the Established and Free churches, together with the African Lakes Company and Buchanan Plantation to draw up a pamphlet to make the case for a British protectorate of Nyasaland, the term English was frequently used in a national context (Waller 1887). Until the period of the 1890s, missionary tales reflected the conventional political usage of "England" for Britain, but after this time, the accounts begin to take on a more distinctively Scottish "national" dimension in line with a growing sense of Scottish "national" as opposed to provincial identity (Goldie 2006). James Jack used the term English in inverted comas (Jack 1900). After the First World War, the national dimension was given pride of place as can be illustrated by this extract by W.P. Livingstone:

Once before Scots had taken part with patriotic pride and high hope in a great overseas undertaking. The Darien Expedition was an attempt to set up a colonial empire which would pour the wealth of tropical America into Scotland, and the bitter ignominy and shame of its failure still haunted the national memory. But Livingstonia would be a noble undertaking, and more in line with the higher genius of the people; it would be an effort, not to secure dividends, but to realize the life-aims of Livingstone, to open up dark Africa, to free a race subject to bondage, and to set up a spiritual kingdom which would exercise a beneficent influence throughout the interior of the continent. All Christian Scotland rallied to the enterprise: subscriptions came from every class and quarter, from city merchant prince and Highland crofter, and the £10,000 required to begin the mission was over-subscribed. (Livingstone 1921: 9)

Although Scotttishness was always part of the missionary tale, its "national" aspect only really assumes significance in retrospective analysis and undoubtedly this was symptomatic of wider changes in Scottish society.

Scottish ecclesiological squabbles were exported overseas. Although the missionary movement acted as a unifier of Presbyterian endeavour on the surface, cracks could and did appear. The settlements of the Established and Free churches in Nyasaland were involved in an unwholesome spat regarding the administration of justice when the Established church had natives flogged for stealing. In Duff Macdonald's account the perpetrator was sentenced to nine dozen lashes in public; "he got five dozen that day and then was led into the stocks. Three days later, he received the remaining four dozen" (Macdonald 1882: 34). Theft was a problem in both the missions in Malawi, but without the establishment of formal colonial control, the administration of justice was a grey area. The Established church believed that it had the right to oversee discipline and operate magistrates, although this was subsequently found to be in violation of the law. A further problem was that if left to native justice, this would often involve the death sentence or slavery for fairly trivial crimes (Macdonald 1882: 40). Indeed, one man died as a result of native flogging for theft (Macdonald 1882: 44). The issue became public and in an endeavour to stem the bad publicity, Macdonald was recalled (Chirnside 1880; Riddel 1880). The Free Church pointed out that such excess was not in keeping with its missionary endeavour while acknowledging that the Established church had no legal authority and that a crime had been committed against the natives. One of the floggers was actually a member of the Livingstonia mission who was helping out with repairs. Both churches used it as evidence of the need to establish a protectorate and tried to play down the unfortunate consequences. Macdonald claimed that the two missions needed one another: "If a minister were to begin by preaching to these poor negroes about theories that separate good Christians at home, he would be a miserable trifler. We believe that one missionary got a hint from Scotland about "distinctive principles", but he replied that he could not find a native word to express these differences and that he did not care to invent one" (Macdonald 1882: 23). Likewise, no matter what the factions said at home, Laws of the Livingstonia mission claimed that "To me the differences in evangelical churches are as of the tartans of different regiments. I care little for the pattern worn by the soldier, but I care much as to how he fights and still more about the issue of the battle" (Livingstone 1921: 38). Try as they might, domestic disputes still could find their way into Africa.

The two churches also became involved in a spat over the issue of idolatry in the established church at Blantyre, and again this was the result of outside agencies. In a nutshell, the Established church was accused of betraying its Presbyterian inheritance by adopting elaborate and ornate architecture for its church and its use of religious iconography. This "High Churchism" involved the use of white gowns or surplices, candles and lamps, and "turning to the east". This smacked of Romanism and was fiercely denounced by its detractors.[15] The defence by the Established church was that the form of worship was adopted to suit the African mind, with the clear implication that as the Africans were more superstitious, the hard and austere form of Scottish worship would not be attractive. For the opposition, there should be no compromise with idolatry. The Foreign Missions Committee of the Established church felt compelled to investigate, and found that most of the complaints were groundless (Livingstone 1931: 90–94). Likewise, when the United and Free churches joined together in 1900 and the House of Lords awarded the property of the latter to the continuing minority of its communion, this put a considerable strain on it financial capacity to fund new missions.

Missionary tales also tapped into the history of Scotland and drew parallels with the history of the Covenanters who fought against oppression and persecution for their religious ideals. Mary Slessor caught this mood of theocratic republicanism:

When Sir Herbert Kitchener, going out to conquer the Soudan required help, thousands of our brightest young men were ready. Where are the soldiers of the Cross? In a recent war in Africa in a region with the same climate and the same malarial swamp as Calabar there were hundreds of officers and men offering their services, and a royal prince went out. But the Banner of the Cross goes a begging. Why should the Queen have good soldiers but not the King of Kings? (Livingstone 1920: 167–68)

---

[15] The fiercest critic was the rather bizarre Pastor Jack Lister who ran his own Conventicles outside Dundee. *Pastor Jack Lister* (no date) has a chapter devoted to the issue.

As has already been mentioned, the theme of persecution and martyrdom was a strong one and echoed through various accounts. Stoic
forbearance was a key theme of missionary endeavours including
strong Calvinist elements in these accounts. The silent killer of disease
was a particular, and arbitrary, danger. The fallen were venerated as
martyrs for the cause of Christ (Robertson 1892). Martyrdom was also
extended to natives and described in language that would not be out of
place in the seventeenth century, as illustrated in this account of
Uganda and the Scottish missionary, Alexander Mackay, who was
working with the English Church Missionary Society:

> Soldiers were sent scouring all over the place in search of converts, and many of the
> brightest Christians were carried off for execution. Eleven were put to death the first
> day, after horrible mutilation. This was, however, but the beginning of the reign of
> terror. Every day fresh batches of Christians, young men and boys chiefly, were first
> tortured and then roasted alive, and hundreds more were waiting the same fate.
> ([Melrose] 1894: 119)

Although not articulated in an explicit manner, the idea of instruments
of God who seek to establish the Godly commonwealth in other parts
of the world chimes with the imperialistic inheritance of seventeenth-
century Presbyterianism where the idea of the Covenant was one that
ought to be exported. British imperial endeavours provided that outlet.

   One theme that does not emerge with much conviction is the idea
of saving souls or redemption. The Calvinist ethos in Scottish
missionary work was bringing others to Christ and expanding the
Godly Commonwealth, but would Africans be saved? While stressing
the benefits of Christianity and the Christian life, the Scottish
Calvinist position precluded the automatic salvation of the converts.
Also, the Scots were very much against nominal conversion and, as
was noted in the World Missionary Conference in Edinburgh in 1910,
required adherents to demonstrate that they had a fairly full
understanding and lasting commitment to the Church before being
granted full membership (World Missionary Conference 1910. Stanley
2009: 152). Arguably, the Calvinist theological commitment of the
Scottish churches could have proved problematic had it been explored
in any depth, and while the churches were softening their positions on
many of the hard-line aspects of Calvinist dogma, the issue is worth
emphasising because it was a distinguishing factor that contrasted the
Scots with other evangelical missionary movements. Missionary tales

did conform to a tradition of the elect in that the missionaries themselves were clearly instruments of God and as such were surely guaranteed a place in heaven. As David Bebbington has shown, the saving of souls was the great cry of the British and American evangelical movement in which Arminianism – the accepting of God's Grace to secure salvation – eroded the old Calvinist ethos of the elect (Bebbington 1989: 15–27). How far this had an impact in Scotland has never been fully explored, but Arminianism was not the doctrinal position of the Scottish churches, even though the Scottish churches took part in the evangelical revival. Why save souls if not all souls are salvable? Yet, missionary endeavour did manage to square the Scottish Calvinist circle of faith and evangelicism. If viewed from the perspective of the individual missionary, the Africans become secondary to the work of the elect. Missionary tales reinforced this picture by using Africa and Africans as the canvas upon which to paint the qualities required of the elect. The complete faith in providence, the willingness to sacrifice all and face death, the promotion of the Kingdom of Christ at whatever personal cost and unquestioning resolution in the face of adversity were all demonstrated. Missionaries were of the same stuff as Scotland's historic Calvinist martyrs. In short, missionary endeavour was the only available road to martyrdom in nineteenth-century Scotland and travelling that road was as close as possible to ensuring membership of the elect.

Although missionary tales emphasised the distinctive Scottish contribution to the Christianisation of Africa, they were also careful to highlight that it was very much a British endeavour. The original settlement at Livingstonia on the lake was set out to replicate the shape of the Union Jack (Livingstone 1921: 73). The collaboration with other British missionary groups was emphasised and the appearance of English missionaries was noted as the stories made a good showcase for British missionary collaboration. The role of the British government and colonial authorities was presented as being of paramount importance in providing the necessary support and protection in a hostile environment. The issue of establishing a British protectorate in Nyasaland was a particular issue that occupied much Scottish public attention. The initial confidence that the missions could operate independently soon evaporated under the strain of native and Portuguese hostility. Also, as has been mentioned, there was the thorny issue of law and jurisdiction. In such a hostile environment, it was unlikely that any mission would succeed and the experience in Malawi demonstrated that colonial authority was a necessary complement to missionary endeavour. As Laws put it:

I fear the British public hardly realize or even think of the task that they ask of these representatives of theirs to perform. They are sent out and expected to do all by moral suasion – that is, they are put into a similar though less favourable position than would be the case if any of the Lords of Court of Justice in Edinburgh were to be commissioned to go to Calton Jail, and by conversation with its inhabitants expect to turn all these criminals into sober well doing citizens. (*Glasgow Herald* 25 February 1888)

The funding of the private war against slavers illustrated the precarious existence of the missions and pressure had to be brought to bear on the government to intervene.[16] As has been mentioned, the issue of slavery was one of the great moral weapons in the missionaries' armoury for greater government intervention. The "Arab war" was presented as a campaign to prevent the establishment of "a powerful Mohammedan Empire in central Africa" (Livingstone 1921: 238). The initial attempt to encourage an annexation failed but the Prime Minister, Lord Salisbury, did agree that the Lake Company and the missions did have the right to defend themselves and the Portuguese were leaned upon to allow the importation of arms and ammunition (Hanna 1956: 79–88). The war spluttered on under the leadership of Captain Fredrick Lugard, but without a decisive outcome. In missionary accounts, however, it was a story that prevented the emergence of a successful slaving empire (Livingstone 1921: 238). Lugard believed that the attack on the missions was "a great moment. And so Karonga's held the gate and Nyasaland, thank God, is today the British Central African Protectorate, instead of a great slave-raiding Mohammedan empire, stretching from Stanley falls to the Zambezi, and embracing both shores of the Nyasa" (Lugard 1893: 210). According to Laws, "Heathenism is bad enough to fight, but heathenism and Islam will be still more dreadful. Portuguese bluster and ambition are bad, but not so bad as the blood and cruelty of Islam" (Livingstone 1921: 239). The suppression of slavery was a crucial moral vindication for the missions. Privately, the British Consul Harry Johnston believed that the African Lakes

---

[16] For an account of the expeditions see Lugard 1893, 1: 45–8.

Trading Company was part of the problem as the "riff-raff of Glasgow is not the best material with which to develop the commerce of British Central Africa" (Hanna 1956: 87). Even Captain Lugard alluded to the fact that the Company had "enlisted a number of desperadoes from the Gold Fields" (Lugard 1893: 21). Before the end of the war, the Lakes Company was in serious financial straits and reported a loss in 1889 (*Glasgow Herald* 13 November 1890). Others were coming to the conclusion that the Scottish missionaries had bitten off more than they could chew:

It is evident that without support of arms, neither British Traders or missionaries will make much further progress there. They are in the centre of Arab intrigues and at the mercy of Arab herders. The missionaries would rather be left to do their best against these than have the supremacy of Portugal established and recognized over the whole Lake. But there is now good reason to think, at any rate hope, that the Portuguese difficulty is on a fair way to removal. If that be so, then it will be comparatively easy to deal in a vigorous manner with the slave trade. That Great Britain will, sooner or later, have to put forth special efforts for the suppression of that traffic, those who watch the signs of the times can hardly fail to perceive. Our entire interests of various kinds in Africa are combining to force the duty on us. (*Glasgow Herald,* 17 April 1889)

In short, the establishment of civilisation required a British imperial presence and force of arms.

What the Nyasa missions demonstrated was that it was near impossible for the Scots to engage in missionary work outside imperial protection and the story was revised to present a picture of the Scots as empire builders who had to combat too-timid politicians. In reality the Scots had stepped into a diplomatic minefield and dragged the British government behind them. It was the action of the Portuguese, and not the native slavers, that tipped the balance in favour of establishing a protectorate. In a complex diplomatic scenario that involved British, Portuguese and German interests, the Scots were a troublesome part of the equation. Undoubtedly, the Portuguese regarded the Scots as a nuisance and suspected them of inciting native rebellion (Newitt 1970; Johnston 1899: 181). Also, the Scots were strategically situated in territory that the Portuguese wanted in order to create a corridor that would link Mozambique and Angola. Without venturing too much into the field of diplomatic history, it was the thwarting of Portuguese ambitions and a threat to British expansion in the north, together with the appearance and ambition of Cecil Rhodes, that forced the government to proclaim a protectorate. Threats of a Portuguese invasion of Blantyre, in what they clearly believed was their sphere of influence, led to an humiliating ultimatum from the British government to back down. Yet, in the popular account of events, pride of place is given to the power of Scottish public opinion in facing down the threat of a Portuguese annexation:

Scotch lives and Scotch treasure have been expended freely for the development of the region, and on the grounds of equity it would have been absurd to hand over the territory to Portugal simply for humouring the whim of the mapmakers of the Portuguese Foreign Office. Moreover, it is possible to take a much higher ground. Portugal is undoubtedly a civilizing power of a kind in Africa; but Portuguese civilization is at best centuries behind that of Britain; and to hand over British territories to a backward power like Portugal would have been a gross neglect of our duty to the native races acknowledging our protection, and an indelible stain upon the honour of Britain. (*Aberdeen Weekly Journal* 22 August 1890)

Initially a proposed treaty between the two powers gave too much to the Portuguese and Scottish opinion was mobilised to combat it ("The Nyassa Missions and the Portuguese", *Glasgow Herald* 26 February 1889). A united declaration by all the Scottish churches, a monster petition signed by all the ministers and elders of all the churches and heavyweight intervention by leading Scottish politicians such as Lord Balfour of Burleigh, Lord Aberdeen and Lord Rosebery gave the appearance of a national movement to make Nyasaland a British protectorate and "not allow those interests to be abandoned to Portugal" (*Glasgow Herald* 18 May 1889). Although newspaper accounts frequently conflated "English" and "British", the propaganda against Portugal was relentless and fell back on that old populist favourite of anti-Catholicism:

The Scotch missionaries in Nyassaland will soon have an enemy to contend with even more formidable than Arab slavers and Portuguese obstructionists. The country explored by Livingstone, and which for twenty years has been the almost exclusive field of work of Scotch missionaries, is about to be flooded by emissaries of Catholicism. Portugal has evidently become alive to the mistake she made in letting Protestant England have her own way. (*Glasgow Herald* 10 July 1889)

The *Glasgow Herald* went as far as to claim that "in truth Nyasaland is less of a British than a Scottish acquisition" (*Glasgow Herald* 21 December 1889). The *Aberdeen Weekly Journal* claimed that the missionaries were pinned down by slavers on one side and the

Portuguese on the other and raised the spectre of another "Gordon and Khartoum" (*Aberdeen Weekly Journal* 22 August 1889). In apocalyptic language it claimed: "There is not a black boy or girl in the Presbyterian schools all over North Nyassaland who does not know that the fall of an outpost means that he or she will be probably outraged and driven under torture as slaves to the coast." Stories of Portuguese anti-British and anti-Scottish statements and the forced removal of the Union Jack on a Nyasa steamship played on sentiments of popular patriotism (*Aberdeen Weekly Journal* 24 Dec. 1889; *Glasgow Herald* 10 July 1889). By the time the story was recounted in the 1920s, Lord Salisbury was a firm ally who used such a unanimous expression of public opinion in Scotland, as evidence that he could not accept Portuguese terms (Livingstone 1931: 52). The road was clear to make Nyasaland a British colony in 1894.

Although there were often disagreements and differences of opinion in which the view of the Scottish missionary mostly wins out, the stories constantly emphasise the benevolence of British rule.[17] At times of potential colonial conflict, such as the Portuguese encroachment in Eastern Africa, the Scots portray their interests as British. Indeed, the Scottish missionary movement in Africa was portrayed as a crucial arm in the expansion of British interests in that part of the world and the extension of British rule was cast as an advancement of civilisation and progress. At the end of the day, as events in Malawi were to prove, fairly extensive military intervention by British authorities was required to secure the area; firstly to tackle the slavers and then to deal with a Ngoni rising in 1895. Mary Slessor was equally as adamant in her view that the formal empire should be extended as far as possible in Nigeria and was constantly pushing at the colonial authorities to extend its reach (Livingstone 1920: 195–97). Scottish missionaries virtually started a rising in Kenya in the late 1920s over the issue of female circumcision (Murray 1976). The Kingdom of Christ did not recognise territorial boundaries.

In conclusion, while Scottish missionary tales are a flawed source of information on African society, they do tell us, however, how the Scots wanted to portray themselves. It was a way of linking the religious inheritance of the past with that of the present, while, at the same time, avoiding the ecclesiological divisions at home. The

---

[17] Harry Johnstone was the villain of the piece in the Nyasa story, *Glasgow Herald* (20 June 1892).

descriptions of African society provide a revealing insight into what formed the core of Scottish assumptions regarding civilisation and its essentials. By highlighting African inferiority, Scottish and British superiority was affirmed to the domestic reading public. The missionary tale was also an effective way to convey the moral right of the imperial mission. The eradication of slavery and the elevation of Africans from a degraded state of humanity to one that encompassed monogamy, work, law, peace and Christianity, was one that few could oppose. Missionary tales created an imperial demonology that encompassed Catholics, Islam and native traditions. Yet, for all its bluster and assurance, at times, it seems that the problems of humanity expressed in an African context by drunken, lawless, heathen savages, were displacements from home.

Bibliography

"Arab Attack on Scottish Missionaries: Severe Fighting Near Lake Nyasa" in *Glasgow Herald* (25 February 1888).

Barr, Rev James. 1943. *Lange Syne: a Memoir*. Glasgow: MacLellan.

Bebbington, David W. 1989. *Evangelicalism in Modern Britain: A History from the 1730s to the 1980s*. London: Unwin Hyman.

Breitenbach, Esther. 2009. *Empire and Scottish Society: The Impact of Foreign Missions at Home, c.1790–c.1914*. Edinburgh: Edinburgh University Press.

—. 1983. *Thomas Chalmers and the Godly Commonwealth in Scotland*. Oxford: Oxford University Press.

Brown, Stewart J. 2008. *Providence and Empire: Religion, Politics and Society in the United Kingdom, 1815–1914*. Harlow: Pearson Longman.

Buchanan, John. 1885. *The Shire Highlands: (East Central Africa) as Colony and Mission*. Edinburgh: W. Blackwood & Sons.

Chirnside, Andrew. 1880. *The Blantyre Missionaries: Discreditable Discoveries*. London: William Ridgway.

Elmsie, Walter Angus. 1899. *Among the Wild Ngoni; being some chapters in the history of the Livingstonia Mission in Central Africa*. Edinburgh: Oliphant & Co.

"Excellent Supplement and Portrait of General Gordon Approved by his Relatives" in *Glasgow Evening Times*. (11 February 1885).

Fields, Karen. 1982. "Christian Missionaries as Anti Colonial Militants" in *Theory and Society* 11 (1): 95–108.

Fotheringham, Lowell Montieth. 1891. *Adventures in Nyassaland: a Two Years Struggle Against Arab Slavers in Africa*. London: Sampson Low & Co.

Fraser, Donald. 1914. *Winning a Primitive People: Sixteen Years Work Among the Warlike Tribe of the Ngoni and the Senga and Tumbuka Peoples of Central Africa*. London: Seeley, Service & Co.

Goldie, David. 2006. "The British Invention of Scottish Culture: World War One and Before" in *Review of Scottish Culture*, 18: 128–48.

Hanna, A.J. 1956. *The Beginnings of Nyasaland and North-Eastern Rhodesia 1859–95*. Oxford: Clarendon

Hunter, R. 1873. *History of the Foreign Missions of the Free Church of Scotland in India and Africa*. London.

Jack, James W. 1900. *Daybreak in Livingstonia: The Story of the Livingstonia Mission*. Edinburgh: Oliphant, Anderson & Ferrier

Johnston, Harry. 1899. *A History of the Colonization of Africa by Alien Races*. Cambridge: Cambridge University Press.

Kingsley, Mary H. [1897] 1965. *Travels in West Africa*. London: Frank Cass & Co.

Livingstone, David, and Charles Livingstone. 1865. *Narrative of an Expedition to the Zambesi and its Tributaries*. London: John Murray.

Livingstone, William P. 1919. *Christina Forsyth of Fingoland: The Story of the Loneliest Woman in Africa*. London: Hodder & Stoughton.

—. 1920. *Mary Slessor of Calabar: Pioneer Missionary*. London: Hodder & Stoughton.

—. 1921. *Laws of Livingstonia: a Narrative of Missionary Adventure and Achievement*. London: Hodder & Stoughton.

—. 1931. *A Prince of Missionaries: the Rev. Alexander Hetherwick of Blantyre, Central Africa.* London: J. Clarke & Co.

Lugard, Frederick. 1893. *The Rise of Our East African Empire.* 2 vols. Edinburgh: W. Blackwood & Sons.

McCracken, John. 2008. *Politics and Christianity in Malawi, 1875–1940: The Impact of the Livingstonia Mission in the Northern Province.* African Book Collective.

Macdonald, Duff. 1882. *Africana; or, the Heart of Heathen Africa. Vol.II. – Mission Life.* London: Simkin, Marshall & Co.

MacKenzie, John M. 1990. "David Livingstone: The Construction of the Myth", in Walker G.&T. Gallagher (eds). *Sermons and Battle Hymns: Protestant Popular Culture in Modern Scotland.* Edinburgh: Edinburgh University Press. 24–33.

Mackie, J.B. 1888. *The Life and Work of Duncan McLaren.* 2 vols. Edinburgh: Thomas Nelson.

Mandler, Peter. 1990. "Tories and Paupers: Christian Political Economy and the Making of the New Poor Law" in *Historical Journal,* 33: 81–103.

[Melrose, Andrew]. 1894. *Alexander Mackay: Missionary Hero of Uganda:By the Author of "The Story of Stanley".* London: Sunday School Union.

Miller, Hugh. 1870. "The Effects of Religious Union on the Colonies", in Davidson, John (ed.). *Hugh Miller: Notes and Essays.* Edinburgh. 221–31.

Moir, Fredrick. 1923. *After Livingstone: And African Trade Romance.* London: Hodder & Stoughton.

"More Details of the Atrocities" in *Glasgow Herald* (27 February 1888).

Murray, Jocelyn. 1976. "The Church Missionary Society and the 'Female Circumcision' Issue in Kenya, 1929–1932" in *Journal of Religion in Africa,* 8(2): 92–104.

Newitt, M.D., D. 1970. "The Massingire Rising of 1884" in *Journal of African History,* 11(1): 87–105.

Porter, Andrew. 1985. "'Commerce and Christianity': The Rise and Fall of a Nineteenth-Century Missionary Slogan" in *Historical Journal,* 28: 597–621.

— (ed.). 2003. *The Imperial Horizons of British Protestant Missions.* Grand Rapids, Michigan: W.B. Eerdmans.

—. 2004. *Religion Versus Empire? British Protestants Missionaries and Overseas Expansion, 1700–1914.* Manchester: Manchester University Press.

Rice, Duncan C. 1981. *The Scots Abolitionists.* Baton Rouge: Louisiana State University Press.

Riddel, Alexander. 1880. *A Reply to the "Blantyre Missionaries: Discreditable Disclosures" by Andrew Chirnside FRGS.* Edinburgh: W. Blackwood & Sons.

Robertson, William. 1892. *The Martyrs of Blantyre: Henry Henderson, Dr. John Bowie and Robert Cleland.* London: J. Nisbet & Co.

Robinson, Ronald, and John Gallagher with Alice Denny. 1970. *Africa and the Victorians: The Official Mind of Imperialism.* London: Macmillan.

Ross, Andrew C. 1971. "Scottish Missionary Concern 1874–1914. A Golden Era?" in *Scottish Historical Review* 51: 52–72.

—. 1996. *Blantyre Mission and the Making of Modern Malawi.* Blantyre: Christian Literature Society in Malawi.

—. 2002. *David Livingstone: Mission and Empire.* London: Hambledon.

"Slavery in Africa" in *The Westminster Review* (April 1876).

Shannon, Richard. 1975. *Gladstone and the Bulgarian Agitation 1876.* Sussex: Harvester.

Smith, George Adam. 1903. *The Life of Henry Drummond.* London: Hodder & Stoughton.

Stanley. Brian. 2009. *The World Missionary Congress: Edinburgh 1910.* Michigan: William B. Eerdmans.

Stevenson, James. 1888. *The Arab in Central Africa.* Glasgow: J. Maclehose & Sons.

Swann, Alfred J. 1910. *Fighting the Slave Hunters in Central Africa.* London: Seeley & Co.

Thompson, T. Jack. 1995. *Christianity in Northern Malawi: Donald Fraser's Missionary Methods and Ngoni Culture.* Leiden: Brill.

Thorne, Susan. 1999. *Congregational Missions and the Making of an Imperial Culture in 19th Century England.* Stanford:.Stanford University Press.

Two Missionary Pioneers in Africa, being an account of the lives and explorations of David Livingstone and Frederick Stanley Arnot. c.1900. Kilmarnock: John Ritchie. 33.

Waller, Rev. Horace. 1887. *The Title-Deeds to Nyassaland.* William Clowes & Sons.

World Missionary Conference, 1910 : to consider missionary problems in relation to the non-Christian world. 1910. Edinburgh: Oliphant, Anderson and Ferrier.

From Slogan to Clan: Three Fragments from the Evolving Scottish/Germanic Literary Relations of the Romantic Period.

Johnny Rodger

As Scotland moved from an eighteenth-century largely feudal and agrarian society to a nineteenth-century industrial powerhouse of the Empire, how were the writings of Scots writers influenced by the Germans, and what influence did they exert in their turn? How, through cultural exchange, were literary tools and concepts refined to deal with an epochal shift in concern from the individual to the masses, the subject to the state, the hero to the mob, or in metaphorical terms here, the slogan to the clan?
Keywords: Romantic; fragment; slogan; individual; mob; Macpherson; Ossian; *Sturm und Drang*; Bards; Carlyle; germanise; Babylonian Dialect; Idealism; Robertson Smith; Freud; Semitic; sacrifice; Bible; totem; clan.

Relations between German nineteenth-century Romantic and Scottish literatures were of such a long, involved and multiform character that it would be difficult to attempt to summarise them in a short chapter. Key elements or exemplary moments are difficult to pin down and can have a deceptive complexity. As authenticity was a perennial question for that age, however, it seems appropriate to make use of a concept whose very name has a certain resonance in the literature: the fragment. Thus this chapter concentrates on fragmented aspects of three Scottish writers whose writing lives spanned more or less 150 years, and examines the ways in which they were influenced by, or exerted an influence upon, German writing. These literary exchanges and reciprocities may indeed allow the careful reader to perceive enduring and significant trends in Scottish culture at large which otherwise would not be apparent.

The fragments presented are from James Macpherson and the effect of the Ossian phenomenon in Germany from 1760 onwards; the influence of certain German writers on Thomas Carlyle in the 1820s and 30s; and from the 1880s the influence exerted by W. Robertson Smith in the field of social anthropology and on Freud, who called Smith a "genius" in his *Moses and Monotheism* (Freud 1964: 1–13). Naturally such an abridged and disjointed presentation of historical material cannot hope to produce a seamless and comprehensive narrative of developments through the period in question. It may be objected that the most glaring omission here is that of Scott and his influence on the Germans; for without an acknowledgement and proper survey of the shaping of attitudes to history and modernity by his work, there is, in effect, no real survey. On the other hand, cannot such "rough cuts" as we propose here, provoke, by simple juxtaposition, new insights about the nature and scale of the epochal shift? The sheer immensity of the task for our understanding is kept palpably before us here, as by two sudden leaps we move from the early Enlightenment, with its concern with the individual subject operating within the historical residue of agrarian, feudal and humanistic layers of organisation, to writings dealing with the complex mass social structures of industrial, imperial and advanced capitalist Britain in the late nineteenth century. Carlyle is, in this sense, a midpoint between these two poles. Not only does he look to Germany as he wrestles in the dark night of his conscience to find an expression suitable – as he sees it – for the rapidly changing society of 1830s industrial revolutionary Britain, but in his obsession both with heroes and mobs, he is precariously balanced between these formal extremes of individualism and social complexity.

The title of the chapter may have aroused some curiosity. I would remind readers that these two words "slogan" and "clan" are two of the most commonly found Gaelic loan words in West European languages. They are of some pedigree: "slogan" (*sluagh ghairm* – battle cry in Gaelic) had its first recorded use in this anglicised form in Scott's *Last Minstrel*; "clan" was first recorded in Scots/English in Douglas's translation of the *Aeneid*, and came into German with the translation of *Humphry Clinker* in the 1770s. I would like to propose however, that "From slogan to clan", given the full complement of meanings and connotations of those words, does encapsulate something of the changing mood from the writings of Macpherson to those of W. Robertson Smith, and the different qualities of influence they exerted.

Macpherson

German literary culture was one of those most immediately and deeply influenced by the Ossian cult that followed the first publication of James Macpherson's translations in 1760. From 1762 onwards various translations and versions appeared in North Germany: in Bremen, Hamburg and Hanover. The first complete translation of Ossian into any language (other than English) was produced by Michael Denis, a Bavarian Jesuit, and the most famous (and arguably the most influential) partial translation is perhaps still Goethe's rendering of the "Songs of Selma" in the novel *The Sorrows of Young Werther* (1774).

What were the Germans looking for, or what did they find in Ossian, that made them so enthusiastic? Tombo, in his short book on *Ossian in Germany* says "there was scarcely a writer of note who did not fall under his spell", and, more specifically, that Ossian himself was "endowed with those qualities that constitute the ideal poet of the Storm and Stress" (Tombo 1901: 67, 75).

An examination of the major translations and what they actually brought over into German might tell us what they found so captivating. The number of different forms used (there are translations completely in prose; also some in rhymed verse; in unrhymed verse; rhythmic prose laid out as verse; free rhythms mixed with odes; and, of course, Denis' translation in hexameters) suggests that the translators found nothing inherently attractive about Macpherson's spare, asyndetic and paratactic prose style. Indeed before beginning his translation from Macpherson's English into German hexameters, Denis had only read and conceived his enthusiasm for Ossian through Cesarotti's Italian translation (Cesarotti 1763) done into *sciolti* – unrhymed hendecasyllabic verse in which the "original" stylistic qualities of Macpherson are already much attenuated by addition of conjunctions and punctuation. Nonetheless some translations like those of Goethe (in *Werther*) and Petersen (Petersen 1782) do preserve some specific and important stylistic qualities from Macpherson, like the inversions (an attempt by Macpherson to give a Gaelic tone to the English) and those aforementioned asyndetic and paratactic qualities.

Yet if it was not principally Macpherson's style that the Germans found so captivating, then neither could the influence of the translations have been based on the subject matter in terms of its strictly historical or geographical content. For, as Tombo points out, some of the German poets claiming the influence of Ossian were quite confused. There was confusion about who the Celts are, or were, and what their relationship was to the Nordic peoples, the Goths and present day Germans. Gerstenberg, for example, has Fingal not only

swearing allegiance to Loda, but praying to Wodan; and in an Ossi-
anic rewriting of the ode *Wingolf*, Klopstock has Orpheus and the
Thracians as a tribe of Celts, which oddly, makes them as much
German as is his Ossian.[1]

In fact it is precisely the simple and rarefied atmosphere of the
Ossian poems in these terms – historical and geographical – which
both guarantee their universality and encourage the sort of fantasies
noted immediately above. As Hugh Blair wrote, it is the "great
advantage of Ossian's mythology that it is not local and temporary"
(Blair 1765: 38). For what does remain in all the translations is the
simple diction, the directness of the poet's voice, the elemental (and
universal) imagery – the trees, the moor, rock, moss, sea; the clouds,
the rain, the snow; and the moon and sun – and the extended similes
and comparisons involving these natural phenomena. This was a
poetry devoid of abstract ideas, one of immediacy and emotion, a
"*Poetry of the Heart*" (Blair 1765: 21) – useful as a slogan, perhaps –
which thus appealed strongly, as Tombo pointed out, to the *Sturm und
Drang* movement with its rebellion against the classical, the
conventional, and the rational. As Howard Gaskill says:

> it could respond to widely shared inferiority complexes and resentments, serving to
> boost the self confidence of Highlands against Lowlands, Scotland against England,
> the barbarous North (Germany, Scandinavia, Russia) against the classical South
> (France, Italy, Greece). And of course equally it could be used to support the claims
> of the original against the derivative, the natural against the artificial, the ancient
> against the modern, the vigorous against the effete, and therefore the young against
> the old, anarchy against order, freedom against enslavement, spontaneity against
> reflection, inspiration against rules, heart against head, feeling against reason; also
> chastity against perversion [...] the (noble) savage against the (corrupt) civilised. It
> could be exploited by the iconoclasts who wished to dispose of the classical canon
> and topple Homer off his pedestal. (Gaskill 1994: 666–67)

If Ossian was thus in danger of being reduced to some sort of symbol,
a slogan for rebellious individuals, then his influence as such would
not be long lived. As W.H. Auden says of *Sturm und Drang*,

> Such a movement has often arisen in history and the consequences have almost
> always been the same; those who embrace it produce some remarkable work at an
> early age but then peter out if they do not, as they often do, take to drink or shoot

---

[1] "Sie sind auch deutschen Stamms". *Wingolf* is a rewriting of the classical Ode "An
meine Freunde" (Klopstock 1887: 5).

themselves. An art which pits Nature against Art is bound to be self-defeating. (Goethe 1970: 11–12)

Goethe did produce some remarkable work at an early age (*The Sorrows of Young Werther* among it), but he neither shot himself nor took to drink. Instead he grew to change his mind on Ossian and his presentation of the poetry in *Werther*. As a more mature writer he claimed that Werther only preferred Ossian to Homer in the second part of the novel i.e. once he had gone mad (Lamport has pointed out that Goethe's position here is textually unsustainable. Lamport 1998: 97). Goethe in his early *Sturm und Drang* years had been encouraged in his interest in Ossian by Herder, and at the same time he took an interest in the Gothic, writing an article on Gothic architecture which was published together with Herder's *Von deutscher Art und Kunst* (later called the "Sturm und Drang manifesto"). When some twelve or thirteen years later in the diary of his *Italian Journey* (an important event in Goethe's conversion to classicism) we find him saying of the Gothic "Thank God, I am done with all that junk for good and all" (Goethe 1970: 95), we must wonder if he does not dismiss Ossian and Werther and everything else connected with that *Sturm und Drang* period in this uncharacteristically vehement outburst.

Tombo tells us that Klopstock's interest in Ossian did not last much longer:

when his enthusiastic admiration for Ossian subsided and took on a saner aspect, when his views on the subject of the relationship of the Celts to the Older German tribes assumed a more scientific character, he could not allow Ossian to occupy the position assigned him at first. (Tombo 1901: 101)

Tombo goes on to say that Klopstock's period of "unbounded admiration" lasted no longer than a decade and that for the other "Bards", of whom Gerstenberg, Denis, and Kretschmann were the most prominent, "the thing passed into a fad through imitation" (Tombo 1901: 103).

It is interesting to note on this head that Schinkel the architect, who sketched Fingal's cave and was at the time an enthusiastic devotee of Gothic architecture, converted to classicism shortly after his trip to Scotland. He developed into Germany's most successful classical architect of the nineteenth century and is said by some to have been an influence on Glasgow's Alexander "Greek" Thomson.

In spite of these evidences of short-lived enthusiasms, the Ossian cult was long lasting in Germany, and there are certain individuals who developed deep and authentic approaches to the poetry. Howard Gaskill (1994) suggests that more work needs to be done on the influence, almost unacknowledged to date (or conveniently forgotten), on Jean Paul (Friedrich Richter), Novalis, and especially Hölderlin. The first ever translations from the so-called Gaelic originals of 1807 were done not into English but into German (in 1811) by a schoolmaster Christian Wilhelm Ahlwardt (Ahlwardt 1811), who also compiled a Gaelic Grammar in German in 1821. It was Herder however, who maintained perhaps the longest and most penetrating critical relationship with the Ossian texts. He had what seems now a most modern insight, and with the twentieth-century ring to his dictum "the thought clings to the expression",[2] he could not fail to be indignant at Denis's translations into hexameters which he reviewed in *Von deutscher Art und Kunst*. He was also able to pick out the most authentic passages of Gaelic folk poetry hidden away in Macpherson's texts[3] (something which many critics contemporary and modern have been unable to do), to compile a glossary of Gaelic terms, and publish some German versions of the poetry himself.

Perhaps the overall situation of Ossian in Germany is best summed up by Gaskill:

> The writers who were profoundly influenced by him matter and are still read. But one imagines that Germany would still have become – for a time – the country of poets, thinkers and indeed Celtic scholars, even if Macpherson had never lived. Nor do I think Herder's aesthetic values are strongly dependent on his reception of Ossian. Without Macpherson he would still have been pursuing the spirit of folk poetry from Latvia to Peru. (Gaskill 1996: 271)

Carlyle

Carlyle, born in 1795, did not learn German until he took private lessons as a twenty-five year old. By the late 1820s and through into the early 30s, however, he had already set himself the task of "germanising the public" (Norton 1888: letter of 4 June 1827 to John

---

[2] "[…] klebt der Gedanke am Ausdruck" (Herder 1877: 16–17).
[3] Gaskill points out that Herder picks the lamentation of the widow of Dargo – "about as genuine as anything in Macpherson's entire Ossianic corpus" – from a Macpherson footnote to send in a sample translation to his fiancé (1996: 265).

Carlyle). He went about this in various ways: by translating Goethe's *Wilhelm Meister's Apprenticeship* (1824), writing a short *Life of Schiller* (1825), by writing numerous critical/biographical essays on German poets and writers for such journals as the *Edinburgh Review*, *Fraser's Magazine* and the *Foreign Review*, and by undertaking to compile a History of German Literature (with the help of Goethe). This was no easy workload, and nor did Carlyle find the path to his literary Valhalla free of grumbling editors and publishers. He had disagreements with Jeffrey at the *Edinburgh Review* about the interest value of the Germans,[4] and Tait abandoned the publication of the History before it was finished on the grounds that "anything German is most specially to be avoided" (Froude 1882–84: 243).

This was of course not the only, nor the greatest, problem that Carlyle faced early in his literary career. For in addition to such German criticism he was also writing essays of socio-political interest such as "Signs of the Times" and "On History", and here he expressed a fear that the world of thought was becoming increasingly polarised. By the late 20s and early 30s Scotland was already moving towards the great intellectual crisis of the 1843 Disruption. So while on one side were those parties getting involved in the schismatic debates concerning faith, religion and its relationship to the State, and who seemed to ignore the massive social upheaval caused by the rapid industrialisation of the country in the nineteenth century, on the other were the Utilitarians, following the lead of Smith, Bentham, and Mill, who advocated material progress as a cure for social ills but paid little if any attention to spiritual or religious questions. Carlyle first tackles this problem in the "Signs of the Times" in the *Edinburgh Review* in 1829, where he designates the two poles as pertaining respectively to the dynamic and mechanical nature of man. As Carlyle sees it there has been too much of a concentration on man's mechanical nature and not enough emphasis placed on the dynamic, or as we might say, spiritual nature. Each of these two poles forms, as he says, "but half a picture" (Carlyle 1839: 250), and Carlyle seems to be seeking a way

---

[4] Bertrand Russell says of this period, "Throughout the period from Kant to Nietzsche, professional philosophers in Great Britain remained almost completely unaffected by their German contemporaries, with the sole exception of Sir William Hamilton, who had little influence. Coleridge and Carlyle, it is true, were profoundly affected by Kant, Fichte and the German Romantics, but they were not philosophers in the technical sense". (Russell 1946: 740)

in which thought and writing can deal with both the material and the spiritual at the same time.

The analysis which Carlyle gives of Mechanism and its one-sided and all-pervasive influence on the culture and society of the time is very lucid and powerful, but unfortunately when he attempts to persuade us of the need for a greater balance and emphasis on the dynamic, he is unconvincing. His method is more to tell us about rather than to show us this dynamic alternative, and it seems, at times, that he doth protest too much. Could he be said simply to fall back on a stereotypically harsh and disapproving Presbyterian heritage in the preachiness of his tone here? And if so, is that because the standard rational prose of the critic, which was rigorous enough to expose the Mechanistic problem, is, in a word, simply not a sufficiently supple and dynamic tool to work up an inspiration in us for his complementary vision? We might indeed say that in this essay we see the first ominous evidence of what A.J.P. Taylor described as Carlyle's "ideas spluttering and half-formed, ideas of revolt and rejection with nothing constructive to follow" (Taylor 1976: 59). In effect, writings as a form of slogan. At any rate, Carlyle himself seems aware of his literary shortcomings here, when at the beginning of the section dealing with the dynamic, he admits to "speak[ing] a little pedantically" (Carlyle 1839: 240).

If "Signs of the Times" was at the least a lucid posing of the problem then the first real answering to the questions it raised could be said to come with the completion of *Sartor Resartus* in 1831 (published in complete form in 1836). *Sartor Resartus* is important not only for what it says, but *how* it says it. Carlyle had by this time developed a poetic, and it must be said, dynamic style which he calls a "Babylonish Dialect". It has cosmic scope, is rhapsodic and affected, makes use of satire, invective and irony, and thus is an answer in itself to the plodding Mechanistic problem. To some extent it can be shown that he developed this style through his readings of German writers (although there are of course other very important influences, such as his strict Presbyterian background, and Biblical influences). Thus with those early essays of the late 1820s and early 30s he may be said not only to have been "germanising the public" but also germanising himself.

Carlyle's reading of German authors was very wide ranging but we may here take a brief look at some of the most important influences, namely Goethe, Novalis, Jean Paul Friedrich Richter and Kant. Goethe was always an inspirational figure for Carlyle, and they carried out a correspondence principally between 1827–31.[5] The spiritual conversion which Carlyle describes as occurring in *Sartor Resartus* between the chapters "The Everlasting No" and "The Everlasting Yea" was effected in him personally by his careful reading and translation of Goethe's Bildungsroman *Wilhelm Meister's Apprenticeship* (1824). Carlyle was going through a spiritual crisis, having doubts and ultimately giving up on his Presbyterian faith, and this book let him see new possibilities of self realisation through an active and socially useful life. Goethe as a pacific, all-encompassing genius who has command of all fields of knowledge and experience can be seen as an inspiration for the character of Teufelsdröckh in *Sartor Resartus*. There we have an all-knowing, all-seeing professor living in a small provincial town: is it Weimar or Weissnichtwo, Teufelsdröckh or Goethe?

Novalis was influenced by Friedrich Schlegel who developed certain Romantic ideas and forms from a reading of the German theorist Wolff. Wolff was one of the first critics to propose that the "Iliad" was not composed by one single poet "Homer" but by many poets acting as poet-critics in a tradition and progressing the body of work through their own critical reading of it and poetic intervention in it (Martin 1994: 82). The Romantics, led by Schlegel, developed two important concepts from this critical reading.

Firstly, that of the Open Work: the literary work as progressive and dynamic, involving the critical and poetic impulses of many hands. Examples include the *Iliad* and the Bible: works that oppose the complete, finished ideal of the single-authored classical literary work. The second concept, which derives from this, is that of the fragment. If individual authority in a work is always limited then it follows that each poet's contribution can only ever be a fragment. The fragment is thus always a key to some ineffable infinite which lies beyond the scope of literary delineation. German Romantic artists from Novalis to Goethe exploited the form of the fragment in working out the ironic stance of a self-contained autonomy as part of a greater totality – it was thus of use to Carlyle in his concern for both heroes

---

[5] A.J.P Taylor noted of Carlyle, that "It sheds a quaint light on the two languages that Goethe, that most classical of German writers, should have inspired the most uncouth writer of English" (Taylor 1976: 59).

and mobs. These German Romantic artists used the form as an opportunity to adopt simultaneously both a subjective and an objective viewpoint. The highest development of the form is perhaps seen in Nietzsche's aphorisms.

A fairly straightforward case can be made for the influence of these ideas on the structure of *Sartor Resartus*. The book is ostensibly about Teufelsdröckh's "Philosophy of Clothes", a philosophy that would explain everything. Yet we never see the whole text, which remains in one sense at least ineffable. Instead we are treated to fragments, contributions critical and poetic, from the editor, from Teufelsdröckh himself, from Teufelsdröckh's friend, from written notes in paper bags, and so on, which all provide a key to that ineffable infinite.

To see how directly Novalis's style might have influenced Carlyle, we need only compare the following opening paragraph of *Novices at Sais* with *Sartor Resartus*, and especially Carlyle's chapter of "Symbols":

Various are the roads of man. He who follows and compares them will see strange figures emerge, figures which seem to belong to that great cipher which we discern written everywhere, in wings, eggshells, clouds and snow, in crystals and in stone-formations, on ice-covered waters, on the inside and outside of mountains, of plants, beasts and men, in the lights of heaven, on scored disks of pitch or glass, or in iron filings round a magnet, and in strange conjunctures of chance. In them we suspect a key to the magic writing, even a grammar, but our surmise takes on no definite forms and seems unwilling to become a higher key. (Novalis [1949] 2005: 3–5)

Here we have the "great cipher", somewhat like the unseen, unseeable, infinite "Philosophy of Clothes". And all these "figures" listed give a "key" to "the grammar", and remind us of Carlyle's statement that "Rightly viewed no meanest object is insignificant; all objects are windows, through which the philosophic eye looks into infinitude itself" (Carlyle 1840: 72).

Jean Paul Friedrich Richter, humorist novelist and critic, might be said to be the Laurence Sterne of German literature. Carlyle wrote two essays on Richter, one for the *Edinburgh Review* in 1827 and another for the *Foreign Review* in 1830, and it is significant that there he places greater emphasis on analysis of style, where in his essays on Goethe and Novalis, for example, he tends to look more for meaning or message. A short passage from each essay may demonstrate this:

There are few writers with whom deliberation and careful distrust of first impressions are more necessary than with Richter. He is a phenomenon from the very surface; he presents himself with a professed and determined singularity; his language itself is a stone of stumbling to the critic; to critics of the grammarian species, an unpardonable, often an insuperable rock of offence. Not that he is ignorant of grammar, or disdains the science of spelling and parsing; but he exercises both in a certain latitudinarian spirit; deals with astonishing liberality in parentheses, dashes, and subsidiary clauses; invents hundreds of new words, alters old ones, or by hyphen chains and pairs and packs them together into the most jarring combination; in short, produces sentences of the most heterogeneous, lumbering, interminable kind. Figures without limit! Indeed the whole is one tissue of metaphors, and similes, and allusions to all provinces of Earth, Sea, and Air; interlaced with epigrammatic breaks, vehement bursts, or sardonic turns, interjections, quips, puns, and even oaths! A perfect Indian jungle it seems; a boundless, unparalleled imbroglio; nothing on all sides but darkness, dissonance, confusion worse confounded! (Carlyle 1855: 10)

and,

Probably there is not in any modern language so intricate a writer; abounding, without measure, in obscure allusions, in the most twisted phraseology; perplexed into endless entanglements and dislocations, parenthesis within parenthesis; not forgetting elisions, sudden whirls, quips, conceits and all manner, yet nowise in what seem military lines, but rather in huge parti-coloured mob-masses. (Carlyle 1855: 197)

Two very important points are clear from these cited passages: Firstly, that here we have Carlyle not only providing a definition of Jean Paul's style but also attempting to create an example of that very style which he seeks to define. Are not Carlyle's own sentences here "intricate" with "the most twisted phraseology", does he not perplex the definition into "endless entanglements and dislocations"? "Figures without limit!" is surely one of these "vehement bursts" itself, and as for "obscure allusions", what about "a perfect Indian Jungle" with an Italian "unparalleled imbroglio" wrapped around it?

This can be read as a definition not only of Jean Paul's style, but also of Carlyle's mature style as it is found in *Sartor Resartus* and the *French Revolution*. For here, in a confusing but planned poetic jumble, "a stone of stumbling to the critic", the author himself, his personal dynamism, is ever-present and linked through figures of "metaphors and similes and allusions" to a cosmic scope of "Earth, Sea and Air". During the year (1830) of the writing of *Sartor Resartus* we see him thus practising again a style which he had first attempted in 1827 and which allows him to charm the Mechanistic Universe, given that "Not our Logical, Mensurative faculty, but our Imaginative one is King over us" (Carlyle 1840: 225).

Carlyle was an enthusiastic expounder of German Idealism, especially in his immature and early mature writings. We find him setting out his versions of that philosophy in the early critical essays, the philosophico-fictive *Sartor Resartus*, and the Histories. Indeed, we only get as far as page six of the three-volume *French Revolution* before he audaciously implies that the whole Gallic affair was underpinned by German philosophy. Carlyle's version of German Idealism consisted more or less of ideas from Kant, conflated with those of Fichte and Schelling, and blended with his own idiosyncratic brand of spiritualism. Indeed while Rene Wellek (1931) admits that Carlyle probably did more than anyone else to make England "receptible" for German idealism, he suggests that what Carlyle expounded as such was more Carlyle than Kant. Wellek implies that Carlyle had never in fact properly read Kant, saying that Carlyle relied "mostly" on "second hand reports" (Wellek 1931: 200). Both Wellek and Froude claim that, in fact, Carlyle never got beyond page 150 of the *Critique of Pure Reason*: starting it in order to "allay his fears" about his impending wedding to Jane Welsh but then abandoning it when it became "too abstruse" for him (Froude 1882–84: 375).

But whatever Carlyle's sources: Kant's writings, other writers' expositions of Kant and German Idealism (notably Novalis), or his own brand of spirituality; and whatever the truth, misrepresentation, and intellectual soundness of Carlyle's "Kanteanism", the fact is that he did not hesitate to exploit his own version of these ideas in all forms of his writings. To take an example first from his early critical essays, that on Novalis in the *Foreign Review* in 1829:

The Idealist, again, boasts that his Philosophy is Transcendental, that is, "ascending beyond the senses"; which, he asserts, all Philosophy, properly so called, by its nature is and must be: and in this way he is led to various unexpected conclusions. To a Transcendentalist, Matter has an existence, but only as a Phenomenon: were we not there, neither would it be there; it is a mere Relation, or rather the result of a Relation between our living Souls and the First Cause; and depends for its apparent qualities on our bodily and mental organs; having itself no intrinsic qualities; being, in the common sense of that word, Nothing. The tree is green and hard, not of its own natural virtue, but simply because my eye and hand are fashioned so as to discern such and such appearances under such and such conditions. (Carlyle 1839: 203)

This essay was written in the same year as "Signs of the Times" in which we see a similar lucid and rational prose style. If we turn now to a couple of excerpts from *Sartor Resartus* completed in 1831, and therefore after the final 1830 essay on Jean Paul's style, we see again an expounding of Carlyle's Kantean ideas, but in a completely different style from their presentation in the 1829 Novalis essay.

But deepest of all illusory Appearances, for hiding Wonder, as for many other ends, are your two grand fundamental world-enveloping Appearances, SPACE and TIME. These, as spun and woven for us from before Birth itself, to clothe our celestial ME for dwelling here, and yet, to blind it – lie all embracing, as the universal canvas, or warp and woof, whereby all minor Illusions, in this Phantasm Existence, weave and paint themselves. In vain, while here on Earth, shall you endeavour to strip them off; you can, at best, but rend them asunder for moments, and look through. […] Believe what thou findest written in the Sanctuaries of Man's Soul, even as all Thinkers, in all ages, have devoutly read it there: that TIME, and SPACE are not God, but creations of God; that with God as it is a universal HERE, so it is an everlasting NOW. (Carlyle 1840: 265–66)

Here we have a presentation of Carlyle's own (spiritualised) version of German Idealism, meshed with "astonishing liberality" in that dynamic style, the "Babylonish Dialect", of which he'd learned so much from Jean Paul. Turning now to the *French Revolution* (1837) we can see how he develops this happy marriage of Kant and Jean Paul to its most mature expression:

For ours is a most fictile world; and man is the most fingent plastic of creatures. A world not fixable: not fathomable! An unfathomable Somewhat, which is Not we; which we can work with, and live amidst, – and model, miraculously in our miraculous Being, and name World. – But if the very Rocks and Rivers (as Metaphysics teaches) are, in strict language, made by those outward Senses of ours, how much more, by the Inward Sense, are all Phenomena of the spiritual kind: Dignities, Authorities, Holies, Unholies! Which inward Sense, moreover, is not permanent like the outward ones, but forever growing and changing. Does not the Black African take of Sticks and Old Clothes (say exported Monmouth Street cast-clothes) what will suffice, and of those, cunningly combining them, fabricate for himself an Eidolon (Idol or Thing Seen), and name it Mumbo-Jumbo; which he can thenceforth pray to, with upturned awestruck eye, not without hope? The white European mocks; but ought rather to consider; and see whether he, at home, could not do the like a little more wisely. (Carlyle 1837: 6)

Here the style has with its "certain latitudinarian spirit" completely stifled any clear expression of content. The "German Idealism" is a substructure clothed in the prose such that it is only exposed in a parenthetical reminder that "Metaphysics" are under all this somewhere. What Carlyle has managed to do is to sublimate completely his own Presbyterian urge to preach, and in effect he has created a dynamic and organic unity of content and style. To attempt a Carlylean-style metaphor: might it not be said that on a certain stylistic level what we have in the *French Revolution* is a warp of Richterian prose woven through the woof of a homespun Kanteanism?

William Robertson Smith

By the 1890s Scotland had moved some way beyond that period of schismatic debates about faith, religion and their relationship to the State that had characterised the era of the Disruption. But it was emerging as a very different country from eighteenth- and early nineteenth-century Scotland: 1872 had brought the Education Act, in 1886 the position of the Secretary of State for Scotland was established in the British Government, and the Scottish Trades Union Congress was to be formed in 1897. This was no longer a nation built around a church that governed the welfare and education of its people, but a Scotland that was more truly a constituent part of the modern British State. However, not everything of these schismatic debates which had seemed to Carlyle to ignore the great social upheavals of the time ("Hebrew Old Clothes" was his characteristic comment) was lost in self-regarding oblivion. In fact one of the great international successes of those years was the contribution of W. Robertson Smith, whose work proves that the Scottish Presbyterian tradition was still able to make a distinct, important and unique contribution to the formation of modern twentieth-century thought.

From the late 1840s onwards many Free Church theologians had started to turn towards Germany for theological guidance. By the 1860s when Robertson Smith was studying, Calvinist theology was under question and students at the New College in Edinburgh were encouraged to attend *Somersemester* and to acquaint themselves with German biblical criticism. Robertson Smith went to Bonn in 1867 and studied under Adolf Kamphausen; in 1869 he was in Gottingen studying metaphysics under Hermann Lotze, theological ethics under Albrecht Ritschl, and Old Testament theology with Ernst Bertheau; and in 1872 he was again in Gottingen to study Arabic with Paul de

Lagarde. An idea of the importance which Robertson Smith himself attached to these studies can be gained from comments in his letters, where he says, "Bonn and Gottingen had quite as much to do with my theological education as the T.M. [Training for the Ministry]" (Kinnear 1995: 95), and, when with reference to the later libel case against him by the Free Church, he calls Ritschl "the *Urvater* of the Aberdeen Heresy" (Rogerson: 1995: 79). A fuller appreciation of the influence of these German thinkers and theologians and others than can be sketched out here is to be found in J.W. Rogerson's *The Bible and Criticism in Victorian Britain*, (1995) where the author establishes that one of the greatest influences on Smith was his reading of *Zur Dogmathik* by the theologian Rothe, who died in 1867.

Smith contributes to modern thought in many important ways, but we will look here in particular at his influence on Sigmund Freud, specifically through his work on the history of the Semitic peoples and religions and on his questioning of Moses' authorship of the Pentateuch. Freud cited Smith's work often and extensively, especially in *Totem and Taboo* and *Moses and Monotheism*. There are three points which may be considered of some significance in this connection.

The first is that while Hume had admitted that it was possible to establish a common sense basis for both a system of morals and of physics, he denied that it was so in the case of organised religion. Both parties at the extremes of the Disruption debates, the Evangelicals and the atheists, agreed with this point, although for different reasons. As a moderate Presbyterian Robertson Smith felt it incumbent upon himself to prove that such a common sense basis could indeed be established. One way to do this was to show the continuities between Presbyterian theology and ancient social practice, which he did by using the Presbyterian rejection of transubstantiation as the basis of his researches into the ancient Totem Meal. Comparisons between Judaism and the Old-Testament-based Scots religion are fairly commonplace (in, for example, Carlyle's comments about "Hebrew Old Clothes" and in writers such as Heine) but Smith's project for a scientific theology bears a particularly strong resemblance to the eighteenth-century Jewish Enlightenment of Moses Mendelssohn, which sets out to establish the rational basis of all Judaic precepts and laws (see Arkush 1994). One might speculate that little of this resemblance would have been lost on Freud, a secularised

Viennese Jew, in his reading of Smith. What is less speculative is the influence of Smith's work in Germany, through friendships and confederacies (notably with Julius Wellhausen), and also later in France through the readings of the sociologist Émile Durkheim. Smith was working to show that religion, and sacrifice in particular, arose not out of an attempt to appease implacable and capricious powers but out of a relationship of love with a benevolent God. The fact that someone like Sigmund Freud could use Smith's results for his own lifelong campaign against organised religion would not, however, have surprised traditionalist Presbyterians such as Dr Alexander Duff (see Walls 1995) who thought Smith's work was undermining a belief in the infallible truth of Scripture,

The second point is that Smith, as a believing critic who held that the Old Testament was a record of progressive revelation of God to the nation of Israel, considered that the study of the historical and social context of the divine action was fundamentally important to understanding the Bible. It was thus that his researches turned to the Holy Land (and the Arabian Peninsula, which he saw as the original territory of the Semitic peoples) and to the religion of the Ancient Semites. One of the results of this research was to show how the structure of relationships between ritual, belief, dogma, and myth in ancient religion differed from that of the positivist faiths.

This can be seen in his *Lectures on the Religion of the Semites* in which Smith contends that " the antique religions had for the most part no creed; they consisted entirely of institutions and practices," and that as a consequence, their rituals were "connected not with a dogma but a myth" (Smith 1889: 16–17). "It must however be remembered", Smith insists, "that in ancient religion there was no authoritative interpretation of ritual. It was imperative that certain things should be done, but every man was free to put his own meaning on whatever was done" (Smith 1889: 399):

Ancient religion was so entirely ruled by precedent that men did not deem it necessary to have an adequate moral explanation of even the most exorbitant demands of traditional ritual; they were content to explain them by some legend that told how the ritual first came to be set up. (Smith 1889: 409)

It is quite a simple step from these findings, which establish rite as more fundamental and chronologically prior to myth, to set up a rough analogy between Smith's analysis of the structure of Ancient Religion and Freud's psychoanalytic theory. In this reading ritual is seen as a sort of collective compulsive neurotic act and myth (like the work of analysis) a retroactive explanation emerging from the collective unconscious. Indeed on the first page of *Totem and Taboo* Freud makes it clear that he is aware of these similarities:

a comparison between the psychology of primitive peoples, as it is taught by social anthropology, and the psychology of neurotics, as it has been revealed by psychoanalysis, will be bound to show numerous points of agreement and will throw new light upon familiar facts in both these sciences. (Freud 1985: 53)

Freud makes extensive use of W. Robertson Smith's research material, and even makes a six-page resume of his findings in the "Return to Totemism" chapter of *Totem and Taboo*. But where Smith organises his work into what might be crudely described as a dialectic of historico-critical character, mapping out man's gradual coming to dominion over the natural world, Freud absorbs the material into his own idiosyncratic mytho-psychoanalytical canon. Robertson Smith follows Julius Wellhausen in seeing the ancient religion, even with its sacrificial feasts, as a joyous thing (see Wellhausen [1885] 1957) in which there is little of guilt or atonement (this comes later with the development of private property, individuality, and in the Hebrew case, with various political disasters). Freud however, asserts both in *Totem and Taboo* and *Moses and Monotheism* that the slaughter of the totem animal and the totem meal are a commemoration in communal guilt of the original slaughter of the tribal father.[6] Freud argues in *Totem and Taboo*, that "Psychoanalysis has revealed that the totem animal is in reality a substitute for the father" (Freud 1985: 202), and in *Moses and Monotheism* that,

---

[6] Durkheim argued in *Elementary Forms of Religious Life* (1915), that although some writers (e.g. Tyler in *Primitive Culture* and Wilken in *Het Animisme bij den Volken van den Indischen Archipel*) saw totemism not as the most elementary religion but as a special form of the cult of ancestors, this is only because they take their evidence from societies which have passed the stage of pure totemism to a decadent form. Freud also seems to believe here that totemism is not an elementary form of religion, but one derived from the cult of ancestors. Durkheim points out for example, that the purest form of totemism is found in Australian societies among whom metempsychosis is unknown. He also points out that in totemism it is not the actual animal or plant that is worshipped, but the emblem or image of the totem, "Now between this religion of the emblem and the ancestor-cult, there is no connection whatsoever" (Durkheim [1915] 2001: 128).

The first decisive step towards a change in this sort of "social" organisation seems to have been that the expelled brothers, living in a community, united to overpower their father and, as was the custom in these days, devoured him raw (Freud 1985: 325)

These assertions fly in the face of Robertson Smith's conclusion from the same material. Namely, that within one totemic clan the same sort of being, or spirit, was seen as belonging equally to the non-anthropomorphic deity, the totem animal, and the worshippers, but that when this Totem system fell into abeyance and was gradually replaced with the institution of property, then the worshippers performing the same prescribed rites could no longer understand the familial or shared blood references to the sacrificial animal. According to Smith:

I apprehend, therefore, that human sacrifice is not more ancient than the sacrifice of ancient animals, and that the prevalent belief of ancient heathenism, that animal victims are an imperfect substitute for a human life, arose from a false inference from traditional forms of ritual that ceased to be understood […] when the full kinship of animals with men (The Totem System) was no longer recognised in ordinary life, all this became unintelligible, and was explained by the doctrine that at the altar the victim took the place of a man. (Smith 1889: 365)

While Robertson Smith can in many ways be seen as the founder of the modern sociology of religion, his almost exclusive advocacy of the totemic system and the joyous sacrifice that goes with it was largely rejected as a model by later scholars. This is the view of T.O. Beidelman:

Undisputably, Smith was a major figure in creating a popular interest in totemism. Freud and Durkheim accepted Smith's data uncritically, even though Smith's scholarly evidence for early mother-right and totemism is very questionable and discredited today. His was a kind of reconstruction based on the worst forms of conjectural history founded on the doctrine of survivals. Certainly his insistence that early man was totemic in religion and never polytheistic, much less monotheistic is now generally rejected. Smith presents his own theory of sacrifice as essentially related to totemism and he relates what he considers the primordial form of sacrifice to communal and commensual rites deriving from a sacrificial devouring of a totem by those who venerate it. (Beidelman 1974: 37–38)

Beidelman then goes on to deal with the question of the "joyous" sacrifice, quoting from Thompson's 1963 study,

In his useful survey Thompson notes: "Most of the scholars reviewed have conceded that expiation had a larger place in early Israelite sacrifice than the Wellhausen school allowed, but none of them have (sic) devoted to it, a systematic and methodological investigation." Indeed he provides an extensive list of recent biblical researchers who have found the joyous sacrifice theory untenable and the theme of solemnity and expiation the dominant one in Old Testament sacrifice. (Beidelman 1974: 55)

In fact in *Moses and Monotheism,* Freud declares that for his earlier *Totem and Taboo* he made use of theoretical ideas put forward by "Darwin, Atkinson, and particularly by Robertson Smith" but specifies that the killing and eating of the patriarch by the sons was an idea he took from J.J. Atkinson (Freud 1985: 379). At any rate Freud here is evidently more closely aligned with the ultimate orthodoxy than with Smith. Durkheim, for example, (whose *Elementary Forms of the Religious Life* was published in its original French version in 1912, a year before *Totem and Taboo*) found that oblation and expiation were as important to sacrifice as communion, and explicitly criticised Smith and his rejection of the theory of animal substitution for original human sacrifice as "false inference". According to Durkheim, "it is inadmissible that beliefs and practices as universal as these, which we find at the basis of the expiatory sacrifice, should be the product of a simple error of interpretation" (Durkheim [1915] 2001: 307).

The final point concerns W. Robertson Smith's use of the word "clan": this aspect of Smith's work remains important, as, in Beidelman's words, "group-held, communal values epitomised primitive life and thought" (Beidelman 1974: 39). Clearly, as an Aberdeenshire Scot, Smith had easy access to this word "clan" and was familiar with the concept behind its native use. It appears however that it was the Americans who were first to employ this word in the anthropological context through Albert Gallatin's studies of North American Indigenous peoples (Gallatin 1836: 109).[7] J.F. McLennan, Robertson Smith's friend and colleague, and a fellow Scotsman, notes Gallatin's use of the term in his seminal article on Totemism in *The Fortnightly Review* (Mclennan 1869: 70). In this context it is adapted as a specifically scientific term, and in a way which may be said to prefigure much of the language and thought of

---

[7] Swiss-born Gallatin was Thomas Jefferson's Secretary of the Treasury, managing the Louisiana Purchase for Jefferson and serving also under Madison. He was also the founder of the American Ethnological Society.

late-nineteenth and early-twentieth century modernism.[8] With Smith
for example, "clan" denotes a specific level of social organisation,
namely one that might be said to be supra-family but sub-tribal:

> the notion that the clan is only a larger household is not consistent with the results of
> modern research. Kinship is an older thing than family life, and in the most primitive
> societies known to us the family or household group was not a subdivision of the clan,
> but contained members of more than one kindred. (Smith 1889: 277)

The word "clan" here signifies that these ancient peoples had complex
social structures, integral in this case to the Totem system. Totemism
as a concept has however been largely discredited by more recent
anthropologists, who regard their predecessors' attempts at defining
and delineating the "primitive" as "abnormal" and separate from
"civilised" man as products of an outdated politics. As such it is surely
no accident that this word "clan" was adapted (or adaptable) for
anthropological use from the language of a marginalised European
people, who for centuries were themselves treated by their nearest
mainstream European neighbours as evolutionary throw-backs. And
given the history of oppression and denial which that people faced, it
is perhaps less than surprising that this lexical borrowing has rarely, if
ever, been explicitly acknowledged in the literature.[9]

    If in his writings Smith confirms the anthropological orthodoxy
of the word "clan" then he uses this word and views the concept in a
very different sense from the eighteenth- (and early nineteenth-)
century Enlightenment or Romantic sense. In the eighteenth century's
gradual working out of bourgeois subjectivity it was the individual
rather than the social structure that generally presented more interest.
Indeed, as John Dwyer has pointed out, there were no "clans" at all in
Macpherson's ideal world of the Gaelic past. Macpherson's attempt to
establish that a society of magnanimous, sympathetic, "feeling" indi-

---

[8]Although Mclennan does at this stage only quote Gallatin using the word "clan", and
himself employs various terms, including *families, gentes, stock, stock-tribes, persons
of one stock, stock-names, bands,* and confusingly, *tribes,* to refer to this social
structure.

[9] It is notable, even shameful, in this respect that although many if not most of the
writers, (including both Durkheim and Freud) give definitions, etymologies and
commentaries on the use of the loan word "totem" (ododem), similar discussion on
the origins of the word "clan" (except sometimes to say that it is an "English" word)
are extremely rare (this writer has never found an adequate one).

viduals like Ossian could exist in a "barbaric" or pre-Enlightenment era meant of course that he had to show that lineage and other formal or legalistic relations "counted for very little and love a lot" (Dwyer 1991: 170). Moderate clergymen like Hugh Blair may have been pleased to see in the image of the Ossianic Bard a role for themselves as one who would temper the ratio-scientific character of the Scottish Enlightenment by discovering "the emotional springs of action" and manipulating "the passions in the interest of a more general benevolence and humanity" (Dwyer 1991: 175).

William Robertson Smith himself may be seen as a later representative of this same moderate tradition, but nonetheless, with the scientific adaptation of the word "clan", his common sense approach takes on a more formalistic, proto-modern aspect. Indeed it is this idea of "clan" as a determinist model in social anthropology, as a complex pre-existing structure which is "always already" there and only within which the discernible primitive "individual" as such can be encountered, that prefigures so much of modernist thought in the early twentieth century. One need only think here of Saussure and the "sign" in structural linguistics; Marxism and "class" in historical materialism; of the "world" and its implemental determinism in Heidegger's existentialism; and of course, Freud and the "unconscious" in psychoanalysis. When Freud himself follows W. Robertson Smith in the use of the word and concept "clan" it is definitely not to be used as a mere slogan but as a significantly more subtle political tool.

Bibliography

Ahlwardt, Christian Wilhelm. 1811. *Die Gedichten Ossians. Aus dem Gaelischen.* 3 vols. Leipzig.

Arkush, Allan. 1994. *Moses Mendelssohn and the Enlightenment.* Albany: State University of New York Press.

Beidelman, T.O. 1974. *William Robertson Smith and the Sociological Study of Religion.* Chicago: University of Chicago Press.

Blair, Hugh. 1765. "A critical dissertation on the Poems of Ossian" in Macpherson, James (ed.). *The Works of Ossian, the Son of Fingal.* 2 vols. London: Becket and De Hondt.

Carlyle, Thomas. 1829. "Sign of the Times" in *Edinburgh Review* 98.

——. 1830. "On History" in *Fraser's Magazine, 10.*[pg. Ref]

——. 1839 *Miscellaneous Essays.* Vol 2. London. Chapman Hall

——. 1855 *Critical and Miscellaneous Essays.* Vol 5. Phillips, Samson & Co.

——. 1899. *Centenary Edition,* Vol. 27. London: Chapman Hall.

——. 1840. *Sartor Resartus; the Life and Opinions of Herr Teufelsdröckh.* New York: J Munroe.

——. 1837. *The French Revolution. A History.* 3 vols. London: Chapman Hall.

Cesarotti, Melchior. 1763. *Poesie di Ossian.* 2 vols. Padua: Comino.

Durkheim, Emile. [1915] 2001. *The Elementary Forms of the Religious Life* (tr. Carol Cosman and Mark Sydney). Oxford: Oxford University Press.

Dwyer, John. 1991. "The Melancholy Savage" in Gaskill, Howard (ed.). *Ossian Revisited.* Edinburgh: Edinburgh University Press.

Freud, Sigmund. 1985. *Pelican Freud Library.* Vol. 13. (eds Albert Dickson & Angela Richards. and tr. James Strachey). London: Penguin Books.

Froude, J.A. 1882–84. *Thomas Carlyle.* 4 vols. London: Longmans, Green.

Galatin, Albert. 1836. "Synopsis of the Indian Tribes" in *Archaeologica Americana.* Cambridge: Cambridge University Press.

Gaskill, Howard. 1994. "Ossian in Europe" in *Canadian Review of Comparative Literature* 21(4): 643–76.

——. 1996. "Herder, Ossian and the Celtic" in Brown, Terence (ed.) *Celticism* [Studia Imagologica 8]. Rodopi, Amsterdam. 257–72.

——. 1998. *From Gaelic to Romantic* (eds Howard Gaskill & Fiona J. Stafford). Amsterdam: Rodopi.

Gay, Peter. 1988. *Freud: A Life For Our Time.* London: Dent.

Goethe, Johann Wolfgang von. 1970. *Italian Journey* (tr. W.H. Auden and Elizabeth Mayer). London: Penguin.

Herder, Johann Gottfried. 1877. *Sammtliche Werke.* Vol 2.(ed. Bernard Suphan). Berlin: Weidmann.

Kinnear, Malcolm A. 1995. "William Robertson Smith and the Death of Christ", in Johnstone, William (ed.), *William Robertson Smith: Essays in Reassessment.* Sheffield: Sheffield Academic Press.

Klopstock, F.G. 1887. *Oden von Klopstock* (ed. Heinrich Duncker). Leipzig: Duncker & Humblot.

Lamport, F.J. 1998. "Goethe, Ossian and Werther" in Stafford, Fiona J. and Howard Gaskill (eds) *From Gaelic to Romantic: Ossianic Translations.* Amsterdam: Rodopi. 97–106.

Mclennan, J.F. 1869. "The Worship of Animals and Plants", in *The Fortnightly Review* 6: 407–27, 562–82.

Norton, C.E. (ed.). 1886. *Early Letters of Thomas Carlyle, 1814–1826.* 2 vols. London: Macmillan.

—. 1888. *Letters of Thomas Carlyle, 1826–36.* 2 vols. London: Macmillan.

Martin, Henri Jean. 1994. *History and Power of Writing* (tr. Lydia G. Cochrane). Chicago. University of Chicago Press

Novalis (von Hardenburg), Friedrich. [1949] 2005. *Novices at Sais* (tr. Ralph Manheim). Archipelago Books: New York.

Petersen, Johann Wilhelm. 1782. *Die Gedichte Ossians neuverteutschet.* Tubinge: Heerbrandt.

Rogerson, J.W. 1995. *The Bible and Criticism in Victorian Britain.* Sheffield: Sheffield Academic Press.

Russell, Bertrand. 1946. *A History of Western Philosophy.* London: George Allen & Unwin.

Sanders, Charles Richard, et al (eds). 1970. *Letters of Thomas and Jane Welsh Carlyle.* Durham, N.C: Duke University Press.

Smith, William Robertson. 1889. *Lectures on the Religion of the Semites.* London.

Taylor, A.J.P. 1976. "Macaulay and Carlyle" in *Essays in English History.* London: Hamish Hamilton.

Tombo, Rudolph. 1901. *Ossian in Germany.* New York: Columbia University Press.

Thompson, R.J. 1963. *Penitence and Sacrifice in Early Israel outside the Levitical Law.* Leiden: E.J. Brill.

Walls, Andrew F. 1995. "William Robertson Smith and the Missionary Movement", in Johnstone, William (ed.), *William Robertson Smith: Essays in Reassesment.* Sheffield: Sheffield Academic Press.

Wellek, Rene. 1931. *Immanuel Kant in England 1793–1838.* Princeton: Princeton University Press.

Wellhausen, Julius. [1885] 1957. *Prolegomena to the History of Ancient Israel.* New York: Meridian Library.

Wilson, D.A. 1923–34. *Life of Thomas Carlyle.* 6 vols. London: Kegan Paul, Trench, Trubner.

Nietzsche in Glasgow: Alexander Tille, John Davidson and Edwin Muir

Ritchie Robertson

Nietzsche's British reception began in Scotland, with strong interest from academics, translators and poets from the late nineteenth into the middle part of the following century. Reflecting debate elsewhere surrounding Nietzsche's philosophical significance, a "brutalist" Nietzsche and a "moralist" Nietzsche can be discerned in the poetic response of John Davidson and of Edwin Muir. Nietzsche is formative in Davidson's imperial views, while Muir's Christianity arises in response to problems about the nature of humanity and of sin that the poet sees Nietzsche giving rise to.
Keywords: Nietzsche; John Davidson; Alexander Tille; Thomas Common; Edwin Muir; Walter Kaufmann; "The Testament of an Empire-Builder" (John Davidson); *We Moderns* (Edwin Muir); Empire; Nazism; Christianity.

Nietzsche himself never visited Glasgow, any more than Hitler – despite Beryl Bainbridge's fantasy in *Young Adolf* – visited Liverpool. But one of the first translations from Nietzsche into English appeared in the *Glasgow Herald* on 18 March 1893. It was an adaptation by John Davidson of an article on Nietzsche by Theodor de Wyzewa, first published in the Paris journal *Revue politique et littéraire* in 1891, and containing several aphorisms from *Human, All-Too-Human* (Sloan 1995: 159).[1] Late in 1894, lectures were given to the Glasgow Goethe Society on "Friedrich Nietzsche: the Herald of Modern Germany" by Alexander Tille, a German *Lektor* and later lecturer at Glasgow University, who in 1895 published an interpretation of Nietzsche entitled *Von Darwin bis Nietzsche*. Tille was appointed editor of the first English translation of Nietzsche's works, which was initiated with *The Case of Wagner*, translated by Thomas Common, and *Thus Spake Zarathustra*, translated by Tille himself. These translations were unsatisfactory, and were superseded by the translation of Nietzsche's collected works, edited by Oscar Levy, which appeared between 1909 and 1913.

Although it is a coincidence that Tille and Davidson propagated Nietzsche in Glasgow, and that Edwin Muir soon afterwards absorbed his writings there, it serves to highlight the fact that Nietzsche's

---

[1] Sloan mistakenly gives "Wynzewa" instead of Wyzeva. See also Thatcher 1970.

British reception began in Scotland. The translator Thomas Common was another Scotsman, who studied for the ministry but abandoned this career in order to propagate Nietzsche. One may ascribe Nietzsche's Scottish reception perhaps to a greater propensity for speculative thought in Scotland than in England. George Davie has described in *The Democratic Intellect* how the nineteenth-century Scottish educational system "made expertise in metaphysics the condition of the open door of social advancement" (Davie 1961: xii). John Davidson wrote in 1898:

When a Scotsman finds himself at cross purposes with life, what course does he follow? – He invariably does one of two things. He either sits down and drinks deeply, thoughtfully, systematically, of the amber spirit of his country, or he reads philosophy. (cited from Thatcher 1970: 68)

Certainly early responses to Nietzsche include some harrumphing about un-English speculation. Thus on Nietzsche's death in 1900, the *London Quarterly Review* wrote:

In this country, despite the efforts of certain devotees, he is but little known, and the practical English mind has small inclination to extract the grain of value from the chaff of speculations which, if ever they came to be generally acted upon, would dissolve society as we understand it. (cited from Thatcher 1970: 35)

John Davidson and Edwin Muir illustrate different possibilities in the reception of Nietzsche. That reception, as Steven Aschheim has shown with respect to Germany, has been extraordinarily diverse (Ascheim 1992). Nietzsche's writings are so multi-faceted, not to say self-contradictory, that they could be appropriated by virtually anyone with an urge for radical renewal. His legacy was claimed by the idealistic *Wandervogel* movement, which sent thousands of young people hiking across pre-1914 Germany, but also by the most brutal anti-semites and Social Darwinists. He was appropriated by Socialists, despite his elitism; by radical feminists like Lily Braun, despite his misogyny; by anarchists like Gustav Landauer, despite his implicit authoritarianism; and by the revolutionary Right around Ernst Jünger, despite his individualism. The widespread view of him as anticipating Nazism, though not wholly false, is hugely over-simplified (see Golomb and Wistrich 2002). It rests not only on a selective reading of his works, but on the activities of his sister, Elisabeth Förster-Nietzsche, who dominated the Nietzsche Archive at Weimar and, among other things, published a selection from his notebooks under the title *The Will to Power*, presenting it as a systematic treatise with emphasis on biological and racial elitism. She deliberately associated her brother's work with Nazism. The famous 1934 photograph by Heinrich Hoffmann, showing Hitler contemplating a bust of Nietzsche in the Nietzsche Archive at Weimar, was an attempt to establish a connection between the two, stage-managed by Förster-Nietzsche to serve her own ambitions (see Sluga 1993). In order to free Nietzsche from the taint of Nazism, Walter Kaufmann published in 1950 a highly influential reinterpretation, stressing Nietzsche as moralist and psychologist. Kaufmann argued that the Will to Power, Nietzsche's central concept, had nothing to do with political domination, but rather implied self-mastery and the sense of security it gives, resulting in an exuberant generosity (Kaufmann 1974; Sokel 1983). Subsequent discussion of Nietzsche has continued Kaufmann's efforts to dissociate Nietzsche from Nazism, sometimes by emphasising the radical scepticism of his later writings, which undermine any positive creed, sometimes by arguing that his "biological" language is to be understood only metaphorically. The most recent research suggests that Nietzsche studied biology carefully in the hope of finding a factual, not metaphorical, basis for his arguments about the Will to Power (Moore 2002). And anyone persuaded by Kaufmann's moral and existentialist account of Nietzsche will have difficulty in coping with such an important passage as this from *Beyond Good and Evil*, about the task of the "new philosophers":

They will teach humans that their future is their *will*, that the future depends on their human will, and they will prepare the way for great risk-taking and joint experiments in discipline and breeding in order to put an end to that terrible reign of nonsense and coincidence that until now has been known as "history" (the nonsense about the "greatest number" is only its most recent form). To accomplish this, new kinds of philosophers and commanders will eventually be necessary, whose images will make all the secretive, frightful, benevolent spirits that have existed in the world look pale and dwarfish. (Nietzsche 1998: 90–91)

In the reception of Nietzsche, especially in the English-speaking world, we can distinguish two important strands, and may loosely associate them with Davidson and Muir respectively. They are the view of Nietzsche as the unashamed advocate of power as domination, and the view of Nietzsche as an analyst of psychology and morals, for whom power is self-mastery. We may call them the brutalist

Nietzsche and the moralist Nietzsche. Each is partial and incomplete, responding to one aspect of Nietzsche's varied and inconsistent œuvre. Davidson perceives, and responds to, the brutalist Nietzsche; Muir focuses on the moralist.

Passages like the one quoted above, along with Nietzsche's hints about breeding a new kind of humanity, supported the brutalist interpretation. They were taken up by Bismarckian adherents of Nietzsche in the English-speaking world such as Levy, the editor of the second and superior English translation of Nietzsche. In his book *The Revival of Aristocracy* (1906), Levy attributes to Nietzsche a practical programme of eugenics designed to breed a new aristocracy. H.L. Mencken, the American sage, wrote an exposition of Nietzsche's philosophy which praised Nietzsche as "the king of all axiom smashers" and assimilated his thought to Social Darwinism (Mencken 1908: ix, 138–42). During the First World War, British propagandists readily though inaccurately associated Nietzsche with the imperialism of the Prussian historian Heinrich von Treitschke and the militarism of the strategist General Friedrich von Bernhardi, and attributed Germany's aggressive entry into the War to the influence of his writings (see Martin 2003).

Alexander Tille, who propagated Nietzsche so energetically in 1890s Glasgow, was an extreme exponent of the brutalist reading. Having studied German, English and Philosophy at Leipzig University, graduating *summa cum laude*, he arrived in Glasgow in 1890 with enthusiastic references, which stressed his reserved and gentlemanly manner.[2] In 1892 he founded the Glasgow branch of the English Goethe Society (established in 1886), serving as its secretary and treasurer. His academic career ended, soon after his promotion to full-time lecturer, when he unwisely published in the Berlin paper *Die Woche* an attack on Britain's conduct of the Boer War, combined with mockery of Britain's military capacity. Extracts in English appeared in the *Glasgow Herald*. Tille was mobbed by students, who manhandled him and tore his gown to pieces. Tille resigned his lectureship and returned to Germany, where he "obtained a lucrative secretarial position with a German business firm" (Thatcher 1974: 24). He died in 1912.

---

[2] "Sein Auftreten und Benehmen ist zurückhaltend und gentlemanlike", from reference by Ernst Elster, quoted in Manz 2003: 97; Manz 2003: 97–108 is an important source of information on Tille.

During his Glasgow years, Tille published not only academic studies of German medieval literature and folklore, but also treatises which, in the view of Alfred Kelly, reveal "[t]he full dehumanizing brutality of radical Social Darwinism" (Kelly 1981: 107). Tille's anonymous *Volksdienst. Von einem Sozialaristokraten* [In Service of the People. By a Social Aristocrat] (1893) maintains, appealing especially to Darwin and Haeckel, that the supposed good of the greatest number must be subordinated to the good of the powerful individual; the law of the stronger is the only law; and the stronger races are entitled to annihilate the weaker.[3] In the same year, an article in the prominent weekly *Die Zukunft*, "Ostlondon als Nationalheilanstalt" [East London as National Asylum], argued that the East End of London served a useful purpose as a dump for incurably degraded human beings who should be segregated from the healthy; according to the statistics collected by the Salvation Army, alcohol abuse and venereal infection ensured a high mortality rate and a low fertility rate, so that these people could be relied on, thanks to natural selection, to become extinct within a very few generations (Tille 1893). The task of segregating the sick from the healthy is the one which, according to Nietzsche in the third book of *The Genealogy of Morals*, is performed by churches. This is Nietzsche's explanation for the otherwise puzzling function of celibate priests in the evolutionary process. Themselves sick, they guard their sick flocks and unwittingly prevent them from interfering with the few healthy specimens in whom the future of humanity is invested.

Tille's Nietzschean concept of "social aristocracy" represents an intervention in German debates about society. His anonymous pamphlet was a riposte to the anonymous, much-read work by Julius Langbehn, *Rembrandt als Erzieher. Von einem Deutschen* [Rembrandt as Educator] (1890), which in turn opposed the levelling-down ascribed to Social Democracy by calling for a social aristocracy which would ennoble the German people.[4] Tille developed the idea of social aristocracy in *Von Darwin bis Nietzsche. Ein Buch Entwicklungsethik* [From Darwin to Nietzsche: A Book on Evolutionary Ethics] (Tille 1895). Here he argues that Christian ideals of brotherly love and

---

[3] Quoted extensively in Theo Meyer's afterword to his edition of Arno Holz's play *Sozialaristokraten* [1896]; see Holz 1980: 178–80.
[4] See the account of Langbehn in Stern 1961. For Tille's place in intellectual debates of the 1890s, see Scheuer 1971: 187–92.

democratic ideals of equality have been refuted by Darwinism, which knows only the fit and the unfit. Natural selection needs to be reinforced by social selection, in order to ensure the survival and enhancement of the most highly developed race. The last chapter of the book quotes extensively from Nietzsche in support of this view. Tille refers to Nietzsche's claim that "life itself is will to power", to his disapproval of compassion, to his attacks on democracy, and his advocacy of sexual selection (Tille 1895: 213–14, 230–34; Nietzsche [1886] 1998: 152–53). Tille regrets only that Nietzsche did not go further by relating these ideas to modern economics and demography.

Although Tille was extreme and one-sided in his reading of Nietzsche, an interpretation focusing on the will to power had many other adherents, including John Davidson. Before he came to Nietzsche, Davidson was already steeped in the egoistic philosophy of Max Stirner and others (Thatcher 1974: 55). His admiration for some of Nietzsche's thought was grafted onto his familiarity (not uncritical) with Carlyle's *Heroes and Hero-Worship*. Davidson left Glasgow in 1890 for a literary career in London. He belonged to the Rhymers' Club, where he inspired some memorable anecdotes recounted by Yeats (Yeats 1955: 315–18), and achieved short-lived success with *Fleet Street Eclogues* (1893) and *Ballads and Songs* (1894). His later volumes of verse sold badly, however, while his plays were rejected by theatre managers. To support his wife and family he had to rely on hack reviewing. Disappointment drove him to elaborate a strange philosophy, indebted among others to Schopenhauer and Nietzsche, composed of atheism, materialism, and the exaltation of the will. He projects his own frustrated will into the recurrent figure of the embattled hero. Thus the hero of the play *Smith: A Tragic Farce* (1888) is "barbarous as a Lapp", but "the kind of man that healthy girls / Yield to at once" (Davidson 1894: 221, 244). He celebrates the modern man of will in the ruthless financier who speaks in the poem "The Aristocrat", where the modern businessman is presented as the successor of the feudal baron:

The warlord and the churchlord stir
The pulses of the world no more;
The trader and the usurer
Have passed the lion-guarded door;
The praise, the prayer, the incensed air
Ascend to us from every shore. [...]

Though Corner, Trust and Company
Are subtler than the old-time tolls,
The Sword, the Rack, the Gallowstree,
I traverse none of Nature's rules;
I lay my yoke on feeble folk,
And march across the necks of fools.
(Davidson 1973: 134–35)

Davidson projected this ideal onto the British Empire, becoming an enthusiastic advocate of Imperialism, under the influence of his friend J.A. Cramb, professor of History in London. Davidson admired Cramb's book of 1900, *Reflections on the Origins and Destiny of Imperial Britain*, which strongly supported the Boer War. This imperial assault on a small nation who had the misfortune to farm on diamond-mines, which now looks like Britain's Vietnam, seemed to confirm the creed Davidson had uttered in the poem "War-Song": "In anguish we uplift / A new unhallowed song: / The race is to the swift; / The battle to the strong" (Davidson 1973: 127). His last long poem, "The Testament of John Davidson" (1908), is prefaced by an imaginary speech addressed to the House of Lords, urges the Lords to reject demands for Irish home rule, workers' rights, and women's enfranchisement, and represents the modern Englishman as the embodiment of Nietzsche's Superman or "Overman" (Davidson 1973: 541).

This poem is one of five long Browningesque blank-verse monologues entitled "Testaments" that Davidson composed in the decade before his suicide. The others are ascribed respectively to a Vivisector, a Man Forbid, an Empire-Builder, and a Prime Minister. All are remarkable, particularly "The Testament of John Davidson", which is a grandiose mythological poem (see Robertson 1983). Here I shall talk only about "The Testament of an Empire-Builder", a poem consisting largely of three dream-visions. The first shows an assembly of beasts discussing their prospective extinction by man, a being higher in the evolutionary chain and therefore destined, by the law of the survival of the fittest, to outlive them. The Hackney describes how "free forgetful stallions", interested only in food and sex, had implanted in them "enduring memory", "an ignominious sense of shame", and "[t]he treacherous fear that undermines the will":

Mnemonics and a discipline adept
In conscience-rearing, Man, the traitor, wrought
With grisly human craft upon Himself.

The thing that never ceases to corrode –
That makes a memory: anguish is the soil,
The root, the stem of conscience and the flower:
The lattice scourged upon the shoulder blades,
The slit snout, eyeless sockets, lettered cheeks,
Cropped ears, maimed members, mouthless, tongueless maws!
(Davidson 1973: 338)

As John Sloan rightly says, this "quotes directly from *The Genealogy of Morals*" (Sloan 1995: 205). In discussing the origin of memory, Nietzsche repeatedly talks about the task of breeding an animal that is able to make promises, and argues that this was accomplished through a long and cruel process in prehistoric times:

"In order to make a thing stay, it must be burned into memory;" only that which never ceases *to hurt*, remains fixed in memory; these are among the fundamental truths of the oldest (unfortunately also longest) psychology on earth. [...] Blood, tortures, sacrifices were indispensable whenever man found it necessary to make a memory for himself; the most frightful sacrifices and pledges (in which category are included the offerings of the first-born), the most abominable mutilations (*e.g.*, castrations) the most barbarous ritual observances in all religious cults (all religions are at the lowest bottom systems of cruelties) – all these things owe their origin to that instinct, which found out pain mental and physical to be the most potent adjutory means of mnemonics. (Nietzsche 1899: 66–67)

Davidson has picked up and developed Nietzsche's analogy (meant perhaps as more than an analogy) between the training of human memory and the training, through cruelty, of animals to serve human purposes.

   We next move to the English countryside for a diatribe on the degrading effects of modern civilisation, and then the speaker is carried aloft by a cloud which leaves him standing on the verge of heaven. Heaven is described with Keatsian sensuousness. But it proves to be not a Christian heaven, but a Nietzschean one. Its denizens include all history's ruthless conquerors, statesmen, millionaires and sensualists. He wonders where hell is. In the midst of heaven he notices a divine figure playing on a jewelled keyboard. This gives him a clue: music results from discipline, and discipline from pain, so the music must emanate from hell. Straining his eyes, he gradually perceives that heaven is surrounded by a prodigious amphitheatre composed of the bodies (not the souls: Davidson is a materialist) of the damned. Their shrieks provide the celestial harmony and add the last spice of pleasure to the bliss of the saved. The membership of hell consists of all the "good" people who submitted to oppression on earth:

> Materials of Hell? The altruists;
> Agnostics; dreamers; idiots, cripples, dwarfs;
> All kinds of coward who eluded fact;
> Dwellers in legend, burrowers in myth;
> The merciful, the meek, and mild, the poor
> In spirit; Christians who in very deed
> Were Christians; pessimistic celibates;
> The feeble minds; the souls called beautiful [...]
> (Davidson 1973: 347–48)

This extraordinary conception was clearly inspired by the passage quoted in *The Genealogy of Morals* from the Church Father Tertullian.[5] In *De spectaculis* Tertullian indulges in a vindictive rhapsody about how the infernal sufferings of play-actors, charioteers and other such will provide the saved with a more pleasant spectacle than any to be seen on earth. This notion that the saved will watch and even enjoy the sufferings of the damned was suggested by the story of Dives and Lazarus (Luke 16: 15–31). It provides material for Nietzsche's debunking of Christian values by suggesting the importance of revenge. Davidson adopts it wholeheartedly, relishing how the saved in his Nietzschean heaven will enjoy sadistically the sufferings of the damned. He quotes sarcastically from the Sermon on the Mount, consigning the "poor in spirit" to Hell, and reverses the fates of Dives and Lazarus:

> Eternal Justice, it was good to see
> Dives in Heaven and Lazarus in Hell
> Maugre two thousand years of Christendom!
> (Davidson 1973: 348)

How much of a Nietzschean was Davidson? He rejected the label, refusing to identify himself with the views expressed by his dramatic speakers such as the Hackney and the Empire-Builder, and claiming that he had held similar ideas long before he encountered Nietzsche's works (Sloan 1995: 206–7). Just how thoroughly he accepted

---

[5] Nietzsche borrowed this quotation from the rationalist historian Lecky, whom he read in German translation; see Lecky 1872: 325.

Nietzsche's ideas may be uncertain; but, since he paraphrases key ideas from *The Genealogy of Morals* at some length, borrowing also Nietzsche's imagery, he evidently found them satisfying. They at least gratified the obsession with violence that is apparent in much of his writing and comes out especially strongly when we see, in the passages quoted above, that he has intensified, with the addition of gruesome detail, the already violent imagery of Nietzsche's original text.

Edwin Muir gives an unreliable account of his Nietzscheanism in his autobiography. Its first version, *The Story and the Fable*, published in 1940 and written after Muir's adoption of an undogmatic, mystical Christianity, is clearly a conversion narrative. Leading up to a decisive turning-point in its author's life, it represents his earlier self as passing through a period of unrelieved spiritual despair, for which Nietzsche is made responsible. He tells us how, isolated from his few surviving relatives and doing a series of dead-end jobs in the Glasgow area, he compensated for his circumstances by buying, reading and annotating the volumes of the translation edited by Levy:

> The idea of a transvaluation of all values intoxicated me with a feeling of false power. I, a poor clerk in a beer-bottling factory, adopted the creed of aristocracy [...]. But I had no ability and no wish to criticise Nietzsche's ideas, since they gave me exactly what I wanted: a last desperate foothold on my dying dream of the future. (Muir 1954: 126)[6]

He also tells us of the notes he wrote for the progressive weekly paper *The New Age* under the heading "We Moderns":

> In these notes I generalised in excited ignorance on creative love and the difference between it and pity, which I unhesitatingly condemned; I pointed out such facts as that humility is really inverted pride, and that the true antithesis of love is not hate but sympathy: whenever I hit upon a paradox which lay conveniently near the surface I took it for the final truth. (Muir 1954: 151)

Muir does much less than justice to the brilliance of *We Moderns*, his book of aphorisms and notes published in 1918. It is understandable that, writing in the aftermath of a spiritual crisis, Muir represents his

---

[6] The earlier parts, including Muir's account of his Nietzscheanism, were first published as *The Story and the Fable* (1940) and reprinted without change.

younger self as compensating for profound unhappiness by an immature imitation of Nietzsche. But if we look at *We Moderns*, we find a much more original book, by no means slavishly dependent on Nietzsche. It owes, in fact, a great deal to the antagonist most often named in it, G.K. Chesterton. Muir attacks the belief in Original Sin which Chesterton had recently put forward entertainingly in such books as *Heretics, Orthodoxy*, and *What's Wrong with the World*. Chesterton is mentioned more often than any writer except Nietzsche. The aphoristic style owes something to Chesterton's love of paradoxes. Another influence that dilutes the Nietzscheanism is Muir's adherence to Guild Socialism (something which actually brought him quite close to Chesterton). Hence a major theme in the book is emancipation. The first stage in the liberation of humanity must be economic emancipation, in order to free man from the economic system which has turned modern society into a "vast machine". Beyond that, Muir refers constantly to the future, and is indeed offering (to quote the subtitle of *Beyond Good and Evil*) a philosophy of the future.

A number of Nietzschean ideas reappear in *We Moderns* and associated texts. Following *The Birth of Tragedy*, Muir exalts tragedy as the supreme art form, and as the supreme affirmation of life. "[I]t is the inevitable, the 'Fate' in Tragedy, that makes of it a heroic and *joyful* thing" (Muir 1918: 157). Tragedy deals in myth, and myth, instead of recording mankind's heroic past, foreshadows man's heroic future. The poet is a liar whose lies are creative and life-giving. Another spur to creativity is pride, which Muir extols against Chesterton's humility. It is the "condition for all fruitful action" (Muir 1918: 73), and is indispensable for artistic creation and for love: "Only Love can create. Pride was fashioned out of a rib taken from the side of Love" (Muir 1918: 83). (This high-flown rhetoric no doubt helped to make Muir feel embarrassed about the book when he looked back at it.) Muir seldom mentions the Will to Power, but he does formulate the notion of self-mastery that Kaufmann was to make so much of: in a somewhat later essay, he answers the question "why do we train our minds at all?" with a diluted version of the Will to Power:

It can only be because we desire to gain greater mastery over life, and in the attainment of that object, and also in the struggle to attain it, a form of happiness is found, perhaps the most stable of all forms of happiness. (Muir 1918: 103)

Nietzsche's distinction between master and slave morality appears also in diluted form:

The few have a conception of life different from that of the many. To the latter still pertain such notions as "do as you would be done by", and so forth. They understand a morality but not the end of morality. The few, however, who also understand both the morality and the reason for it, who have a conception of Life more difficult and unyielding, seem to the many cold and a little inhuman. The lives of the many, on the other hand, appear to the few as a naively happy, narrow and absurd form of existence. (Muir 1917: 429)[7]

Muir thus imagines an intellectual and moral elite. This underlies his talk of inequality. Opposing Chesterton's praise of democracy, Muir denounces equality as a reductive and ungenerous concept, a way of viewing man "through the eyes of the serpent" (Muir 1918: 61):

To those who believe in the future, inequality is a holy thing; their pledge that greatness shall not disappear from the earth; the rainbow assuring them that Man shall not go down beneath the vast tide of mankind. All great men are to them at once forerunners and sacrifices; the imperfect forms which the Future has shattered in trying to incarnate itself; the sublime ruins of *future* greatness. (Muir 1918: 62)

After looking back regretfully to the Renaissance, a time when great men were permitted to flourish, Muir concludes: "Well, we must weigh men again; we must deny equality; we must affirm aristocracy – in everything but commerce and production, where democracy is really a return to the aristocratic tradition" (Muir 1918: 161). This cryptic parenthesis presumably alludes to the Guild Socialism that places industry under the control of workers' guilds. Muir may mean that such institutional democracy would give free play to the natural aristocracy of the specially talented. His conception of aristocracy seems remote from that of Nietzsche, who went so far as to extol the Indian caste system, and close to that of E.M. Forster, who was later to affirm "not an aristocracy of power, based upon rank and influence, but an aristocracy of the sensitive, the considerate and the plucky" (Forster 1951: 82).

Muir responds particularly to Nietzsche's ambivalent assessment of Christianity. As is well known, Nietzsche, especially in *The Genealogy of Morals* and *The Antichrist*, attacks Christianity for

---

[7] This is among the aphorisms that Muir did not reprint in book form.

promoting slavish qualities under the guise of virtues. This charge lies behind Muir's many assaults on the concept of Original Sin as espoused by Chesterton. But Nietzsche also admits that two thousand years of Christianity have, by driving man's impulses inwards, developed his inner life and made him, though still an animal, an interesting animal. Muir agrees with Nietzsche about the profound psychological (rather than moral) effect of Christianity:

Not that Man has been forced into the mould of Christian morality, but that in the process he has undergone the most unique convulsions, adaptations and permutations, that an entire new world of conflict, pain, fear, horror, exaltation, faith and scepticism has been born within him, that Life, driven within itself, has deepened, enriched and invested him – *that* is from the standpoint of human culture the most important thing, beside which what is usually understood by the Christianizing of Europe is relatively insignificant. Not Christian morality, but the effects of Christian morality it is that now concern us. And these effects are not themselves Christian; rather the contrary. Chrsitianity has made Man more complex, contradictory, sceptical, tragic and sublime; it has given him more capacity for good and for evil, and has added to these two qualities subtlety and spirituality. (Muir 1918: 86–87)

However, where Nietzsche, especially in *The Genealogy of Morals*, argues that man's natural cruelty has merely been disguised by Judaeo-Christian morality and herd civilisation, Muir thinks that man's instincts are joyful and loving: "There is one region in man where innocence and a good conscience still reign – in the unconscious. Love and the joy in Love are of the unconscious" (Muir 1918: 179). Man's natural innocence can be regained through Creative Love, a subject to which Muir devotes one-sixth of *We Moderns*. This is a demanding emotion, which brings both rapture and pain, and hence the opposite of sympathetic love, or humanitarianism, whose aim is merely the alleviation of suffering. (Here we detect a faint echo of Nietzsche's warnings against compassion.) In affirming the innocence of Creative Love, Muir uses the Nietzschean phrase "beyond Good and Evil" (Muir 1918: 209). He is certainly indebted to Nietzsche's demand for a non-moral vision of the world and for its affirmation. Nietzsche wants to apply to all phenomena the non-judgemental view taken by the scientist, and he also wants to shake off the Judaeo-Christian sense of sinfulness, of bad conscience. In *Thus Spake Zarathustra* Nietzsche talks of the metamorphoses of the spirit. The third metamorphosis, in which the spirit becomes a child, signifies the rediscovery of innocence, and hence the possibility of affirming life. In Thomas Common's translation:

> Innocence is the child, and forgetfulness, a new beginning, a game, a self-rolling wheel, a first movement, a holy Yea.
> Aye, for the game of creating, my brethren, there is needed a holy Yea unto life: *its own* will, willeth now the spirit; *his own* world winneth the world's outcast. (Nietszche 1909: 27)[8]

The world must be affirmed, even though it is not only amoral but also meaningless. The Superman is to give a new meaning to the intrinsically meaningless process of life. The severest test for Zarathustra's affirmative attitude towards life is his realisation that life consists of an infinite repetition of identical events. Nevertheless, he manages to affirm even the doctrine of Eternal Recurrence.

Although this idea seems later to have become important for Muir, he mentions it only once, and briefly, in *We Moderns*. The theory of Eternal Recurrence hovers uneasily between a thought-experiment and a cosmological theory. Even now, Nietzsche's best readers, such as Alexander Nehamas and Robert Holub, are not sure how to take it (see Hehamas 1985: 141–69 and Holub 1995: 62–67). This quasi-doctrinal side of Nietzsche appeals to Muir least. For him, even in *We Moderns*, Nietzsche is not primarily a theorist but rather a visionary whose visions have poetic rather than logical truth:

> The only modern who has dared to be a poet through and through, that is, a liar in the noble and tragic sense, is the author of the Superman. In Nietzsche, again, after centuries of divine toying, the poet has again appeared in his great *rôle* of a creator of gods. (Muir 1918: 171)

Some years later, when marriage, psychoanalysis, and foreign travel had widened Muir's horizons, he expressed a more detached and sceptical view of Nietzsche in an essay, "A Note on Friedrich Nietzsche", published in his collection *Latitudes*. Nietzsche now seemed a dated thinker, very much of a past generation:

> We shall probably have to throw away half the more systematic part of Nietzsche's thought. It may be said of him, as Matthew Arnold said of Emerson, that "he was a man of great thoughts, but not a great thinker." What did not come to him in pure

---

[8] This version is quite different from (and much better than) Common's original translation, published in 1898.

intuition was generally unreliable and sometimes absurd. His transvaluation of values; his interpretation of morality in terms of the Will to Power; his particular definition of decadence; these have, in spite of the passion with which he stated them, an appearance a little pedantic. The belief, prevalent for some time in a little circle, and held by Nietzsche himself, that Christianity had sustained an irreparable reverse, a defeat which would alter the fate of the world for the next two thousand years, in "The Will to Power" and "Also Sprach Zarathustra", is for us now only a curious piece of literary history. The Superman is no longer an ideal, but a character in fiction. All this may be freely admitted. Yet how much poorer our vision of life to-day would be had Nietzsche never written about Christianity, morality and the Superman. He brought a new atmosphere into European thought, an atmosphere cold, glittering and free; and any thinker in our time who has not breathed in it has, by that accident, some nuance of mediocrity and timidity which is displeasing. (Muir 1924: 85–86)

Muir criticises Nietzsche for confusing his intuitions with intellectual constructions; for offering, through Zarathustra, a new kind of love which is an intellectual theory rather than a feeling; and for the self-deception which made him hope for "the appearance of a set of natural aristocrats capable of binding the monster Europe" (Muir 1924: 91). "As a shaper of Europe", he concluded, "Nietzsche has been less effectual, it is certain, than the late Lord Northcliffe, a man whom he would hardly have approved" (Muir 1924: 90–91).

Nietzsche's presence in Muir's poetry is less obvious than in Davidson's, but perhaps more pervasive. The few statements of Nietzschean doctrine are matched by explicit opposition to Nietzsche. The concept of Eternal Recurrence is memorably expressed in "The Road", where the ever-turning road signifies earthly life as an inescapable prison. It receives a reply in "The Recurrence", beginning "All things return, Nietzsche said", where the vision of earthly life as having nothing beyond itself, and hence as a futile series of repetitions, is contradicted by the unique fact of the Incarnation (Muir 1984: 102–4). However, although Muir affirms that life in time derives its meaning from something outside time, his poetry also insists on the value of earthly existence, and here we may surmise the continuing influence of Nietzsche's visionary affirmation of earthly life in *Zarathustra:* "I conjure you, my brethren, *remain true to the earth*, and believe not those who speak to you of superearthly hopes!" (Nietszche 1909: 7).

Hence the emphasis that Muir places throughout his religious poetry on earthly life. In "The Annunciation", inspired by a picture of Mary and the Archangel Gabriel that Muir saw in Rome, he asserts:

The angel and the girl are met.
Earth was the only meeting place.
For the embodied never yet
Travelled beyond the shore of space. (Muir 1984: 223)

Similarly, in "The Transfiguration" we have a vision of a redeemed Earth, not of another, discarnate reality (Muir 1984: 198–200). However, Muir gradually moves from imagining earthly life transfigured, freed from its impurities, to accepting it in all its complexities. In a crucial poem, "The Three Mirrors", written soon after the acceptance of Christianity which forms the climax of his first autobiography, the third mirror is said to disclose "evil and good / Standing side by side / In the ever standing wood" (Muir 1984: 141). Muir commented that this vision was available only to the greatest poets and mystics; but it strongly resembles also the affirmation of necessity that Nietzsche called *amor fati*. Again, in one of Muir's most famous poems, "One Foot in Eden", the primeval unfallen state is dismissed as incomplete, as not worth regaining, by comparison with the mixture of good and evil in the existence we know:

Strange blessings never in Paradise
Fall from these beclouded skies. (Muir 1984: 227)

Here the moralist Nietzsche has been overlaid by the visionary Nietzsche, and both together, but especially the latter, have paradoxically placed their stamp on Muir's Christianity.

Bibliography

Aschheim, Steven E. 1992. *The Nietzsche Legacy in Germany 1890–1990*. Berkeley: University of California Press.

Carey, John. 1989. *The Intellectuals and the Masses*. London: Faber.

Cramb J.A. 1900. *Reflections on the Origins and Destiny of Imperial Britain*. London: Macmillan.

Davidson, John. 1894. *Plays*. London: Elkin Matthews & John Lane.

—. 1973. *The Poems of John Davidson* (ed. Andrew Turnbull). Edinburgh and London: Scottish Academic Press.

Davie, George. 1961. *The Democratic Intellect*. Edinburgh: Edinburgh University Press.

Forster, E.M. 1951. *Two Cheers for Democracy*. London: Arnold.

Golomb, Jacob and Robert S. Wistrich (eds). 2002. *Nietzsche, Godfather of Fascism? On the Uses and Abuses of a Philosophy*. Princeton and Oxford: Princeton University Press.

Holub, Robert C. 1995. *Friedrich Nietzsche*. New York: Twayne.

Holz, Arno. [1896] 1980. *Sozialaristokraten* (ed. Theo Meyer). Stuttgart: Reclam.

Kaufmann, Walter. 1974. *Nietzsche: Philosopher, Psychologist, Antichrist*. 4th edn. Princeton: Princeton University Press.

Kelly, Alfred. 1981. *The Descent of Darwin: The Popularization of Darwinism in Germany, 1860–1914*. Chapel Hill: University of North Carolina Press.

Lecky, W.E.H. 1872. *History of the Rise and Influence of the Spirit of Rationalism in Europe*, 5th edn. London: Longman, Green, & Co.

Levy, Oscar. 1906. *The Revival of Aristocracy* (tr. Leonard Magnus). London: [no publisher].

Manz, Stefan. 2003. *Migranten und Internierte: Deutsche in Glasgow, 1864–1918*. Wiesbaden: Franz Steiner.

Martin, Nicholas. 2003. "'Fighting a philosophy': the figure of Nietzsche in British propaganda of the First World War" in *Modern Language Review* 98: 367–80.

Mencken, Henry L. 1908. *The Philosophy of Friedrich Nietzsche*. London: T. Fisher Unwin.

Moore, Gregory. 2002. *Nietzsche, Biology and Metaphor*. Cambridge: Cambridge University Press.

Muir, Edwin. [Edward Moore]. 1917. "We Moderns" in *New Age* 21 (13 September 1917).

—. [Edward Moore]. 1918. *We Moderns: Enigmas and Guesses*. London: George Allen & Unwin.

—. 1922. "Causerie de Jeudi" in *New Age* 32 (14 December 1922).

—. 1924. *Latitudes*. London: Andrew Melrose.

—. 1954. *An Autobiography*. London: Faber.

—. 1984. *Collected Poems*. London: Faber.

Nehamas, Alexander. 1985. *Nietzsche: Life as Literature*. Cambridge, MA: Harvard University Press.

Nietzsche, Friedrich. 1899. *A Genealogy of Morals; Poems* (tr. William A. Haussmann and John Gray). London: T. Fisher Unwin.

—. 1909. *Thus Spake Zarathustra: A Book for All and None* (tr. Thomas Common). Edinburgh and London: T.S. Foulis.

—. [1886] 1998. *Beyond Good and Evil* (tr. Marion Faber). Oxford and New York: Oxford University Press.

Robertson, Ritchie. 1983. "Science and myth in John Davidson's *Testaments*" in *Studies in Scottish Literature* 18: 85–109

Scheuer, Helmut. 1971. *Arno Holz im literarischen Leben des ausgehenden 19. Jahrhunderts (1883–1896): Eine biographische Studie.* Munich: Winkler.

Sloan, John. 1995. *John Davidson, First of the Moderns: A Literary Biography.* Oxford: Clarendon Press.

Sluga, Hans. 1993. *Heidegger's Crisis: Philosophy and Politics in Nazi Germany.* Cambridge, MA: Harvard University Press.

Sokel, Walter H. 1983. "Political uses and abuses of Nietzsche in Walter Kaufmann's image of Nietzsche" in *Nietzsche-Studien* 12: 436–42.

Stern, Fritz. 1961. *The Politics of Cultural Despair.* Berkeley: University of California Press.

Tille, Alexander. 1893. "Ostlondon als Nationalheilanstalt" in *Die Zukunft* 5 (11 November 1893): 268–73.

—. 1895. *Von Darwin bis Nietzsche. Ein Buch Entwicklungsethik.* Leipzig: C.G. Naumann.

Thatcher, David S. 1970. *Nietzsche in England 1890–1914: the Growth of a Reputation.* Toronto: University of Toronto Press.

Yeats, W.B. 1955. *Autobiographies.* London: Macmillan.

"The great affair is to move": Stevenson's Journeys

Kenneth Simpson

The pioneering impulse was strong in Stevenson: travel prompted self-exploration, investigation of the human psyche, and significant innovation in narrative strategies. His "kinetic method" identifies him as a harbinger of Modernism and, with his agnosticism, locates his work in the movement from Absolutism to Relativism, which is further reflected in his engagement with the concept of evolution – of humankind, of the earth, and of fiction itself. Stevenson's writing throughout is characterised by the interplay of values of motion and stasis. Sophisticated techniques such as fragmentary form and free indirect narration require the reader's alertness on the journey through the text.

Keywords: kinetic; Relativism; Modernism; narrative experimentation; reader response; Scottish writer-adventurers; evolutionary theory; stream of consciousness; duality; free indirect narration; *Travels with a Donkey in the Cevennes; The Strange Case of Dr Jekyll and Mr Hyde; Weir of Hermiston;* "On Some Technical Elements of Style in Literature"; Henry James

Movement is everywhere in Stevenson. His life was a compulsive quest, his style honed yet fluid, his narratives characterised by their momentum. He is kinesis personified. Restless physical energy is paralleled in challenge to orthodoxies. In both his agnosticism and the shifting perspectives of his narratives Stevenson is in the vanguard of the shift in values from Absolutism to Relativism which dominated mid- and late-nineteenth century thought.

In *Travels with a Donkey in the Cevennes* (1879) Stevenson offers a forthright statement of what he is about: "For my part, I travel not to go anywhere, but to go. I travel for travel's sake. The great affair is to move" (Stevenson 2004: 35); to which in *The Cevennes Journal*, the diary whose material forms the basis of *Travels*, he adds, "and to write about it afterwards, if only the public will be so condescending as to read it" (Golding 1978: 54). The implications for the practice of fiction of this emphasis on motion and flux are evident from Stevenson's comment on Balzac's technique: "I wish I had his fist – for I have already a better method – the kinetic – whereas he continually allowed himself to be led into the static" (Smith 1948: 267). In his essays and his exchanges with Henry James, Stevenson gives direction to theorising about fictional practice; in his experi-

ments with narrative and formal strategies as means of shaping reader
response he points forward to Modernism (Sandison 1999).

Stevenson is one of a line of Scottish writers motivated by
personal restlessness, the desire to extend their horizons, whether in
the quest for health abroad or liberation from the constraints of life in
the homeland: Smollett spends much of his latter years in France and
Italy; Boswell espouses the cause of Corsican nationalism; Galt sails
the Mediterranean with Byron, is a pioneer in eastern Canada, and
combines literary and mercantile careers. There may be a case for
viewing such Scottish adventurism – both physical and cultural – as
both a response to the competitiveness which the Union of 1707
engendered and a challenge to Presbyterianism's emphasis on life as a
"given", a reluctance to surrender to a brooding fatalism bred of
Calvinism. Equally, account should be taken of precedents such as the
numbers of Scottish scholars in the Low Countries in the later Middle
Ages or the remarkable example of William Lithgow who spent
nineteen years (1609–28) wandering in Europe, North Africa, and
Asia. His *Peregrinations* (1632) includes illustrations depicting
Lithgow in the Libyan desert; in the ruins of Troy wearing Turkish
apparel; tied to a tree by thieves in Moldavia; and strapped to the rack
in Spain. Less adventurous physically, William Drummond explored a
range of cultures via the books in seven languages which his library
housed. These precedents were there to inspire Stevenson, confirming
Muriel Spark's shrewd assessment a century later that for the Scot
exile was "a calling" (Dunn 1992: 8).

From adolescence Stevenson had been a rebel, challenging
conventional values. With his cousin Bob Stevenson, Charles Baxter,
and others, he founded a youthful society whose motto was
"Disregard every thing our parents taught us". Declining to follow
family tradition and become a lighthouse engineer, he opted instead
for Law, but never practised. Reacting against the values of Victorian
middle-class Edinburgh, he became an agnostic, grew his hair long,
took to wearing capes, and ultimately married an American divorcee,
Fanny Osbourne. To the rebel the lure of the imagination is strong: the
imagination is the means of creating an alternative world.

Yet Stevenson's early prose work mainly took the form of travel-
writing. As Andrew Noble observed, "his underestimated travel books
[…] in their direct response to contingent reality drew the best out of
Stevenson" (Noble 1983: 7). The Stevenson family had travelled

widely; Robert had visited France as a child; and his uncle Alan had spent some time in that country. When Fanny Osbourne returned to the United States in August 1878, the love-sick Robert conceived of the solitary journey through the Cevennes, which he completed in twelve days (22 September – 3 October 1878), recording experiences in his journal and depicting scenes in his sketch-book. In his introduction to a welcome new edition Christopher MacLachlan comments, "the experiences in *Travels with a Donkey* and *The Amateur Emigrant* (a memoir of 1879–80) feed into the novels that were to make his reputation less than a decade later" (Stevenson 2004: xxxiv). Movement, journeys, exile and return are characteristic of his novels, with *Kidnapped* (1886) and *The Master of Ballantrae* (1889) the most notable examples; so much so that Stevenson is widely regarded as a pioneer in the action novel.

Stevenson's own dismissive comment on *Travels* – "lots of it is mere protestations to F. [Fanny Osbourne]" (Booth & Mehew 1994–95: 2: 313) – seems to have given commentators their cue for underestimating his achievement. The normally astute biographer, J.C. Furnas, dismisses *Travels* as "a youthful journeyman work" (Furnas 1952: 381), while later critics have favoured a psycho-biographical approach, Robert Holmes terming the journey "a physical trial, a piece of deliberate 'adventurism', a bet undertaken against himself" (Holmes 1985: 38). Quite the most helpful comment is that of John Wilson who praised:

the mastery and flexibility of the first-person narrative, the skilful introduction of comment and supposition, the ways in which he achieves fluidity by varying the length of his sentences [...]. He is the master of the active sentence. (Wilson 1983: 80)

Stevenson's energetic but carefully modulated prose mimics both the sometimes haphazard progress of his journey and the fluctuating emotional responses it stimulates.

For Stevenson the appeal of travel is that it breeds incident and offers the potential for adventure. Throughout the journey in the Cevennes he is motivated by "the old unwearied hope of finding something new in a new country" (Stevenson 2004: 64); and he acknowledges, "I have been after an adventure all my life, a pure dispassionate adventure, such as befell early and heroic voyagers" (Stevenson 2004: 32). He sees himself responding to the need to

234   *Kenneth Simpson*

"come down off this feather-bed of civilisation, and find the globe granite underfoot and strewn with cutting flints" (Stevenson 2004: 35). High Victorian energies, as exemplified in the lighthouse Stevensons, were directed to shaping the world. Robert's response is to emulate in a personal way, dictated by his reading, personality, and individual gifts. From the outset he is aware of the ambivalent status his journey bestows on him:

A traveller of my sort was a thing hitherto unheard-of in that district. I was looked upon with contempt, like a man who should project a journey to the moon, but yet with a respectful interest, like one setting forth for the inclement Pole. (Stevenson 2004: 7)

This ambivalence is also reflected in the ironic juxtaposition of epigraphs to the first section, "Velay": "'Many are the mighty things, and naught is more mighty than man […]. He masters by his devices the tenant of the fields.' Sophocles", and "'Who hath loosed the bands of the wild ass?' Job". There could be no clearer signal to the reader as to the hybrid perspective in which the "heroic voyager" is to be viewed.

Stevenson is at pains to emphasise the distinction which the undertaking of such a journey brings: the route from Velay to Gevaudan "was a cheerless prospect, but one stimulating to a traveller" (Stevenson 2004: 22). After his short residence in the monastery he concedes there are points "in which the Trappist order appeals […] as a model of wisdom", but he concludes, "I blessed God that I was free to wander, free to hope, and free to love" (Stevenson 2004: 45, 47); hence, ironically, his admiration for one of the monks, Father Apollinaris: "[he] had made the road which we were following […] with his own two hands within the space of a year" (Stevenson 2004: 40). From within the constraining religious order the monk has built the route thence, but he can only pursue it to its limits and no further. Stevenson's respect for him may have been evoked by recollection of his own grandfather. Bella Bathurst notes, "As Louis recognised, there were two competing forces at work in Robert [RLS's grandfather], an unashamed pleasure in adventure, and a ruthless need for order" (Bathurst 1999: 136). As the civil engineers who were his immediate ancestors had encountered dangers in illuminating and hence controlling nature's energies, so Stevenson, sometimes almost despite himself, finds imaginative momentum subject to the ordering constraints of form.

In *Travels* the quest for adventure is not without its frustrations. With wry amusement Stevenson records the obstacles to progress. Until he learns the donkey-driver's cry of "Proot" he is at the mercy of Modestine's waywardness:

> I had a vision ever present to me of the long, long roads, up hill and down dale, and a pair of figures ever infinitesimally moving, foot by foot, a yard to the minute, and, like things enchanted in a nightmare, approaching no nearer to the goal. (Stevenson 2004: 12–13)

Of Modestine he notes "The tendency of lost travellers to go round in a circle was developed in her to the degree of passion" (Stevenson 2004: 26). There are further impediments from human agencies. Finding himself at Bouchet St Nicolas, Stevenson comments, "Thither, about a mile south of my destination, and on the other side of a respectable summit, had these confused roads and treacherous peasantry conducted me" (Stevenson 2004: 18). It is more than coincidental that *The Pilgrim's Progress* provides the epigraph to "Upper Gevaudan". Evocations of Bunyan's work abound: confronted by an apparent infinity of roads, Stevenson exclaims "It was the most pointless labyrinth. I could see my destination overhead, or rather the peak that dominates it, but choose as I pleased, the roads always ended by turning away from it"; the road opted for "had the air of being a road which should lead everywhere at the same time" (Stevenson 2004: 17).

Stevenson stops short of the allegorical representation of the road characteristic of Bunyan, of JamesThomson in *The City of Dreadful Night* (1874), and of Kafka and his translator, Edwin Muir. There is, though, undeniably a psychological dimension to the significance of the journey: it functions as a quest for self. Paradoxically, physical movement is motivated by a desire to bring stability to the fluidity of personal identity. Poignantly Stevenson remarks that "some thoughts, which sure would be the most beautiful, vanish before we can rightly scan their features" (Stevenson 2004: 92). In contrast with his experience of crowded inns, it is when alone at night and responsive to the natural world that he finds "I have not often enjoyed a more serene possession of myself, nor felt more independent of material aids" (Stevenson 2004: 58).

The natural world provides more than a mere backcloth to the quest for self-identification: in itself it exudes energy and movement. Stevenson's landscapes are rarely static. At an early point in *Travels* he enthuses over "a fine, busy, breathing rustic landscape" (Stevenson 2004: 23). Natural energies manifest in ways vibrantly aural, testifying to Stevenson's acute responsiveness to sound, a dimension which fascinated him. After a vivid description of a stormy night in the open air he states, "Night after night, in my own bedroom in the country, I have given ear to this perturbing concert of the wind among the woods" (Stevenson 2004: 31). In what follows, the shifting perspective of the observer finds a correlative in the dynamism inherent in the natural world:

All around there were bare hill-tops, some near, some far away, as the perspective closed or opened, but none apparently much higher than the rest. The wind huddled the trees. The golden specks of autumn in the birches tossed shiveringly. Overhead the sky was full of strings and shreds of vapour, flying, vanishing, reappearing, and turning about an axis like tumblers, as the wind hounded them through heaven. (Stevenson 2004: 32)

Frequently Stevenson's landscapes are personified, effectively usurping his role as traveller. Here his own erratic progress is projected on to his environment:

Hill and valley followed valley and hill; the little green and stony cattle-tracks wandered in and out of one another, split into three or four, died away in marshy hollows, and began again sporadically on hillsides or at the borders of a wood. (Stevenson 2004: 25)

The legacy of his family's preoccupation with illumination is evident from Stevenson's descriptions. Light, for Stevenson, is ambivalent in its function. Storm-bound, he lights his spirit-lamp, and the result bespeaks both constancy and flux, while the effect foregrounds relativity: "The light was both livid and shifting; but it cut me off from the universe, and doubled the darkness of the surrounding night" (Stevenson 2004: 30). Just as his uncle Alan had adapted the work of the French brothers Fresnel on lighthouse lenses for use in Scotland, just as his father had studied Atlantic storms and North Sea swells to identify wave frequencies, so Stevenson was keenly attuned to the movement of light. Waking at dawn after a starless night, he observes that "Nothing had altered but the light, and that, indeed, shed over all a spirit of life and of breathing peace, and moved me to a strange exhilaration" (Stevenson 2004: 59).

As John Wilson noted, Stevenson's fondness for the pictorial was reflected in his interest in photography and the fact that he regularly depicted in his sketch-book the scenes that he encountered (Wilson 1983: 76). There is a sense in which Stevenson is both an observer and the operator of a slide-show, ever keen to move on to the next slide. Stevenson stresses that the momentum is essential for full appreciation of what is witnessed. Recording the Sabbath observances in St Martin de Frugeres, he affirms, "It is only a traveller, hurrying by like a person from another planet, who can rightly enjoy the peace and beauty of the great ascetic feast. The sight of the resting country does his spirit good" (Stevenson 2004: 14). Here, as so often with Stevenson, there is an essential inter-relatedness: fixity and flux are interdependent. Likewise, the need to move on elicits a hybrid response: taking leave of a priest and an Irishman, Stevenson comments, "I parted first from one and then from the other with unfeigned regret, but yet with the glee of the traveller who shakes off the dust of one stage before hurrying forth upon another" (Stevenson 2004: 53).

For Stevenson, setting is the location for event, and the traveller is motivated by the quest for it. In "A Gossip on Romance" Stevenson expands as follows:

One thing in life calls for another; there is a fitness in events and places. The sight of a pleasant arbour puts it into our mind to sit there. One place suggests work, another idleness, a third early rising and long rambles in the dew. The effect of night, of any flowing water, of lighted cities, of the peep of day, of ships, of the open ocean, calls up in the mind an army of anonymous desires and pleasures. Something, we feel, should happen; we know not what, yet we proceed in quest of it. And many of the happiest hours of life fleet by us in this vain attendance on the genius of the place and moment. It is thus that tracts of young fir, and low rocks that reach into deep soundings, particularly torture and delight me. Something must have happened in such places, and perhaps ages back, to members of my race; and when I was a child I tried in vain to invent appropriate games for them, as I still try, just as vainly, to fit them with the proper story. Some places speak distinctly. (Norquay 1999: 54)

Such is the kaleidoscopic nature of travel: it hosts events, prompting the mind either to seek them out or to conjure others by association. Physical movement stimulates mental energies, creating levels of expectation which, if failed by life itself, will be fulfilled by the imagination. "Some places speak distinctly [...] there is a fitness in events and places": at Luc the inn has "the very model of what a kitchen ought to be; a melodrama kitchen, suitable for bandits or noblemen in disguise" (Stevenson 2004: 36).

As Kenneth Graham has pointed out, Stevenson readily engaged with "the perception and the pressure of life's shapeless variety" (Graham 1983: 31). To relish the randomness of experience, freed from the constraints of institutionalised living, is precisely what he seeks from his travels, sleeping under the stars and delighting in being mistaken for pedlar or vagabond. Contemplation of the galaxy in "A Night among the Stars" prompts "the reflection that we share the impulse with all outdoor creatures in our neighbourhood, that we have escaped out of the Bastille of civilisation, and are become, for the time being, a mere kindly animal and a sheep of Nature's flock" (Stevenson 2004: 57). If in such comments Stevenson seems to be yet another Scottish writer seduced by the lure of Primitivism, it is worth recognising that his attempt at Noble Savagery is compromised by proof of the pervasiveness of "civilised" mores: he leaves money on the grass as payment for the revelation of his oneness with nature but, aware of the irony, does so in a "half-laughing way" (Stevenson 2004: 59). This is far from being the only instance of Stevenson's subjecting his experiences and behaviour to ironic observation; his relations with Modestine, for instance, provide further exemplification.

At times there is a cosmic dimension to Stevenson's perspective; witness, for instance, the comment, "it is always daylight in the fields of space" (Stevenson 2004: 83). In the created world itself the elemental force is that of flux and change, as this description – early testimony to Stevenson's interest in evolutionary theory – indicates: "The stony skeleton of the world was here vigorously displayed to sun and air. The slopes were steep and changeful [...] I have never seen a river of so changeful and delicate a hue" (Stevenson 2004: 64–65). Stevenson's fondness for the motif of the river, with the implicit analogy with the movement of the mind by means of association, plainly accords with William James's coining of the term, "stream of consciousness": the river, like consciousness (except in sleep) is constantly present but constantly in motion; hence it is the perfect embodiment of contraries.

But memory and the forces of history inevitably exert a constraining influence by contextualising. Stevenson's vaunted sense of pioneering individualism is habitually confronted and compromised by the recognition that he is treading the paths of his ancestors. The subtly modulated rhythms of this sentence reflect the tension between assertion and qualification:

There was not a sign of man's hand in all the prospect; and indeed not a trace of his passage, save where generation after generation had walked in twisted footpaths, in and out among the beeches, and up and down upon the channelled slopes. (Stevenson 2004: 38)

The "twisted footpaths" might be said to represent for Stevenson, anticipating the symbolism of Edwin Muir, the adult's awareness of the loss of a personal Eden. Stevenson's breadth and depth of reading and his knowledge of history repeatedly remind him of precedents for his experience; and – again manifesting an ambivalence – he acknowledges, "I own I like definite form in what my eyes are to rest upon" (Stevenson 2004: 38). So, on his reaching the highest summit on his journey, the vista moves him to boast, "I took possession, in my own name, of a new quarter of the world" (Stevenson 2004: 62), but this is just after quoting Keats's lines on Cortez in "On first looking into Chapman's Homer"; likewise, he acknowledges that the stars "had looked not otherwise to Roland or Cavalier" (Stevenson 2004: 82). Despite the emphasis on adventurism, Stevenson plainly derives comfort from the validation of his experience by the precedents offered by history.

Stevenson had an intense interest in "how we are shaped by culture and geography" (Stevenson 2004: xxxiii), so his sense of his place in history inevitably assumes a Scottish dimension. A dinner-table discussion of religion "was tolerantly conducted, and surprised a man brought up among the infinitesimal and contentious differences of Scotland", prompting the further claim that "the true work of Bruce and Wallace was the union of the nations" (Stevenson 2004: 86). Habitually comparing and contrasting, Stevenson cannot evade his consciousness of being a Scot. From Cheylard to Luc is "one of the most beggarly countries in the world [...] like the worst of the Scottish Highlands"; in the valley of the Tarn he finds "a pass like that of Killiecrankie" (Stevenson 2004: 35, 71). The new is identified in relation to the known. Encountering "a tall, ill-made, sombre, Scottish-looking man" and his foul-mouthed mother, he replies to her question "in the Scottish manner" with a question. Two of the priests in the monastery "were bitter and upright and narrow, like the worst of Scotsmen" (Stevenson 2004: 17, 18, 49). Though he initially terms the Camisards "those southern Covenanters", Stevenson notes that, though memories of the religious wars are keen, in Florac at the heart of Camisard country "Protestant and Catholic intermingled in a very easy manner" (Stevenson 2004: 67, 79). Yet, having previously proclaimed his "Protestant education", he acknowledges that he meets the Protestants "with delight and a sense of coming home" (Stevenson 2004: 38, 80). During his penultimate dinner, spent in the company of two Catholics, discussion of marriage between a Protestant and a Catholic leads one of them to assert that "It's a bad idea for a man to change". Revealingly, and perhaps surprisingly after Stevenson's celebration of the extension of personal horizons, he now states categorically, "it is the current philosophy in these parts. I have some difficulty in imagining a better" (Stevenson 2004: 92). The linear progression – albeit haphazard – charted in the account of the journey has culminated in circularity: there is no escape from the formed self.

In his mature works of fiction such as *The Master of Ballantrae* and – most especially – *The Strange Case of Dr Jekyll and Mr Hyde* (1886) Stevenson plays effectively on the tension between linearity and circularity, using narrative technique to shape reader response. The compartmentalisation of the material and the range of narrative perspectives are integral to Stevenson's purpose in that they disrupt the conventionally linear progression to full understanding which fiction traditionally engenders. *Jekyll and Hyde* begins with Utterson and Enfield taking a walk. Stevenson's narrative then precipitates the reader into a textual journey on which alertness is essential and there is no guarantee of access to absolute truth.

The very title of the first section – "Story of the Door" – signals the interactive role of the reader by arousing interest and creating a level of expectation: doors lead to something, as do stories; closed doors conceal, as does the author until the end of the story. So, too, the building containing the door is part of a court; hence it is "hard to say where one [building] ends and another begins" (Stevenson 1987: 12). With justification Emma Letley designates the first section of *Jekyll and Hyde* "a masterpiece of narrative unease", adding that "unease and uncertainty are caused by the nature of the men who are called upon to tell the story, to bear witness" (Stevenson 1987: xiii). Utterson and Enfield seem to represent rational civilised man, but there is a limit to what they can understand or, perhaps, want to understand: they have agreed that it is a good rule not to enquire further about the place with the door.

In the initial description of Utterson, the difference between public appearance and private self is brought out. In the figures of Utterson and Enfield, ostensibly pillars of Victorian society, Stevenson highlights the disparity between inner and outer man, an ironic foreshadowing of the more extreme exemplification in the Jekyll-Hyde duality. In the reluctance of Utterson and Enfield to probe further he is questioning the extent and effectiveness of rational enquiry. Jekyll's will, naming Hyde as sole beneficiary, has offended Utterson "both as a lawyer and a lover of the sane and customary sides of life, to whom the fanciful was the immodest" (Stevenson 1987: 14). Similarly, Dr Lanyon comments, "It is more than ten years since Henry Jekyll became too fanciful for me [...]. Such unscientific balderdash would have estranged Damon and Pythias" [legendary for the strength of their bond of friendship] (Stevenson 1987: 15). Jekyll's experiments evoke Faustus, the definitive over-reacher who sells his soul to the Devil in the belief that he will gain access to absolute knowledge. The reactions of Utterson, Enfield, and Lanyon imply that Jekyll threatens the supposed stability of their world with its basis in what is assumed to be rational enquiry.

In a tellingly ironic juxtaposition, Enfield's tale of the "human Juggernaut [that] trod the child down" engrosses Utterson and stimulates the "fanciful": "Hitherto it had touched him on the intellectual side alone; but now his imagination was engaged or rather enslaved" (Stevenson 1987: 16). He visualises "a figure to whom power was given, and even at that dead hour, he must rise and do its bidding". The figure is "in two phases" (Stevenson 1987: 16), foregrounding the series of dualities with which Stevenson's novella engages. But the foremost irony is this: the involvement of the imagination ensures that Utterson becomes the slave of his curiosity and he begins "to haunt the door" (Stevenson 1987: 17). Imagination has been charged with threatening the rational basis of society; and Stevenson is using all the resources of the imagination to identify the dualities in the human psyche.

The figure of Hyde, the metamorph of Jekyll, is an embodiment of contradiction. Enfield concedes that he can't describe him; and – even more revealingly – Hyde has never been photographed

(Stevenson 1987: 12, 29). With its accuracy of representation, photography supplanted portrait-painting as the prime medium for realistic representation, thereby encouraging art and literature towards Impressionism. Thus the unphotographed Hyde arouses in Enfield "a strong feeling of deformity" for which he cannot account; and for Utterson, "out of the shifting, insubstantial mist that had so long baffled his eye, there leaped up the sudden presentment of a fiend" (Stevenson 1987: 12, 14). While "the few who could describe him differed widely […] only on one point were they agreed; and that was the haunting sense of unexpressed deformity with which the fugitive impressed his beholders" (Stevenson 1987: 29). Moreover, encounters with Hyde prompt a common reaction, inducing the individual to recognise or even give vent to the evil side within them. Speculating that Jekyll is paying the price of "some old sin, the cancer of some concealed disgrace", Utterson "brooded awhile on his own past, groping in all the corners of memory, lest by chance some Jack-in-the-Box of an old iniquity should leap to light there" (Stevenson 1987: 20–21). Similarly, the policeman's eye "lighted up with professional ambition"; and in Hyde's landlady's response – "'Ah' said she, 'he is in trouble! What has he done?'" (Stevenson 1987: 26, 28) – the oxymoronic "odious joy" of her facial expression emphasises duality.

In sharing Utterson's perspective, the reader joins his quest to identify the truth behind the mystery. The formal fragmentation and staccato narration have a function analogous to that of clues in the detective story or mystery thriller, genres then in vogue. The text requires the reader to become involved in piecing things together by navigating the subtle ironies and juxtapositions embedded within it. In "Dr Jekyll was Quite at Ease", for instance, the disparity between the section-title and the initial description of Jekyll on the one hand, and his subsequent words and behaviour on the other, conveys economically the fact that he too exemplifies the inner-outer duality: the former is how he wishes to be seen, the latter the observable reality. "Incident of the Letter" is replete with individual interpretations, subjective versions of the truth. Jekyll's assertion, "I bind my honour to you that I am done with him [Hyde]. It is all at an end […] he is quite safe; mark my words, he will never more be heard of" (Stevenson 1987: 31), is highly ironic in that it reflects the extent to which he is trying to convince himself of its truth.

Increasingly through the language of dialogue Stevenson reinforces the sense of the essential subjectivity of response. Poole the butler, for instance, is a master of understatement: witness his summation of his master, Jekyll: "It seemed as if he had something on his mind" and "There is something wrong" (Stevenson 1987: 38, 41). Stevenson's mastery of the discrimination of character through idiolect is further confirmed in the ensuing exchange. Utterson offers a tortuous explanation beginning, "Your master, Poole, is plainly seized with one of those maladies that both torture and deform the sufferer". Its formality is offset, and its authority qualified, by the butler's matter-of-fact response: "Sir, that thing was not my master, and there's the truth" (Stevenson 1987: 45). The ironies informing the quest for the truth are underpinned by Stevenson's skill in the use of telling detail: the key, the drug, the "pious work, annotated in his own hand, with startling blasphemies" (Stevenson 1987: 50), and – above all – the cheval glass, an especially significant detail in that it has offered the mirror-image not of fixity, but of flux and duality; appropriately so, since Jekyll has been both appalled and fascinated by the reflection of his metamorphosis.

This section, "The Last Night", concludes with the discovery of Jekyll's letter, which directs Utterson to Lanyon's narrative and then to Jekyll's own confession. In so doing, the letter dictates the direction of the narrative and, with the increased momentum, raises reader expectations of closure, which have been already signalled by the section's title. However, in a further foregrounding of duality, Utterson goes off "to read the two narratives in which this mystery was now to be explained" (Stevenson 1987: 52). But, consistent with the emphasis on subjectivity, in "Dr Lanyon's Narrative" Jekyll's viewpoint, as represented in his letter, is contained within Lanyon's account. Lanyon records that Hyde had offered him the alternatives – duality once more – of letting him go, and thereby knowing nothing of the truth, or succumbing to "the greed of curiosity" (Stevenson 1987: 58). Jekyll/Hyde, the over-reacher in pursuit of absolute knowledge, tempts another with a comparable prospect. But, having read thus far, the reader, too, has succumbed to "the greed of curiosity"; which leads to the disconcerting possibility that s/he, too, will suffer the fate of the over-reacher if s/he pursues matters further. This is arguably the subtlest of Stevenson's many ironies: the text is ironising its reader.

"Henry Jekyll's Full Statement of the Case" is certainly "full" and demonstrates acute insight into the nature of his experience. Both sides of his intelligence, moral and intellectual, lead him to the conclusion that "man is not truly one, but truly two"; and he predicts that others will come to recognise the multiplicity of the self. His moral side permits him to see that "if I could rightly be said to be either, it was only because I was radically both" (Stevenson 1987: 61). He has taken pleasure from contemplation of the possible separation of the two so "life could be relieved of all that was unbearable", and as man of science he has set out to find a way of dissociating them. The vivid description of the experience of taking the potion and his awareness of the relationships of mind, body, and soul reveal the over-reacher as fully conversant with the moral implications of his actions. There is an obvious tension between his moral sense and his spirit of scientific enquiry. Jekyll alternates between knowing acceptance of his condition (on the basis of scientific evidence and looking in the mirror) and moral repugnance which leads him to attempt to abnegate responsibility, referring as he does to "the infamy with which I thus connived (for even now I can scarce grant that I committed it)" (Stevenson 1987: 66). Jekyll's statement conveys very clearly the fluctuation between his confidence and his terror. On waking, he thinks he is not where he seemed to be: "I smiled to myself, and, in my psychological way, began lazily to inquire into the elements of this illusion" (Stevenson 1987: 66). Looking round, he sees that his hand is that of Edward Hyde. The "psychological way" – and a remarkable one indeed – is that of Stevenson. In this last section in particular, Stevenson extends the expressive thresholds of language in terms of its capacity for investigation of the human psyche. In particular Jekyll's alternating between his name and Hyde's and the pronoun alternation between "I" and "he" reinforces the sense of the schizoid, a condition which Jekyll claims is universal, writing "Strange as my circumstances were, the terms of this debate are as old and commonplace as man" (Stevenson 1987: 68).

It might be argued that Stevenson over-endows Jekyll with understanding of the significance of his experiences. Yet his comprehension of his situation may be read ambivalently. On one hand, the degree of knowledge of which he is possessed serves to underline the irony of his powerlessness, his inability to halt the momentum of the process which his experiment has established.

Equally, the very fullness of his statement is such as to suggest that he has usurped the omniscience of his creator, Stevenson; which plainly cannot be, given that he is a character within a fiction. Hence one is led to the conclusion that Jekyll's authority as revealed in his certainty of understanding is itself ironised, thereby ensuring that, in the manner of some Modernist and Postmodernist fiction, Stevenson's text resists closure. Thus the reader's journey, motivated by the "greed of curiosity", culminates in recognition of the impossibility of certainty.

In *Jekyll and Hyde*, his most sophisticated finished work, Stevenson extended the expressive capacity of fiction in its investigation of the human psyche. But his novella also offers exemplification of the extent to which the background of ideas in which a novel is set increases in influence with the approach of Modernism, in effect moving to the foreground. Demonstrating the inseparability of narrative technique and values, *Jekyll and Hyde* fully substantiates Stevenson's claim in his essay "On Some Technical Elements of Style in Literature" that "the idea and the stylistic pattern proceed hand in hand" (Norquay 1999: 98). Interest in fantasies of the creation of human life intensified after the publication in 1859 of Charles Darwin's *On the Origin of Species*. If, rather than being the creation of God, man evolved from the animal, how readily, it was wondered, might he regress? It is in the context of such speculation that the recurrent use of animal analogies in relation to Hyde is to be read; likewise the inference from Hyde's violent conduct that the veneer of civilisation is fragile indeed if man's alter ego is so bestial.

Darwin's *Origin of Species* propelled the shift in values from Absolutism to Relativism. If the Christian account of the Creation was open to challenge, how valid as absolutes were such concepts as good and evil? In countenancing such issues, Stevenson employs in *Jekyll and Hyde* a narrative technique which presents various ways of seeing, offering possibilities in place of previously conventional certainties. Paradoxically, the traditional authority of the author is exercised with the result that the authority that is subject to question is not only theological certainty but the very omniscience of authorship itself.

That such conventions should have been interrogated by Scottish authors such as Smollett, Mackenzie, Galt, Hogg, Oliphant, and Stevenson with the development of narrative strategies which test the validity of the single version of truth and challenge the notion of authorial omniscience as a given, that too is richly paradoxical: their foregrounding of subjectivity in their fiction, it might be suggested, is at least in part a reaction to the certainties of the religion in which they were raised.

Stevenson's cultural roots ran deep. "That is the mark of the Scot of all classes: that he stands in an attitude to the past unthinkable to Englishmen" (Stevenson 1987: 131): the words of the narrator of *Weir of Hermiston* might be applied to its author. Henry James accurately observed that "in *Weir of Hermiston* and *Catriona*, the predominant imaginative Scot reasserts himself after gaps and lapses, distractions and deflections superficially extreme" (Smith 1948: 273). In *Weir* the recurrent motif and the central theme is that of judgement. Most obviously judged is the protagonist, Archie Weir, but there is a sense in which judgement is invited of the other principal characters – his mother, whose "philosophy of life was summed in one expression – tenderness" (Stevenson 1987: 90); the manifestly devious Frank Innes; the Borders family of Elliott for whom justice is something to be personally exacted; and – pre-eminently – Archie's father, Lord Justice-Clerk Weir, a character modelled on the infamous "hanging judge", Lord Braxfield. Scrupulous in administering the steel of justice and deeply imbued with the legacy of Calvinism ("Na, there's no room for splairgers under the fower quarters of John Calvin" (Stevenson 1987: 114) he informs his artistically inclined son), Weir exemplifies the duality of public and private: in the words of the narrator, "My Lord Justice-Clerk was known to many; the man Adam Weir perhaps to none" (Stevenson 1987: 97). There is an undeniable irony in the fact that judgement is passed and justice dispensed by someone who so embodies contradictions.

Ironically juxtaposed with the thematic centrality of judgement is Stevenson's chosen narrative technique, which is characterised by fluidity rather than fixity of perspective. The locus of narration fluctuates between external observation and replication of the perspective of the individual character by means of identification, sometimes sympathetic, sometimes hostile. Stevenson proves the equal of writers such as Austen, Dostoevsky, and Henry James in the subtle use of narration by means of Free Indirect Speech (Simpson 1983: 215). This technique offers a double perspective: as Roy Pascal has noted, it both evokes the individual character and places him in a context of judgment by the narrator (Pascal 1977: 74–75).

A comparable ambivalence informs Stevenson's attitude to Scotland and its enduring impact on him: his homeland is evoked and also judged. That Stevenson was aware of the irony of his situation is evident from his writing from Samoa while working on *Weir*, "Singular that I should fulfil the Scots destiny throughout, and live a voluntary exile, and have my head filled with the blessed, beastly place all the time" (Colvin 1969: 4: 249). That oxymoronic conjunction of "blessed, beastly" accords with recent investigations of the complexities of Stevenson's relationship with Scotland. In a short but acutely perceptive analysis of the theme of exile in *Kidnapped*, Caroline McCracken-Flesher comments: "Whereas the modernist tradition Stevenson anticipates focuses on the difficulty of situating the self, Stevenson suggest that Scots should refuse to situate themselves"; and she concludes, "Memory can only operate to dissociate us: it cannot get us there from here, and our failure only shows us how far we do not fit into its conventions" (McCracken-Flesher 2007: 5).

"Out of my country and myself I go": these words appeared in quotation marks in Stevenson's early travel work, *An Inland Voyage* (1877), and also later in *The Amateur Emigrant* (Stevenson 1924: 17: 88; 18: 55). For all the spirit of brash adventurism that first motivated him, he must have known how doubly impossible this was. Stevenson experiences *in extremis* the sense of dislocation natural to the *émigré*. About his last Scottish texts, *Weir of Hermiston* (published in 1896) and the equally promising, but also incomplete *Heathercat*, there is more than a hint of the apopemptic: it is as if Stevenson is attempting to finally "nail" Scotland before discharging it from his mind into limbo. Self-exiled, however, it is he who is in limbo.

Bibliography

Bathurst, Bella. 1999. The *Lighthouse Stevensons: The extraordinary story of the building of the Scottish lighthouses by the ancestors of Robert Louis Stevenson.* London: Flamingo.

Booth, Bradford A., and Ernest Mehew (eds). 1994–95. *The Letters of Robert Louis Stevenson.* New Haven: Yale U.P.

Colvin, Sidney (ed.) 1969. *The Letters of Robert Louis Stevenson.* New York: Scribners.

Dunn, Douglas (ed.) 1992. *Scotland.* London: Fontana

Furnas, J.C. 1952. *Voyage to Windward: The Life of Robert Louis Stevenson.* London: Faber & Faber.

Golding, Gordon (ed.) 1978. *The Cevennes Journal: Notes on a Journey through the French Highlands.* Edinburgh: Mainstream; New York: Taplinger Publishing, 1979.

Graham, Kenneth. 1983. "Stevenson and Henry James: A Crossing" in Noble, Andrew (ed.) *Robert Louis Stevenson.* London and Totowa, NJ: Vision and Barnes & Noble.

Holmes, Richard. 1985. *Footsteps.* London: Hodder and Stoughton.

McCracken-Flesher, Caroline. 2007. "Cross-Channel Stevenson: David Balfour and the Problem of Scottish Return" in *International Journal of Scottish Literature* 2. [http://www.ijsl.stir.ac.uk/issue2/cmf.htm, accessed 30/08/2009]

Noble, Andrew (ed.) 1983. *Robert Louis Stevenson.* London and Totowa, NJ: Vision and Barnes & Noble.

Norquay, Glenda (ed.) 1999. *R L. Stevenson on Fiction: An Anthology of Literary and Critical Essays.* Edinburgh: Edinburgh U.P.

Pascal, Roy. 1977. *The Dual Voice.* Manchester: Manchester U.P.

Sandison, Alan. 1996. *Robert Louis Stevenson and the Appearance of Modernism: A Future Feeling.* Houndsmills: Macmillan Press.

Simpson, K.G. 1983. "Author and Narrator in *Weir of Hermiston*" in Noble, Andrew (ed.) *Robert Louis Stevenson.* London and Totowa, NJ: Vision and Barnes & Noble, 202–27.

Smith, Janet Adam (ed.) 1948. *Henry James and Robert Louis Stevenson: A Record of Friendship and Criticism.* London: Rupert Hart-Davis.

Stevenson, Robert Louis. 1924. *The Works of Robert Louis Stevenson* (ed. Lloyd Osbourne and F. Van de G. Stevenson). 35 vols. London: William Heinemann.

—. 1987. *The Strange Case of Dr Jekyll and Mr Hyde* and *Weir of Hermiston* (ed. Emma Letley). Oxford & New York: Oxford U.P.

—. 2004. *Travels with a Donkey in the Cevennes* and *The Amateur Emigrant* (ed. Christopher MacLachlan). London: Penguin Books.

Wilson, James. 1983. "Landscape with Figures" in Noble, Andrew (ed.) *Robert Louis Stevenson.* London and Totowa, NJ: Vision and Barnes & Noble. 73–95.

The Enchanted Worlds of Scott, Scotland, and the Grimms

Sarah Dunnigan

This chapter explores the imaginative, cultural, and intellectual affinities between the Grimm brothers and Walter Scott, an overlooked facet of the relationship between early nineteenth-century Scottish and German Romanticism. The Grimms' fascination for Scottish traditional belief is also mediated through the work of the Irish antiquary, Thomas Crofton Croker, who published their essay on "The Elves in Scotland". Here, Scott's position as Scotland's most eminent "fairy historian" appears supplanted by another collector of "enchantment", W.G. Stewart. Unravelling the connections between Scott, Croker, Stewart, and the Grimms helps to illuminate shared aspects of cultural nationalism, popular antiquarianism, and neomedievalism which emerge out of fairy belief and the idea of enchantment in early nineteenth-century Europe. Keywords: Jacob Grimm; Wilhelm Grimm; Walter Scott; Thomas Crofton Croker; William Grant Stewart; neomedievalism; Thomas of Erceldoune; fairies; elves; folk revival; antiquarianism.

Jacob Grimm (1785–1863), the German philologist, folklore collector and, most famously, with his beloved brother, Wilhelm (1786–1859), compiler of the most enduringly popular collection of European folk and fairy tales, once confessed that "For a long time, I have felt the immense advantage that is granted to those who occupy themselves with their native works" (Brill 1963: 489). The brothers' complex emotional and intellectual fascination for the stories "der Heimat" was, of course, imprinted on their *Kinder- und Hausmärchen* [Tales for Children and the Household], first printed in 1812. Jacob's sense of what he terms the peculiar "security" (Brill 1963: 289) fostered by the study of "native works" binds him to some key movements of European Romanticism: to antiquarianism, folk revivalism, and cultural nationalism, for example. But what is less well known is that it binds him to Walter Scott, who also sought "to contribute somewhat to the history of my native country" (Scott 1902: 175) and, in Jacob's words, to the discovery of "songs [...] oral sagas and fairy tales" (Brill 1963: 497), those "traditional materials" (Crick 2005: 7) in which he believed Scottish culture to be especially rich. Jacob Grimm's "enchantment" with Scottish tradition, and his interest in the antiquarian offshoots of a broader Scottish Romanticism, is perhaps unsurprising.

Edward V.K. Brill, Richard Dorson and Ruth Michaelis-Jena have
commented briefly on the series of letters exchanged between Scott
and Jacob Grimm from 1814 until 1815; but implications of the
correspondence for studies of early nineteenth-century Scottish culture
and its European contexts have not been explored in detail. This
chapter returns to those letters (first published by Brill in 1963)[1] to
explore some possible affinities, both cultural and intellectual,
between these two great architects of Romantic cultural nationalism.
This exchange, however, does not encompass the whole of the
Grimms' relationship with Romantic Scotland. Another alliance, this
time forged through the Irish antiquary Thomas Crofton Croker
(1798–1854), reveals the extent of their particular fascination for how
"belief in a people of spirits invisibly filling all nature" (Croker 1825–
28: 3: 53) is manifest in Scotland. The essays Croker publishes in his
Fairy Legends and Traditions of the South of Ireland (1825–28) attest
how the Grimms reach beyond Scott's work to a far less well known
work on the Scottish occult by W.G. Stewart. In so doing, what might
be termed the Grimm enchantment with an enchanted Scotland finds
its fullest expression. Such correspondences between the Grimms,
Scott, Croker, and Stewart – not just literal, but intellectual and
imaginative, too – can help to refine our understanding of the
interrelated worlds of Scottish and German Romanticism at the
beginning of the nineteenth century, and the role played by the
influence of German literature in Scott's own creative development.

The correspondence between Scott and Jacob Grimm is one
particular link in a long-established chain of Scottish-Germanic
cultural influences and inspirations. In the later part of the nineteenth
century, the fairy-tale fantasies of George MacDonald owe much of
their mystical and spiritual impulses to the poetic philosophies of
Novalis (the pseudonym of Friedrich von Hardenberg (1772–1801)).
German philosophical currents are, of course, most deeply embedded
in the work of Thomas Carlyle who was clearly an avid reader of the
German *Künstmarchen*, or literary fairy tale, exemplified by his
translations published in 1827 of Karl August Musaeus and Ludwig
Tieck, inventors of artful and esoteric fairy tales. To earlier

---

[1] The English translation provided here of Grimm's German letters (based on Brill's
transcription) is provided by Stefanie Lehner. I am enormously grateful to Dr. Lehner
for all her generous assistance and advice. Further archival information about the
source and provenance of these letters can be found in Brill 1963.

generations of German artists, the particular Ossianic vein of northern Romanticism proved especially productive in fostering a "cult of melancholic sublimity" (Littlejohns 2004: 63; see also Gaskill 2004), while the rediscovery of *Volkspoesie,* most famously by Herder, but supplemented by the work of Gottfried August Burger (1747–94) and others, was in part nurtured by Percy's *Reliques.*

Against this background Scott's own artistic journey into German literature unfolds, though it grows into a rather ambivalent relationship. Henry Mackenzie's lecture on German literature to the Royal Society of Edinburgh on 21 April 1788 (Lockhart 1900: 174; see also Hewitt 2006) is seen as pivotal: "The literary persons of Edinburgh […] were then first made aware of the existence of works of genius in a language cognate with the English, and possessed of the same manly force of expression" (Lockhart 1900: 174). J.G. Lockhart writes that the "German class", of which Scott was a member, was "formed before the Christmas of 1792" (Lockhart 1900: 174), adding that Scott was one of the members of the group who more eagerly turned to "the popular Belles Lettres of Germany", rather than to study of the Kantian philosophical movement. Finding assistance in German from his friend, James Skene (Lockhart 1900: 224), Scott began to translate German ballads: from Bürger's "Der Wilde Jager" and "Lenore", he produced "The Chase" and "William and Helen" in the late 1790s. Scott's early engagement was therefore with a vein of German balladic literature shaped by the influences of the *Sturm und Drang* movement and its aesthetically innovative and politically revolutionary energies. In his "Essay on Imitations of the Ancient Ballad", Scott marvels at the work of poets such as Bürger, Goethe, and Schiller which, compared to the "low ebb" of recent British poetry, is charged with a rebellious, transcendent potential: "a race of poets who had the […] lofty ambition to spurn the flaming boundaries of the universe, and investigate the realms of chaos and old night" (Scott 1902). Significantly, Scott's most direct engagement with Goethe is with the writer's *Sturm und Drang*-influenced period of creativity: he translates his drama *Goetz of Berlichingen* in 1799 and his poem "Der Erl-König", which he sent as "The Erl-King" to his aunt Christian Rutherford in 1797, was "a goblin story […] [t]o be read by a candle particularly long in the snuff" (Lockhart 1900: 239–40). Scott's interests mirror the broader patterns of German literary influence exerted on British writers and readers, which saw the *Sturm*

und Drang works of Goethe (*Werther*) and Schiller (*The Robbers*)
find most popularity (Bohm 2004: 35). Bürger's ballad, "Lenore"
enjoyed a far higher reputation in Britain than in Germany (see Bohm
2004). Scott remarked that his ballad translations "sunk unnoticed",
though they drew fulsome praise from John Ramsay in 1796: "your
translations excite mingled emotions of pity and terror [...] it reminds
me [...] of the magic of Shakspeare" (Lockhart 1900: 220). Lauber's
perception that Scott's engagement with Burger helped to direct "his
attention towards the ballad style and toward the poetic possibilities of
traditional lore" (Lauber 1989: 8) is a fair assessment of its artistic
influence.

Another strong Germanic imprint stamped on Scott's early poetic
work was drawn from the Gothic movement. Scott's ballad
translations seem almost gleefully to delight in their Germanic super-
naturalism ("uncouth sounds [are] heard in the depth of a German
forest" (Scott 1831: 456)). Scott himself would rather apologetically
come to refer to poems such as "William and Helen" as a "youthful
essay" (Scott 1831: 457), as if his early encounters with German
Romanticism perhaps echoed in some sense his literary childhood
experiences of "the wonderful and the terrible" (Lockhart 1900: 1:
21). He later expressed critical reservation about this particular Gothic
inflection of German influence, both in his essay on E.T.A. Hoffmann
in the *Foreign Quarterly Review* of 1827, and in his arch, rather than
admiring, comment that Matthew Lewis (author of *The Monk*)
"wanders through the whole enchanted land of German faery" (Scott
1902: 25; Parsons 1964: 57); Scott had contributed ballads to Lewis's
Tales of Terror after William Erskine had met Lewis in 1798 and
showed him Scott's versions of 'Leonore' and the 'Wild Huntsman':
"when he mentioned that his friend had other specimens of the
German *diablerie* in his portfolio, the collector anxiously requested
that Scott might be enlisted in his cause" (Lockhart 1900: 253).
Perhaps in echo of the criticism Bürger (and translations of his work)
had already garnered (in 1806, for example, the *Edinburgh Review*
complained about his "outrageous sensibility [which] disgraces most
German poetry"), Scott is privately as well as publicly anxious about
how the supernatural is easily abused: in a letter to Currie in 1801,
Scott writes that "I think the Marvellous in poetry is ill-tuned and
disgusting when not managed with moderation" (cited from Parsons
1964: 57).

In spite of this, Gothic influences remained a staple element of Scott's artistic practice, and often a constituent irony of his fiction. Scott's simultaneous fascination with, and yet distaste for, the artistic and psychological excesses of "German faery" is perhaps best seen in the figure of the White Lady in *The Monastery* (1820), an otherworldly visitant loosely based on the water spirit of Friedrich de la Motte Fouqué's *Undine* (1811). In a preface to the novel, Scott confesses that his protagonist fails to realise the eroticism or the pathos of Fouqué's sylph: "The ingenious Compte de la Motte Fouqué composed, in German, one of the most successful productions of his fertile brain, where a beautiful and even afflicting effect is produced by the introduction of a water-nymph" (Preface to *The Monastery*).

This vein of what might be termed Scott's half-hearted German Romanticism is, however, more deeply tapped in his portrayal of, and writing about, fairy belief. The Gothic fairy landscapes of the *Lady of the Lake*, for example, find a counterpart in the essay "On the Fairies of Popular Superstition": the "more harsh and terrific [...] character of the Scottish Fairy" (Scott 1902: 351), compared to "the elves of our sister kingdom", is attested by accounts, for example, "of a conflict of a mysterious and terrible nature, between mortals and the spirits of the wild" (Scott 1902: 322).

By 1814, then, the year in which Scott and Jacob Grimm began to correspond, Scott had been both immersed in, and then tentatively detached from, particular strands of German Romantic writing. Yet, as with all of Scott's artistic views and practices, they remain complex. His library at Abbotsford shows that Scott was a voracious collector, if not reader, of German materials; by the 1820s, he himself "enjoyed a vogue of quite sensational proportions in Germany" (Tymms 1955: 371); and years after the relationship with Grimm had ended he was still writing to Goethe, though he did not manage to visit the German writer before he died in 1832. That it was Jacob who initiated the correspondence seems most probable. By January 1814, the date of Jacob's first extant letter (at that time he was secretary to the Hessian Legation and, until June of that year, frequently based in Paris), Scott's reputation was firmly sealed after the successful publication of the *Minstrelsy of the Scottish Border* (in 1802, 1806, 1810 and 1812) and the major narrative poems. In turn, the first volume of the *Kinder- und Hausmärchen* had appeared in 1812, for which the Grimms began collecting materials seriously in 1806. Individually, Jacob had published *Über den altdeutschen Meistergesang* [On the Old German Mastersong], and Wilhelm, librarian in Kassel where they had attended school, a translation of *Altdänishe Heldenlieder, Balladen und Märchen* [Ancient Danish Heroic Songs, Ballads, and Tales]. It is perhaps unsurprising that Jacob, and not Wilhelm, should be Scott's correspondent; as Crick notes, "[o]f the two, Jacob was the initiator of their joint antiquarian and academic projects and the greater scholar" (Crick 2005: xvi). Just as Scott in his reply generously acknowledges what Jacob's work has so far "done for ancient German literature", so Jacob confesses his familiarity with the *Lady of the Lake, Marmion* and, after "manifold toils", the *Minstrelsy of the Scottish Border*. Interestingly, in 1813 Wilhelm had published three "altschottische Lieder", with translations: "Lord Randal" and "O gin my love were yow red rose" from the *Minstrelsy*, and "The twa brothers" from Robert Jamieson's *Popular Ballads and Songs* (1806) (Brill 1963: 490, 506).[2] Scott assures Jacob of his "familiar[ity] with *Der alte Hildebrand*", an edition of the *Song of Hildebrand*, the Old High German legendary, heroic poem, which the brothers had published in 1812, and that he "was much flattered by finding the Scottish Ballads had been of use to your researches" from their contribution to the journal *Zeitung für Einsiedler* (1808) (published by Clemens Brentano and Achim von Arnim in Heidelberg, a copy of which Scott owned). Scott seems not to have seen the first edition of their *Kinder- und Hausmarchen,* though he "should like much to possess" it (Grierson 1932–37: 439); Jacob's subsequent letter suggests Scott did not receive the copy he had sent, though he eagerly awaits Scott's opinion of their "children's fairytales".[3]

---

[2] In her commentary on the tale of "The Singing Bone", Crick draws attention to a note made by Wilhelm "in his copy of the first edition" (Crick 2005: 317) where he lists "at least six other variations on the motif of fratricide" (Crick 2005: 317), including the ballad of "The Cruel Sister" taken from Scott's *Minstrelsy.*

[3] In fact, Scott's view of their collection is best seen in a letter he wrote to Edgar Taylor, the earliest English translator of their *Märchen:* "When my family were at the happy age of being auditors to fairytales I have very often endeavoured to translate to them in such an extempore manner as I could and was always gratified by the pleasure which the German fictions seemed to convey. In memory of which our old family cat still bears the foreign name of Hinze which so often occurs in the little narratives. In a great number of these tales, I can perfectly remember the nursery stories of my childhood, some of them distinctly and others like the memory of a dream" (Grierson 1932–37: 7: 310; see also Michaelis-Jena 173–75).

In none of the letters does Jacob make any qualitative judgement about Scott's creative and scholarly work. This leads to a broader point which should perhaps be made about the correspondence in general. These are neither personal nor candid letters. Given that they only wrote for just over the space of a year, and that long periods of time intervened between letters, it is hardly surprising that formality of discourse is seldom breached. The use of letters as a basis from which to reconstruct any relationship or to draw inferences presents challenges for the reader or interpreter; one can never be sure of the extent to which the epistolary voice has been carefully crafted, shaped, or disguised. Despite this, in Jacob's first letter an anxious sense of propriety can be sensed: "it was important to me to justify my first letter to you through citations of my works and projects" (Brill 1963: 492). Each correspondent is also apologetic about their choice of language: Jacob confesses that "the English language, which I am well capable of reading, I dare not attempt to write and I have written to you in German [...] with the conviction that a poet, of which England is proud as its first living one, has read the works of Göthe [Goethe] in the original" (Brill 1963: 493); in turn, Scott responds, somewhat disarmingly, that he "read[s] the German language with facility, as you are so good as to use the Latin characters, but I dare not attempt to write it" (Grierson 1932–37: 439).

While their letters are not obviously "personal", what does seem transparent is that Jacob perceives Scott's antiquarian and editorial work as a strong point of affinity: "The English and Scottish antiquities are closely related to my study of Old German and Icelandic poetry and history" (Brill 1963: 491); Scott can help him glean "more precise information" (Brill 1963: 491) about the former subject. Jacob's desire to renew, strengthen, and expand his knowledge of Scottish and English folk collecting and transcription also appears keenly felt in the wake of his country's gradual political re-emergence from Napoleonic domination:

Now after God and our faithfully kept courage have dissolved the disgrace [*Schmach*] from us and we are more at liberty in all things [lit. we breathe freely again in all things], we can soon catch up on the English books and on a subject that is recently both in Germany and England eagerly pursued. (Brill 1963: 492)

Although the Grimms' collecting had extensive precedent, not only in Herder's work, but in that of Arnim and Brentano (the Grimms had contributed to their important folksong collection, *Das Knaben Wunderhorn* [The Boy's Magical Horn]), it finds renewed impetus in the political struggles imposed by French occupation (Zipes 2002: 10). In the letters, Jacob makes clear that the scholarly endeavour of gathering up "ancient folk traditions" in Germany (not then a unified country, but a collection of principalities) is a collective one: "in our country", he writes, it acts as a "bitter solace from the past over the present" (Brill 1963: 492). While the *Minstrelsy* is not presented as an explicitly politicised endeavour, it too finds its lineage in a collecting practice that may be considered as such: in the recovery and discovery of tradition (folk-song, tale, and custom) that has strong linguistic, cultural, and intellectual import after the Union of 1707. The threat the Grimms and their co-collectors confronted during the Napoleonic occupation, of course, was violently militaristic; but the politicised thread that runs through Scottish Romantic folk collection may still have prompted a form of recognition or kinship in Jacob. Jacob's letter to Scott certainly communicates the urgency, as well as the optimism, of his enterprise: having outlined what he and Wilhelm have achieved so far, he observes that there must be "many precious things still contained in manuscripts" (Brill 1963: 492).

Although Scott is evidently a means for Jacob to discover information about British collectors and their recent work, he already has a reasonably extensive knowledge. In that first letter, Jacob states that he possess copies of "Ritson's and Weber's collections", referring to *A select collection of English songs*, edited by the English antiquary, Joseph Ritson (1752–1803); and *Metrical romances of the thirteenth, fourteenth, and fifteenth centuries*, edited by Henry Weber (1783–1818), who had for the last seven years acted as secretary and amanuensis to Scott. In fact, it was Scott who encouraged Weber to contact Jacob:

I have requested him to write to you, because while all I know is most sincerely at your service, he being *utriusque linguae* doctor and an enthusiast in German literature, may be able to communicate much that is curious and interesting which might escape me". (Grierson 1932–37: 436)[4]

In addition to knowledge of Francis Douce's *Illustrations of Shakspeare and of ancient manners* (London, 1807) – Douce (1757–1834) had assisted Scott in preparation of his edition of *Sir Tristrem* – and Ellis's *Specimens of Early English Metrical Romances* (1805; 1811), Jacob shows familiarity with the Scottish ballad collections of Scott's friend, Robert Jamieson (1772?–1844), in particular the *Popular Ballads and Songs* of 1806. Though Jacob initially confuses him with the Jamieson of the *Dictionary* (Scott points out the error), Jamieson's scholarship on the affinities between Scottish and Danish ballads would have mirrored Jacob's enduring interest in Scandinavian folk traditions. Wilhelm shared his fascination and, in a letter written from him to Jamieson in 1818 which Ruth Michaelis-Jena published in 1975, remarks that he values Scottish ballads (those printed by Scott and Jamieson) "not only for their own poetical worth, but equally for their affinity to the Danish ballads, and even our own German ones" (Michaelis-Jena 1975: 46; see also Crick 2005: 318–19). Jacob is clearly knowledgeable about these antiquarian networks – where the threads of association almost uniformly wind back to Scott – but he is not unreservedly positive: "How often have I wished that, instead of several insignificant Old English rhymeries, they would have printed those [that are] for the history of poetics the most important ones". However, Scott assures Jacob that he will send him a copy of Weber and Jamieson's *Northern Antiquities* (to which he himself had contributed "an abridgment of the Eyrbiggia Saga"; Grierson 1932–37: 436). He tells Jacob unhappy news about Douce whom he "fear[s] [...] will do no more for literature. His health is not good" (Grierson 1932–37: 438); about Ritson, who "died in a melancholy manner, having first, in a fit of insanity, destroyed all his

---

[4] Two letters between Jacob and Weber are published in Brill 1963: 500–505. Weber would have been an interesting correspondent for Jacob: his father was from Westphalia, and he studied medicine at the University of Jena in 1806. Both his edition of medieval romances (1810) and his essay on medieval Germanic and Scandinavian romance for *Illustrations of Northern Antiquities from the Earlier Teutonic and Scandinavian Romances* (1814), a volume on which he collaborated with Scott and Robert Jamieson, attest his formidable learning and devotion to the subject. Two years after Jacob and Weber corresponded, the latter was admitted to York Lunatic Asylum, where he would tragically die in 1818.

curious transcripts and manuscripts" (Grierson 1932–37: 437); and, most poignantly, about John Leyden, who had died three years earlier of fever in Batavia. The death of Leyden, a prodigiously gifted and diverse writer from Roxburghshire who was also a linguist as well as a surgeon, was an "incalculable [...] loss" (Grierson 1932–37: 436) to Scott, who had benefited from Leyden's help in assembling material for the *Minstrelsy* (especially in regard to the "Essay on the Fairies of Popular Superstition"; Leyden had also contributed to Lewis's *Tales of Wonder*). Jacob appears particularly interested in Leyden's edition of the *Complaynt of Scotland* in 1801, which brought this compellingly odd allegorical, visionary, and political early modern text to the attention of antiquaries. In particular, Jacob's attention has been caught by the litany of titles found early on in the work which suggests, in tantalisingly fragmentary and incomplete form, the richness of a late medieval Scottish folk ballad and tale tradition. Whilst Leyden had prefaced his edition by a "Preliminary Dissertation" of 287 pages in which he speculates on the provenance and identity of these often fragmentary titles, Jacob is still intrigued: "At times [...] Leyden invokes peculiar fragments, and must surely have written more" (Brill 1963: 493).

This sense of potential and promise – of what a collective European work of recovery and discovery might unearth – underpins many of Jacob's comments about the particular texts and antiquaries which interest him. Some of this potential is in danger of being lost due, rather prosaically, to an erratic postal service: he writes that "I was [...] unlucky with Sir Tristrem by Thomas of Erceldoune, of which two copies were lost" (Brill 1963: 491). In return, Scott assures Jacob that he will send him a copy of his edition of *Sir Tristrem*, which had appeared in 1804, only two years after the *Minstrelsy*, and about which he boldly asserts that "I put out my strength as an antiquary". Jacob's particular keenness to read his edition of *Sir Tristrem* might have gratified Scott, for whom the late thirteenth-century romance embodied immeasurable potential; not least to serve as the foundation stone of a Scottish medieval romance tradition (see Johnston 1964). And since Scott believed this version of the Tristan and Isolt legend was the work of Thomas the Rhymer, or Thomas of Erceldoune – seer, prophet, and communicant with the fairies – it was further enriched for Scott by representing a literary origin which is identified with the idea of enchantment itself. The ascription to

Thomas is, of course, unfounded, though Jacob clearly echoes it in his letter to Scott. Scott himself devoted a great deal of care to the project, providing a detailed textual apparatus for the poem (found in the late fifteenth-century Auchinleck Manuscript, which Scott knew from the Advocates Library in Edinburgh, and a rich repository of other Middle English romance). The volume was not, as David Hewitt suggests, "an editorial success" (Hewitt 2006); inaccuracies and misassertions have long been pointed out, some of which may in fact stem from Scott's flawed linguistic abilities (Jerome Mitchell suggests that Scott did not read the German romances in the original and was therefore heavily indebted to Weber; Mitchell 1987: 23). Still, Scott roundly asserts the significance of the Scottish *Tristrem* as the source of other European versions.

It is this point of connection, and the possibility of "a close comparison" between *Sir Tristrem* and Gottfried von Strassburg's *Tristan* – for the Grimms the most beautiful of the Tristan stories – which "excites" Jacob. In this respect, the actual scholarly errors Scott perpetuates are secondary to the significance of the broader mythopoeic vision he creates: the seed of the great German Tristan legend takes first root in the region of the Scottish Borders. While Thomas of Erceldoune's authorship of the poem was in fact suggested to Scott by Ritson (an ascription with which "Leyden and Scott were eager to concur", Hewitt 2006; Lockhart 1900: 289), Scott's loving elaboration and exposition of its significance reveal a pool of shared interests and sympathies with the work of the Grimms. Scott's fascination with *Sir Tristrem* partly reflects his more general fascination for "the medieval". The cult of the medieval was, of course, an important dimension of Romantic aesthetics, as well as a stimulus to the task of the archival and scholarly recovery which led eighteenth- and early nineteenth-century antiquaries to medieval textual sources. Thomas Wright's comment that "The fables and legends now current among the peasantry are the fictions of the Middle Ages" (cited from Dorson 1968: 64) typify the period's pervasive belief in the medieval provenance of traditional materials. Scott and Jacob, too, are united in their conviction, however differently manifested, of the "legitimising" power of medieval literature: it offers a cultural origin and source that arises out of a secure, politically stable identity. The recovery of medieval romances, folktales, and ballads yields up their political and mythic, as well as aesthetic, powers. For the Grimms, along with Brentano, Arnim, and other members of the Heidelberg group of Romantics, the *Volk* culture of medieval Germany offered, in the language of organicism which they often used, a purer and more natural source from which contemporary culture could be artistically and spiritually renewed. As Zipes comments, "Germany's medieval past became a utopian symbol for the Grimms – the recovery of the 'natural essence' of Germans was the foundation on which they hoped to build a more authentic Germany" (Zipes 2002: 7).

Scott was therefore keen to tell Jacob about two "ancient Scottish" poems, "both classical, and almost epic" (Grierson 1932–37: 437): John Barbour's *Bruce* and Blind Hary's *Wallace* which had recently been reprinted. Scott disparagingly refers to John Pinkerton's edition of the Bruce printed in 1790 ("by no means a good one": Grierson 1932–37: 437), but directs Jacob to the importance of each work: Barbour's poem "relates to the exploits of Robert the Bruce, who recovered Scotland from the English yoke, and is well-nigh historical in its details"; Hary's is

[…] legendary, but makes up in a high spirit of poetry what it wants in historical authenticity. Both [of] them being till late great favourites with the common people have been repeatedly reprinted, but in a very degraded and corrupted state". (Grierson 1932–37: 437)

Scott recommends to Jacob David Macpherson's edition of Wyntoun's *Orgynale Cronykil of Scotland* (1795). Jacob confirms that he "own[s] Pinkerton's edition of Bruce; I know Winto from the Gottinger Library; however, I do not know Wallace" (Brill 1963: 498), a remark which interestingly points to the broader, European circulation and currency of Scottish antiquarian publications. The survival of the *Bruce* and the *Wallace* enables Scott to present them as Scotland's pre-Ossianic national epics. It is worth bearing in mind that the propensity of some German Romantic writers such as Fouqué to create their own pseudo-medieval epic arose in part from what Goethe acknowledged in his "Dichting und Wahrheit" [Fiction and Truth] (1811–14; 1833) as the problematic lack of German national epic (Bohm 2004: 44). Certainly what Scott's mythopoeic elaboration of the Thomas-Tristan association speaks of, even in the face of authorially authenticated material such as the *Wallace* and the *Bruce*, is a similar desire to created consolatory "magical" fictions of cultural origin. Leith Davis observes how in the *Minstrelsy* Scott "builds on Percy's hint about the creative potential of the Borders", creating "a much more elaborate place for the Borders in British history" (Davis 1998: 153), adding that he offered "if not an epic of Scotland, then at least a series of sketches that would suggest epic possibilities" (Davis 1998: 153). One might also suggest that, for Scott, *Sir Tristrem* becomes Scotland's own national *märchen*.

Despite these points of intellectual sympathy and accord between Scott and Jacob, their friendship (if it can be called that) was relatively short-lived. Jacob's letter from Vienna on 24 May 1815, to which Scott does not seem to have replied, is the last material evidence of their association. In this brief letter, Jacob encloses a copy of the *Kinder- und Hausmärchen*, noting optimistically "what a success should the execution of the same have in England, Scotland, and Ireland!", and promises to send further material. He also observes, rather diplomatically, that "[p]resumably, there has been no opportunity offered to you to send the books that you promised me in your last letter" (Brill 1963: 500). There are no obvious reasons why they ceased to correspond; at least none explicitly stated in extant letters or journals. Perhaps the common ground between Scott and Jacob may not have been so deeply founded in other ways. The Grimms' essay that appeared in Crofton Croker's *Fairy Legends* (1825–28), discussed in detail below, remarks that they made far more use of W.G. Stewart's *Popular Superstitions* than Scott's work, which might suggest a change of opinion regarding Scott's importance. If so, it may have arisen from a difference in how editorial procedures and collecting practice should be conceptualised. Jacob and Wilhelm continually subscribed to the ideals of veracity and authenticity in their practice. Even in the letters to Scott, Jacob makes several comments which support this: the best tales in their *Märchen*, for example, are those which are "the most accurate and elaborate ones" (Brill 1963: 498); he refers to the vital importance of folk traditionality or authenticity [*Volksmassigkeit*], and the accuracy of transcription. Ironically, and as subsequent scholarship has attested in detail, the Grimms exerted often quite considerable editorial powers in reshaping material for both artistic and moral effect, and their informants were sometimes ingenuously presented. (The Grimms also removed material from subsequent editions of the *Kinder- und Hausmärchen*, which was not sufficiently Germanic; this included, as

Crick notes, a version of a Gaelic story translated into English by Anne Grant, and then translated into German by Jacob, removed because "it was too directly Scottish, not German" (Crick 2005: 289–90)). Perhaps, then, Jacob simply grew to see Scott, and his collection of "romantic lore" (Grierson 1932–37: 435–36), in a different light. A difference of artistic opinion was, after all, expressed in the letters. Scott had written of his particular fondness for the fairy tales of Karl August Musaeus in which he "recognise[s]" some of "the outlines of the stories of our nurseries and schools" (Grierson 1932–37: 439), a sentiment shared by Leyden, who noted the similarity between the Scottish folktale, "The Black Bull of Norroway" and "one of Musaeus' *Popular Tales of the Germans*" in his *Complaynt* (Leyden 1801: 235). Jacob responds that he intends his own work to mirror Musaeus "as little as possible", whose apparent modernity of style he clearly dislikes (especially so, perhaps, since it was inspired by the French courtly fairy tale tradition).[5] In 1825 the Grimms received a copy of Thomas Crofton Croker's *Fairy Legends of the South of Ireland*, and a new alliance was forged between them and the interests of antiquaries and collectors in Britain and Ireland. Even though the direct connection with Scott had dissolved, the connection between the Grimm brothers and the idea of Scotland did not. The symbolic enchantment possessed by Scott's Tristrem-Thomas myth was pursued by the brothers in their fascination with Scottish traditional belief in the otherworld and, in particular, with fairies. The Grimms therefore play a role in the Romantic transcription, and idealisation, of a Scotland in which the culture of the magical and the numinous has tenacious root.

Croker's Irish *Fairy Legends* provided the means by which the Grimms' fascination could be made known to an English-language readership: their earlier belief that "no other nation contains as rich an oral tradition as this one [Scotland]" (Brill 1963: 489) could be mediated through a work devoted to the preservation of Irish oral tale and legend. Croker enjoyed an eclectically diverse career (his various ethnographical, archaeological, and historical publications ensured his election to the Society of Antiquaries of London and the Royal Irish

---

[5] It is interesting that in his letter to Jacob, Weber remarks on the apparent diminution of traditional folktales and songs in Scotland and England because their 'nurseries are all occupied with French fairy tales' and 'old wives' have now been 'civilised' (Brill 1963: 504); there is a shared assumption of anti-French cultural sentiment.

Academy), but it was his *Fairy Legends and Traditions of the South of Ireland*, published between 1825 and 1828 in three volumes, which established his popular reputation. (The first volume appeared anonymously, but such was its success that the subsequent volumes were commissioned by the publisher John Murray). The work garnered praise, in the words of Croker's contemporary, Thomas Wright, for teaching "people the real importance of the legends themselves, and their interest [was] taken, not only philosophically, but in a historical and ethnological point of view" (cited from Schacker 2005: 47). Wilhelm wrote a positive review of it in the journal *Göttingische Gelehrte Anzeigen* (Schacker 2005: 76). In 1826, the Grimms translated the first volume into German [*Irische Land- und Seemärchen,* or Irish Elf Tales], which, according to Croker's frontispiece, presented "Tales [...] written in the style in which they are generally related by those who believe in them; [...] it is the object of the Compiler to illustrate, by their means, the Superstitions of the Irish Peasantry – Superstitions which the most casual observer cannot fail to remark powerfully influence their conduct and manner of thinking" (Croker 1825–28). Croker's claim that he had faithfully transcribed the stories of his informants most probably appealed to the Grimms,[6] professed adherents to the practice of "authentic" collection: witnesses and victims of the supernatural are named; there are family testimonies of perennial spirit haunting; and there is a particular named topography of haunting and visitations. Dorson remarks that Croker's work:

represent[s] the first international field collection to be made in Great Britain, in that sense paralleling the Grimms' *Household Tales.* Their contents differed, embracing not märchen nor fictional fairy tales, but traditional stories about demonic beings rife among the Irish peasantry. It was Jacob Grimm of the *Deutsche Mythologie*, not of the *Kinder- und Hausmarchen*, who was fascinated by the Irish legends. (Dorson 1968: 45)

Schacker, while commenting on the lack of critical attention paid to the relationship between Croker and the Grimms (Dorson 1968: 76), agrees with Hennig's view that the Grimms regarded the *Fairy*

---

[6] Thomas Keightley challenged the authenticity of the material in his *Tales and Popular Fictions* (1834); in response, Croker removed ten stories from the 1834 edition, hoping that 'this curtailment will be regarded as an essential improvement' (Croker 1834: 4).

Legends as a way of learning about Irish history and culture, echoing their own perception of how folk collecting can reveal the "true and ancient origins" of "our poetry [...] history [...] language" (Crick 2005: 295).

Part of the book's success, however, was due to the engaging vitality of the tales' narration and their beguiling orality (however much "editorially" crafted): "for I was fairly bothered out of my senses with eagles, and men of the moon, and flying ganders, and whales, driving me through bogs and up to the moon, and down to the bottom of the green ocean" ("Daniel o Rourke": Croker 1825–28: 1: 290). Croker also provides scholarly annotations for these folk stories. Collecting "long after the days of the fairies" (Croker 1825–28: 1: 3), Croker has frequent recourse to Milton, Shakespeare, and Spenser, and to established medieval sources of the occult (e.g. Croker 1825–28: 1: 260–62). Croker's comment that "It is curious to observe the similitude of legends and of ideas concerning imaginary beings, among nations that for ages have had scarcely any communication" (Croker 1825–28: 1: 44) reflects the desire to discover associations and affinities between traditional cultures which was seen in the letters between Jacob and Scott. It is not surprising therefore that Croker should have struck up a correspondence not just with the Grimms, but with Scott too; as Dorson observes "Friendship and exchange of information with the Grimms and Scott were a fruitful byproduct of Fairy Legends" (Dorson 1968: 47). A letter from Scott (dated 27 April 1825), containing "news from fairy land", was printed in Croker's volume, bestowing his seal of approval. Having observed the "extreme similarity of your fiction to ours in Scotland" (Croker 1834: 342), Scott then relates how he recently heard, before "all the solemnities of a court of justice" (Croker 1834: 343), the testimony of a young shepherd who had witnessed a fairy gathering in some woods near the River Ettrick. He contrasts this with another anecdote about a recent "fair-day at Selkirk", where a puppeteer, performing with his show of "fantoccini", was accosted by villagers, angrily intent on discovering the secret of the puppets' animation. Such an incident, Scott argues rather wryly, shows how "the spirit of science [...] slightly stimulated by that of malt whisky" (Croker 1834: 344), has destroyed the spirit of "wonder" – that spirit which, by implication, the believing storytellers of Crofton's book retain.

A year later on 20 October 1826, Scott and Croker met in London (where Croker had moved from Cork); in his journal entry, Scott writes of "the author of the Irish fairy tales – little as a dwarf, keen eyed as a hawk and of easy prepossessing manners". In turn, Croker describes how he:

> really had not the power of speaking [...] he mentioned my Fairy Legends, and hoped he should soon have the very great enjoyment of reading the Second Volume. "You are our – I speak of the Celtic Nations (said Sir Walter) – great authority now on Fairy Superstition, and have made Fairy Land your Kingdom; most sincerely do I hope it may prove a golden inheritance to you. To me (continued Sir Walter) it is the land of promise of much future entertainment. I have been reading the Grimms' very elaborate Introduction". (cited from Dorson 1968: 49)

This reciprocal generosity was reflected in print. In the first volume of the *Fairy Legends*, Croker had made use of Scott's "valuable" (Croker 1825–28: 1: 78) essay on fairy belief (from the *Minstrelsy*), citing Scott's own detailed annotations on material in the collection as evidence of affinities between Irish and Scottish folktales. Dedication of the second volume to Scott (the third was to the Grimms), "in admiration of his genius, and in gratitude for his kindness", publicly sealed their shared sympathies. It was, too, an alliance between Irish and Scottish antiquarianism, belief, and tradition which pointedly excluded England, where belief in the supernatural had already disappeared (except in some "northern counties": Croker 1825–28: 3: xii), and where "these 'shadowy tribes' will live only in books" (Croker 1825–28: 1: 325).

Of course, both Croker and Scott, in putting "the twilight tales of the peasantry before the view of the philosopher" (Croker 1825–28: 2: vii), can be said to have assembled works which buried living tradition in print. Yet, for the Grimms, the work of Scott and, especially, Croker evinced a vitality and importance that bound Scottish and Irish folk culture to the Scandinavian traditions which they also studied. In that sense, the Grimm essays that appeared in Croker's volumes – "The Elves in Ireland", "The Elves in Scotland", and "On the Nature of the Elves"[7] – helped nurture a particular vein not just of northern, but of "Celtic" Romanticism. Significantly, Croker's third volume also includes a section on Welsh fairy legends, based on material

---

[7] It is highly likely that Croker produced the English translation of the Grimms' essays for his volume, but this supposition still needs to be verified.

about the Mabinogi, the Welsh romances, from William Owen Pughe (1759–1835), thereby intensifying the popular strain of "gothically or supernaturally endowed Celticism" (Carruthers and Rawes 2004: 5) on which it draws. That their essay on the Scottish fairies, or elves, however, is significantly longer than that on the Irish is noted by Dorson (1968: 48); the Grimms explain that they prefer the term "elf" as "the most general expression in our (the German) language for these spiritual beings [...] evident from the examination of every dialect of the German" (Croker 1825–28: 3: 56). Characteristically anchored in various literary and scholarly authorities, their apprehension of the "more intimate connections between mankind and the fairies" in "Scotch [and] Danish traditions" (Croker 1825–28: 3: 111) suggests the brothers' particular responsiveness to the occult beliefs and stories of Scottish traditions. Their comments on the physical, social, and psychological propensities of Scottish fairies, as evidenced in traditional belief and tale-telling, are also scattered through their third, more general essay printed in Croker's volume. The Grimms are clearly able "fairy historians" of Scotland, to use Croker's phrase (Croker 1825–28: 3: xx). The physical beauty of the "Scotch Shians" (Croker 1825–28: 3: 14) – or "the good people, good neighbours, men of peace" (Croker 1825–28: 3: 108) – aligns them with the similarly beautiful fairies of Irish, Danish, and Swedish traditions (Croker 1825–28: 3: 72), though their combination of both "heavenly and terrestial" qualities can make them seem both beautiful and young as well as old and ugly. Fairy traditions drawn from the Borders, the Highlands, and the Shetland isles show their "illusive splendour", love of revelry and music, skill in trades and crafts, as well as the variety of their "elfin animals". Their peculiar "dexterity" – in metamorphosing shape, prophesying truths, and in stealing children – is seen through anecdotes and stories that repeatedly attest mortal vulnerability to fairy powers. The fairies speak softly, envy "the more pure and perfect happiness of man" (Croker 1825–28: 3: 16), and "handsomely [...] reward" the singing of "old Gaelic song[s]" (Croker 1825–28: 3: 91, 33). The Grimms' exposition of Scottish fairy belief is therefore compellingly detailed and conscientiously illustrated, testament to the intellectual seriousness with which they regarded belief in spirit worlds.

Their account is stitched together not, however, from their own observation or recording, but from the scholarly and creative work of other Scottish writers from which allusions and references are conspicuously taken: they cite Graham's *Sketches of Picturesque Scenery*; Jamieson's *Illustration of Northern Antiquities*; Allan Cunningham's *Traditional Tales*; Scott's notes to the *Lady of the Lake* and the second volume of the *Minstrelsy*. But none of these exert the "considerable" influence of William Grant Stewart's *Popular Superstitions* (1823). The Grimms assert that they are drawn to study of the "Scotch traditions" because they "contain the most complete system" of belief in spirits; they may admire Stewart's work because of its avowedly systematic and comprehensive impulses, its analysis of categories of ghosts, fairies, and "festive amusements" through "firsthand spirit stories", to use Dorson's phrase (1968: 156). The Grimms may have leaned towards its classificatory, Enlightenment spirit, but Stewart's work also mirrors the peculiarly hybrid form of what might best be conceived as the late Romantic travel book; "Tour writing", as one contemporary described it, "is the very rage of the times" (cited from Piggott 1976: 124). These are not just travel books, charting moral and psychological, as well as literal paths, but often encyclopaedias or miscellanies of folklore, natural history, geology, superstitions, beliefs, stories; the authorial traveller in question is a historian, an archivist, a collector. Stewart, or rather his traveller-narrator, apologises for the imperfect nature of his "gleanings", but asserts, rather more confidently, that its "literary" merit is perhaps less debatable, a self-declared "branch" of an interest in "national peculiarities" already explored by Burns, Ramsay, Scott, "and others of lesser note" (Stewart 1823: ix). His work is defined as part of a well-exemplified fascination with the "unexplored recesses" of the Highland landscape, which has generated "some of the most splendid works which adorn the circle of British literature" (Stewart 1823: viii). Stewart's work reflects the language of eighteenth-century primitivism, and also draws on the Romantic cult of the picturesque and sublime. He is keenly aware of the fashionability of his subject; the Highlands and islands have "of late attracted so much attention" (Stewart 1823: vii, with reference to the cult of Ossian, and to Johnson too). This leads to a fluid sense of temporal boundaries: a sense of the contemporary moment is always bound up with the world of "pastness" evoked by the literal and cultural "relics" (Stewart 1823: xi) he discovers: the ghostly memories of the Jacobite Rebellions, as well as accounts and stories about fairies.

Stewart's work may therefore have appealed to the Grimms through its interesting engagement with the cultural, philosophical, and spiritual worlds on which such traditions impinge. They do seem, at any rate, conscientious readers of the work. While the *Minstrelsy* is the obvious source for some stories (the story of Godfrey MacCulloch, for example, which is also illustrated), others belong to the *Popular Superstitions*, such as the fairy abduction of Donald and Rory Macgillivray, the Strathspey fiddlers who emerge out of a fairy hill after a hundred years only to crumble into dust; as the Grimms comment elsewhere, "[t]he dead belong to the fairies" (Croker 1825–28: 3: 121). They repeat at length Stewart's account of Michael Scot, the thirteenth century philosopher and alchemist whose "wizardry" Scott had famously celebrated in the *Lay of the Last Minstrelsy*. Stewart acknowledges "the notices of him written by the Minstrel of Minstrels", but suggests that it "is not yet quite complete" (Stewart 1823: 78). His account of "the wonderful exploits of Michael Scott's fairies" (Stewart 1823: 85) in helping to carve the landscape of the Grampians is retold by the Grimms (their ropes "may carry me to the moon [...] make them of slime and sea-sand", Croker 1825–28: 3: 30), as is his description of the wizard's miraculous death: his heart, placed upon a pole, is stolen by a white dove rather than a black raven, thereby enabling him to escape an eternal damnation in hell. And in the story about the fisherman who killed a seal near John o' Groats only to be taken down to the kingdom of "those wonderful beasts" (Stewart 1823: 65) in order to atone, the Grimms even echo the somewhat odd cadences of his prose: seals, claims Stewart, are "neither dogs nor cods, but downright fairies" (Stewart 1823: 65); "Sea-Elves", claim the Grimms, are "neither seals nor fish, but are properly Elves" (Croker 1825–28: 42). At the beginning of their essay, the Grimms note that Stewart's work was unknown in Germany; but, despite the second and last reprint of the book in 1851, in which a preface claimed that it was "very favourably received by the Public on its original publication", it never attained the popularity and reputation of Croker's *Fairy Legends*. In making their own contribution to the Romantic collecting of Scottish tradition and belief, the Grimms made visible Stewart's *Popular Superstitions*: a significant and interesting work which pre-dated Croker's far more celebrated volume by two years. Although Croker had not cited Stewart's book in his own work, it appears in the catalogue of his library, as Dorson notes "no doubt acquired after the Grimms' comment on its omission!" (Dorson 1968: 52). But just as these essays give prominence to Stewart, so they announce a disagreement with Scott's scholarly practice in the *Minstrelsy*. Though their comments are confined to a handful of remarks, they nonetheless imply their firm severance from the *Minstrelsy*'s approach to tradition: its assertions about fairy belief are "[t]oo arbitrary [...] being founded on mere superstition, to elucidate various parts of this belief in spirits" (Croker 1825–28: 3: 53). The implied incompleteness of the evidence on which Scott's assertions are based contrasts, the essay declares, with their own approach to the analysis of belief. Such belief forms part of "a complete and connected whole" (Croker 1825–28: 3: 54); in other words, belief in fairies belongs to broader, interrelated philosophical and spiritual belief systems which are themselves historically shaped: "By not confounding different ages, but, on the contrary, separating each, and showing the great influence of Christianity in affecting changes in it, we think that we preserve the right of historical investigation" (Croker 1825–28: 3: 54). The Grimms' essay therefore implies that Scott's method lacks both the historical exactitude and conceptual breadth of their own. In this way, the Grimms' presentation of Scottish fairy belief to an English readership already curious about Irish legend diminishes Scott's importance as a "fairy historian" (Croker 1825–28: 3: xv) while extolling Stewart in the role instead.

This chapter has sought to unpick one thread of the early nineteenth-century Romantic movement that binds Scotland to Germany. The brief correspondence between Scott and Jacob Grimm is an emblem of how the practices of Romantic antiquarianism, "medievalism", and folk revivalism – seen in the collecting of folktale and belief, the editing of medieval texts and, in Scott's case, the creation of the Thomas-Tristrem *mythehistoire* – both converge and differ in two of the movement's most eminent exponents. Though their relationship had foundered earlier (perhaps more Scott's fault than Jacob's), it found more public "closure" in the Grimms' essay on Scottish fairy belief, which disagreed with his methodology. Still, a broader perspective can illuminate some similarities: the desire to recover aesthetic roots that also carry political significance; and to collect and preserve traditional song, legend, and romance as a means of shoring up the less secure cultural identities of the present. Both see the occult – and in particular fairies – as especially rich bearers of national identity, culture, and language. The Grimms were not as scrupulous as they professed to be; in that sense, their work, as much as Scott's, arose out of an investment in the past which was imaginative and emotional as well as intellectual; they too recreate as well as preserve. The Grimms' essays in Croker's *Fairy Legends* pay tribute to the rich endurance of Scottish fairy belief; Scotland's vestigial enchantments are, for the Grimms, exemplary. The role of the Irish *Fairy Legends* suggests the way in which this aspect of early nineteenth-century Scottish Romanticism could be further unlocked: the reciprocal interests of Scott, Stewart, Croker, and the Grimms are a precursor to the more well-known "Celticism" of the later nineteenth-century. It is interesting to know that the brothers Grimm, still the most famous of fairy tale creators, perceived Scottish traditions and cultures of the otherworld to be richly "complete". In turn, the work of both Scott and Stewart helped to shape the contours of a Scottish otherworld which was not merely collected and annotated, but was powerful enough to offer imaginative nourishment to other strands of European Romantic art such as ballet and opera. The "whole enchanted land of [...] faery", to use Scott's phrase, would remain open for quite a while.

Bibliography

Alexander, J.H. and David Hewitt (eds.) 1983. *Scott and his Influence*. ASLS: Occasional Papers Number 6. Aberdeen; Association for Scottish Literary Studies.

Barclay, David E. 1993. "Medievalism and Nationalism in Nineteenth-Century Germany" in Workman, Leslie J. (ed.) *Medievalism in Europe* [Studies in Medievalism 5]. Cambridge: D.S. Brewer. 5–22.

Bayne, T.W.. 2004; 2006. "Leyden, John (1775–1811)" (rev. Richard Maxwell) in H.C.G. Matthew and Brian Harrison (eds) *Oxford Dictionary of National Biography*. Oxford: Oxford University Press.

— .2004. "Jamieson, Robert (1772–1844)" (rev. Harriet Harvey Wood) in H.C.G. Matthew and Brian Harrison (eds) *Oxford Dictionary of National Biography* Oxford: Oxford University Press.

Bohm, Arnd. 2004. "Goethe and the Romantics" in Mahoney, Dennis F. (ed.) *The Literature of German Romanticism* [The Camden House History of German Literature, 10 vols. Vol 8]. Rochester, NY.: Camden House. 35–60.

Brill, Edward V.K. 1963. "The Correspondence between Jacob Grimm and Walter Scott" in *Hessische Blätter für Volkskunde* 54: 489–509.

Carlyle, Thomas. 1827. *Translations from the German. Vol 3: Musaeus, Tieck, Richter*. 3 vols. London: Chapman and Hall.

Carruthers, Gerard and Alan Rawes (eds.) 2004. *English Romanticism and the Celtic World*. Cambridge: Cambridge University Press.

Crick, Joyce (ed.) 2005. *Jacob and Wilhelm Grimm. Selected Tales*. Oxford: Oxford University Press.

Croker, Thomas Crofton. 1825–28. *Fairy legends, and traditions of the South of Ireland*. 3 vols. London: John Murray.

—. 1834. *Fairy Legends and Traditions of the South of Ireland*. London: John Murray.

—. 1846. *Fairy Legends and Traditions of the South of Ireland*. London: John Murray.

—. 1882. *Fairy Legends and Traditions of the South of Ireland*. London: John Murray.

Davis, Leith. 1998. *Acts of Union. Scotland and the literary negotiation of the British nation, 1707–1830*. Stanford, CA: Stanford University Press.

Davis, Leith, Ian Duncan and Janet Sorensen (eds). 2004. *Scotland and the Borders of Romanticism*. Cambridge: Cambridge University Press.

Dorson, Richard. 1968. *The British Folklorists. A History*. London: Routledge & Kegan Paul.

Goslee, Nancy Moore. 1988. *Scott the Rhymer*. Lexington, KY: University Press of Kentucky.

Grierson, Herbert (ed.) 1932–37. *The Letters of Sir Walter Scott*. 12 vols. London: Constable.

Grimm, Jacob and Wilhelm. 2005. "Preface to the Second Edition (1819)" in Crick, Joyce (ed.) *Jacob and Wilhelm Grimm. Selected Tales*. Oxford: Oxford University Press. 3–10.

— . "Circular Letter Concerning the Collection of Folk Poesy" in Crick, Joyce (ed.) *Jacob and Wilhelm Grimm. Selected Tales.* Oxford: Oxford University Press. 294–97.

Haase, Donald. 1993. *The Reception of Grimms' Fairy Tales. Responses, Reactions, Revisions.* Detroit: Wayne State University Press.

Hayden, John O. (ed.) 1970. *Scott. The Critical Heritage.* London: Routledge & Kegan Paul.

Hennig, John. 1956. "Goethe's translation of Scott's criticism of Hoffmann" in *MLR* 51(3): 369–77.

Hill, David (ed.) 2003. *Literature of the Sturm und Drang* [The Camden House History of German Literature, 10 vols. Vol 6]. Rochester, NY: Camden House.

Hughes, Glyn Tegai. 1979. *Romantic German Literature.* London: Edwin Arnold.

Johnston, Arthur. 1964. *Enchanted Ground. The Study of Medieval Romance in the Eighteenth Century.* London: Athlone Press.

Koelb, Clayton and Eric Downing (eds). 2005. *German Literature of the Nineteenth Century, 1832–1899* [The Camden House History of German Literature, 10 vols. Vol 9]. Rochester, NY: Camden House.

Lampart, Fabian. 2004. "The Turn to History and the *Volk*: Brentano, Arnim, and the Grimm Brothers" in Mahoney, Dennis F. (ed.) *The Literature of German Romanticism* [The Camden House History of German Literature, 10 vols. Vol 8]. Rochester, NY: Camden House. 171–90.

Lauber, John. 1989. *Sir Walter Scott.* Boston: Twayne Publishers.

Leyden, John. 1801. *The Complaynt of Scotland: written in 1548. With a preliminary dissertation and glossary.* Edinburgh: Archibald Constable.

Littlejohns, Richard. 2004. "Early Romanticism" in Mahoney, Dennis F. (ed.) *The Literature of German Romanticism* [The Camden House History of German Literature, 10 vols. Vol 8]. Rochester, NY: Camden House. 61–78.

Lockhart, J.G. 1893. *The Life of Sir Walter Scott, bart., 1771–1832.* London : A. & C. Black, 1893.

— . 1900. *Memoirs of Sir Walter Scott.* London: Macmillan.

McCormack, W.J. 2004; 2006. "Croker, Thomas Crofton (1798–1854)" in H.C.G. Matthew and Brian Harrison (eds) *Oxford Dictionary of National Biography.* Oxford: Oxford University Press.

Michaelis-Jena, Ruth. 1970. *The Brothers Grimm.* London: Routledge & Kegan Paul.

— . 1975. "Early exchanges in oral traditions: two unpublished letters by Robert Jamieson and Wilhelm Grimm" in *Folklore* 86(1): 42–47.

Mitchell, Jerome. 1987. *Scott, Chaucer and Medieval Romance. A study in Sir Walter Scott's indebtedness to the literature of the Middle Ages.* Lexington, KY: University Press of Kentucky.

Needler, George Henry. 1950. *Goethe and Scott.* Toronto: University of Oxford Press.

Neumann, Siegfried. 1993. "The Brothers Grimm as Collectors and Editors of German Folktales" in Haase, Donald (ed.) *The Reception of Grimms' Fairy Tales. Responses, Reactions, Revisions.* Detroit: Wayne State University Press. 24–40.

Ochojski, Paul M. 1965. "Sir Walter Scott's continuing interest in Germany" in *Studies in Scottish Literature* 3: 164–73.

Parsons, Coleman O. 1964. *Witchcraft and Demonology in Scott's Fiction. With chapters on the Supernatural in Scottish Literature.* Edinburgh and London: Oliver & Boyd.

Pierce, Frederick E. 1930. "Scott and Hoffmann" in *Modern Language Notes* 45(7): 457–60.

Piggott, Stuart. 1976. *Ruins in a landscape: essays in antiquarianism.* Edinburgh: Edinburgh University Press.

Pittock, Murray. 2008. *Scottish and Irish Romanticism.* Oxford: Oxford University Press.

— . (ed) 2006. *The Reception of Sir Walter Scott in Europe.* London: Continuum.

Reitemeier, Frauke. 2006. "The reception of Sir Walter Scott in German literary histories, 1820–1945" in Pittock, Murray (ed.) *The Reception of Sir Walter Scott in Europe.* London: Continuum. 95–116.

Ross, Margaret Clunies and Amanda J. Collins. 2004; 2006. "Weber, Henry William (1783–1818)" in H.C.G. Matthew and Brian Harrison (eds) *Oxford Dictionary of National Biography.* Oxford: Oxford University Press.

Schacker, Jennifer. 2005. *National Dreams. The Remaking of Fairy Tales in Nineteenth-Century England.* Philadelphia: University of Pennsylvania Press.

Scheck, Ulrich. 2004. "Tales of Wonder and Terror: Short Prose of the German Romantics" in Mahoney, Dennis F. (ed.) *The Literature of German Romanticism* [The Camden House History of German Literature, 10 vols. Vol 8]. Rochester, NY: Camden House. 101–24.

Schulz, Gerhard. 2004. "From 'Romantick' to 'Romantic': The Genesis of German Romanticism in Late Eighteenth-Century Europe" in Mahoney, Dennis F. (ed.) *The Literature of German Romanticism* [The Camden House History of German Literature, 10 vols. Vol 8]. Rochester, NY: Camden House. 25–34.

Scott, Walter. 1804. *Sir Tristrem, a metrical romance.* Edinburgh.

—. 1831. *Poetical Works.* Paris: A. and W. Galignani.

—. 1902. *Minstrelsy of the Scottish Border.* Edinburgh: Oliver & Boyd.

—. 2000. *The Monastery.* (ed. Penny Fielding). Edinburgh: Edinburgh University Press.

Stewart, William Grant. 1823. *The popular superstitions and festive amusements of the Highlanders of Scotland.* Edinburgh: Archibald Constable and Co.

—. 1851. *The popular superstitions and festive amusements of the Highlanders of Scotland.* London.

Tatar, Maria. 2003. *The Hard Facts About the Grimms' Fairy-Tales.* Princeton, NJ; Oxford: Princeton University Press.

Thomson, Douglass H. 2007. "The Scottish-German Connection" in *The Walter Scott Digital Archive.* Edinburgh University Library. http://www.walterscott.lib.ed.ac.uk [accessed 29 October 2011].

Tymms, Ralph. 1955. *German Romantic Literature.* London: Methuen & Co. Ltd.

Weber, H.W., Jamieson, Robert, and Scott Walter (eds) 1814. *Illustrations of northern antiquities, from the earlier Teutonic and Scandinavian romances; being an abstract of the Book of heroes, and Nibelungen lay; with translations of metrical tales, from the Old German, Danish, Swedish, and Icelandic languages; with notes and dissertations.* Edinburgh: J. Ballantyne.

Whiting, B.J. 1934. "Scott and Wyntoun" in *Philological Quarterly* 13(3): 296.

Zipes, Jack. 2002. *The Brothers Grimm. From Enchanted Forests to the Modern World*. Basingstoke: Palgrave Macmillan.

Index

19ᵀᴴ CENTURY SCOTTISH LITERATURE

The Cottagers of Glenburnie
and other educational writings
by Elizabeth Hamilton
Edited by Pam Perkins
£9.95   Paperback   978-0-948877-86-5   2010

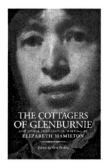

The Cottagers of Glenburnie (1808), with its vivid depictions – and biting satires – of Scottish peasant life, is a lively and entertaining tale that skilfully discusses and dissects class issues, British imperialism, and war. Edited by Pam Perkins, this edition comes with a glossary and notes for scholars and students.

Kirsteen
by Margaret Oliphant
Edited by Anne M. Scriven
£9.95   Paperback   978-0-948877-99-5   2010

Kirsteen's options, as a Scotswoman from an old but poor family, appear to be unpaid drudgery at home, or a loveless marriage. Rejecting both, Kirsteen escapes to London where she begins to make her own living through her own craft and skill. Though looked down upon by her family for choosing to work, Kirsteen becomes independent and successful in the life she makes for herself. *Kirsteen* (1890) is a startlingly modern novel in its treatment of women and work.

Literary Tourism, The Trossachs and Walter Scott
Edited by Ian Brown
£9.95 / $15.95   Paperback   978-1-908980-00-7   2012

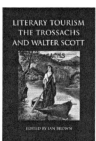

Exploring the potent appeal that links books, places, authors and readers, this collection of eleven essays examines tourism in the Trossachs both before and after 1810, and surveys the indigenous Gaelic culture of the area. It also considers how Sir Walter's writings responded to the landscape, history and literature of the region, and traces his impact on the tourists, authors and artists who thronged in his wake.

Traditional Tales
by Allan Cunningham
Edited by Tim Killick
£12.50   Hardback   978-1-906841-08-9   2012

Originally published in 1822, Allan Cunningham's *Traditional Tales* is a selection of folk stories steeped in the traditions and popular literature of southern Scotland and northern England. Operating within the debateable land between fact and fancy, mixing the natural and supernatural, they blur the distinction between the oral traditions of the distant past and emerging ideas of literature and modernity.

THE ASSOCIATION FOR
SCOTTISH LITERARY STUDIES
www.asls.org.uk

Lightning Source UK Ltd.
Milton Keynes UK
UKOW050029100912

198690UK00001B/93/P

9 789042 035621